India Public Finance and
Policy Report

India Public Finance and Policy Report: Health Matters is an excellent report, analyzing the pressing (public) health policy issues in India, with high level of academic rigour, supplemented by robust data tables, yet very reader friendly. The book deals with a wide range of topics, including access and affordability of health services, government funded social health insurances, and the cost of medicines, each being highly relevant and topical. In ongoing discourse on 'universal health coverage', the policy makers—at both union and state levels in India—need an in-depth understanding of each of these issues to make informed policy choices to improve access, reduce inequities, and make health services affordable. This book will be a must read for anyone who wishes to get insight into current health challenges in India and desires to evaluate potential solutions. It would be immensely useful for policy makers, the academic community, as well as researchers of social policies, development, public health, and finance.

—Chandrakant Lahariya
Senior Public Health Specialist and National Professional Officer,
World Health Organization India

This is a timely volume analyzing the pros and cons of providing social insurance for affordable, reliable, and effective healthcare in India. The evidence-based economic perspectives offered by the authors are sure to be useful for researchers and policy makers of the field.

—Kajal Lahiri
Distinguished Professor of Economics, and
Health Policy, Management & Behavior, University at Albany, SUNY

This is a very extensive and informative document. The amount of hard work gone into it by so many experts is quite evident.

—Satinath Mukhopadhyay
MD (Internal Medicine), DM (Endocrinology), FRCP (London), FAMS (India)
Endocrinology & Metabolism
Institute of Post-Graduate Medical Education and
Research and Seth Sukhlal Karnani Memorial Hospital, Kolkata

India Public Finance and Policy Report

Health Matters

Edited by

Jyotsna Jalan, Sugata Marjit, and Sattwik Santra

OXFORD
UNIVERSITY PRESS

Oxford University Press is a department of the University of Oxford.
It furthers the University's objective of excellence in research, scholarship,
and education by publishing worldwide. Oxford is a registered trademark of
Oxford University Press in the UK and in certain other countries.

Published in India by
Oxford University Press
22 Workspace, 2nd Floor, 1/22 Asaf Ali Road, New Delhi 110 002, India

ISBN-13 (print edition): 978-0-19-012115-0
ISBN-10 (print edition): 0-19-012115-7

ISBN-13 (eBook): 978-0-19-099054-1
ISBN-10 (eBook): 0-19-099054-6

Typeset in 11/13.6 Adobe Garamond Pro
by Tranistics Data Technologies, New Delhi 110 044
Printed in India by Replika Press Pvt. Ltd

Contents

Acknowledgements   vii

List of Tables, Figures, and Boxes   ix

List of Abbreviations   xiii

Overview   1

1. Social Health Insurance Schemes   4
   Arjun S. Bedi, Arpita Chakraborty, Sisir Debnath, Tarun Jain, Anagaw Derseh Mebratie,
   Pradeep Panda, E. van de Poel, Wameq Raza, Frans Rutten, Zemzem Shigute, Robert Sparrow,
   Revathy Suryanarayana, and Getnet Alemu Zewdu

2. Inexpensive and Effective Healthcare?   50
   Koushik Kumar Hati, Kalyan Khan, and Biswajit Mandal

3. Health Inefficiencies: A Statistical Profile   75
   Sandip Sarkar

Statistical Appendix: A Compendium of Health-Related Statistics   85

Blogspeak: Cross-Section of Opinions among Different Stakeholders   153

About the Editors and Contributors   165

Acknowledgements

This report was prepared by a team led by Jyotsna Jalan, Sugata Marjit, and Sattwik Santra. The team comprised (in alphabetical order) Arjun Bedi, Sisir Debnath, Koushik Hati, Tarun Jain, Kalyan Khan, Binod Kumar, Biswajit Mandal, Tushar Kanti Pathak, and Sandip Sarkar. The team was ably assisted by Sumit Datta, Elsoma Dey, Jharna Panda, and Santosh Sarkar. A special mention needs to be made of Devika Chirimar, who worked tirelessly and spent long hours to put the final version of the report together. The team also benefitted from comments received in the India Public Finance and Policy Report (IPFPR) Conference organized by the Centre for Training and Research in Public Finance and Policy (CTRPFP) in January 2018.

We gratefully acknowledge the generous support from the CTRPFP research budget for the preparation of the report.

Aside from the above contributions, we have received advice and comments from many people. The list is too long to thank them individually.

Tables, Figures, and Boxes

TABLES

1.1	Categories of Beneficiaries Enrolled in *Swasthya Sathi*	6
1.2	Summary Statistics	19
1.3	Effect of Village Characteristics on Utilization under *Aarogyasri*	21
1.4	Features of Different Community-Based Health Insurance Models	30
1.5	List of Papers Included in the Review	31
1.6	Description of Benefit Packages under the CBHI Schemes (in INR)	39
1.7	Renewal Rates for Individuals over the Years	40
1.8	Effects of Randomized Offer (ITT) and Uptake of Insurance (ATET) on Healthcare Utilization and Financial Protection (data pooled across three intervention sites)	41
1.9	Effects of Randomized Offer (ITT) and Uptake of Insurance (ATET) on Healthcare Utilization and Financial Protection: Site Specific Estimates	42
2.1	Component-Specific (in-hospitalization) Average Health Expense in India (INR)	52
2.2	Component-Specific (non-hospitalization) Average Health Expense in India (INR)	53
2.3	Component-Specific (in-hospitalization) Average Health Expense in West Bengal (INR)	53
2.4	Component-Specific (non-hospitalization) Average Health Expense in West Bengal (INR)	54
2.5	Health Expenditure as Percentage of Household Consumption Expenditure (per capita terms)	54
2.6	Percentage of Patients Using Private/Public Facilities in Rural/Urban Centres for Different Prognosis in West Bengal (in-hospitalization)	55
2.7	Percentage of Patients with Health Insurance	55
2.8	Cost Comparison of Common Surgical and Non-surgical Procedures (in INR)	57
2.9	Availability of Drugs (percentages in brackets)	69
2.10	Distribution of Maximum Retail Prices (in INR) over Drugs	70
2.11	Distribution of Prices (in INR) across Diseases	71

3.1   List of Dependent and Independent Variables and Their Sources   80
3.2   Statistics of the Outcome Variables and Some Input Variables   81
3.3   Estimation Results   82

A1   District-Wise Estimates of Inefficiencies (statistical estimates obtained from the statistical
     model described in Box 3.2)   85
A2   State-Wise Estimates of Inefficiencies (statistical estimates obtained from the statistical
     model described in Box 3.2)   96

B1   Out-of-Pocket Expenses as a Percentage of Monthly Consumption Expenditure (MCE)
     across Religion, Social Group, and Quartiles of Usual MCE for NSS 60th (2004)
     and 71st (2014) Rounds   97
B2a Out-of-Pocket Expenses as a Percentage of Monthly Consumption Expenditure across States
     and Sectors for NSS 60th Round (2004)   98
B2b Out-of-Pocket Expenses as a Percentage of Monthly Consumption Expenditure across States
     and Sectors for NSS 71st Round (2014)   99
B3a Average Days of Hospitalization across Perception of Absolute State of Health over
     Sectors and Quartiles of Usual Monthly Consumption Expenditure   100
B3b Number of Persons (aged 60 and above) across Perception of Absolute State of Health over
     Sectors and Quartiles of Usual Monthly Consumption Expenditure   101
B4a Total Per Day Loss of Income Due to Ailment across Usual Monthly Consumption
     Expenditure Quartiles for NSS 60th Round (2004) (in INR at 2004 prices)   102
B4b Total Per Day Loss of Income Due to Ailment across Usual Monthly Consumption
     Expenditure Quartiles for NSS 71st Round (2014) (in INR at 2004 prices)   102
B5a Total Loss of Per Day Income Due to Ailment across Sectors and States for NSS 60th Round (2004)
     (in INR at 2004 prices)   102
B5b Total Loss of Per Day Income Due to Ailment across Sectors and States for NSS 71st Round (2014)
     (in INR at 2004 prices)   103
B6   Median Usual Monthly Per Capita Consumption Expenditure across Sectors and States
     (in INR at 2004 prices)   104

C1   Knowledge about Male Contraceptive Methods across Age Groups: National Family Health Survey-4
     (2014–15)   105
C2   Knowledge about Female Contraceptive Methods across Age Groups: National Family
     Health Survey-4 (2014–15)   106
C3   Knowledge about Male Contraceptive Methods across Number of Children: National
     Family Health Survey-4 (2014–15)   107
C4   Knowledge about Female Contraceptive Methods across Number of Children: National
     Family Health Survey-4 (2014–15)   108
C5   Knowledge about Male Contraceptive Methods across Quintiles of Frequency of Reading
     Newspaper, Listening Radio, and Watching Television: National Family Health
     Survey-4 (2014–15)   109
C6   Knowledge about Female Contraceptive Methods across Quintiles of Frequency of Reading
     Newspaper, Listening Radio, and Watching Television: National Family Health
     Survey-4 (2014–15)   110

C7   Knowledge about Male Contraceptive Methods across Educational Attainments: National
       Family Health Survey-4 (2014–15)   111
C8   Knowledge about Female Contraceptive Methods across Educational Attainments:
       National Family Health Survey-4 (2014–15)   113
C9   Knowledge about Male Contraceptive Methods across Religion: National Family Health
       Survey-4 (2014–15)   115
C10   Knowledge about Female Contraceptive Methods across Religion: National Family
       Health Survey-4 (2014–15)   116
C11   Knowledge about Male Contraceptive Methods across Social Groups: National Family
       Health Survey-4 (2014–15)   117
C12   Knowledge about Female Contraceptive Methods across Social Groups: National Family
       Health Survey-4 (2014–15)   118
C13   Tuberculosis: National Family Health Survey-4 (2014–15)   119
C14   Knowledge about Tuberculosis across Highest Educational Level Attained: National
       Family Health Survey-4 (2014–15)   120
C15   Knowledge about Cure for Tuberculosis across Highest Educational Level Attained:
       National Family Health Survey-4 (2014–15)   122
C16   Willingness to Disclose Tuberculosis across Highest Educational Level Attained: National
       Family Health Survey-4 (2014–15)   124
C17   HIV/AIDS: National Family Health Survey-4 (2014–15)   126
C18   Knowledge about HIV/AIDS across Quintiles of Frequency of Reading Newspaper,
       Listening Radio, and Watching Television: National Family Health Survey-4 (2014–15)   128
C19   Knowledge about HIV/AIDS across Educational Attainments: National Family Health
       Survey-4 (2014–15)   130
C20   Knowledge about Cure for HIV/AIDS across Educational Attainments: National
       Family Health Survey-4 (2014–15)   132
C21   Attitude towards HIV/AIDS across Educational Attainments: National Family Health
       Survey-4 (2014–15)   134
C22   Willingness to Disclose HIV/AIDS across Educational Attainments: National Family
       Health Survey-4 (2014–15)   136
C23   Female Sample Observations across Age Groups: National Family Health Survey-4 (2014–15) 138
C24   Female Sample Observations across Number of Children: National Family Health
       Survey-4 (2014–15)   139
C25   Female Sample Observations across Quintiles of Frequency of Reading Newspaper,
       Listening Radio, and Watching Television: National Family Health Survey-4 (2014–15)   140
C26   Female Sample Observations across Educational Attainments: National Family
       Health Survey-4 (2014–15)   141
C27   Female Sample Observations across Religion: National Family Health Survey-4 (2014–15)   142
C28   Female Sample Observations across Social Groups: National Family Health Survey-4 (2014–15) 143
C29   Male Sample Observations across Age Groups: National Family Health Survey-4 (2014–15)   144
C30   Male Sample Observations across Number of Children: National Family Health
       Survey-4 (2014–15)   145
C31   Male Sample Observations across Quintiles of Frequency of Reading Newspaper, Listening
       Radio, and Watching Television: National Family Health Survey-4 (2014–15)   146
C32   Male Sample Observations across Educational Attainments: National Family Health
       Survey-4 (2014–15)   148

C33   Male Sample Observations across Religion: National Family Health Survey-4 (2014–15)   150
C34   Male Sample Observations across Social Groups: National Family Health Survey-4 (2014–15)   151

FIGURES

1.1   Distribution of Hospitals between Public and Private Sector   9
1.2   Composition of Healthcare Providers   10
1.3   Hospitalizations per 1,000 Enrolled   11
1.4   Percentage of Total Amount Blocked in Each District   12
1.5   Departments Most Utilized under *Swasthya Sathi* (as per cent of total admissions)   12
1.6   Sub-district-wise Claims under *Aarogyasri*   17
1.7   Cumulative Surgeries from 2007 to 2015   17
1.8   Cumulative Claim Amount from 2007 to 2015   18
1.9   Inpatient Out-of-Pocket Expenses (per cent of usual consumption expenditure as defined by NSSO)   44
1.10   Outpatient Out-of-Pocket Expenses (per cent of usual consumption expenditure as defined by NSSO)   44
1.11   Total Out-of-Pocket Expenses across Consumption Wealth Quartiles (per cent of usual consumption expenditure as defined by NSSO)   45

3.1   Spatial Distribution of Technical Inefficiencies across States   83

BOXES

1.1   Features of the *Swasthya Sathi* Scheme   8
1.2   Conducting the Review   26

2.1   Criteria for Inclusion and Deletion of Medicines from the National List of Essential Medicines 2015   68

3.1   SDG Health Score across Countries   76
3.2   The Formal Stochastic Model   79

Abbreviations

2SLS	Two Stage Least Squares
ACCORD	Action for Community Organization, Rehabilitation and Development
ADMHS	The Department of Alcohol, Drug, and Mental Health Services (Ghana)
AHS	Annual Health Survey
AIDS	Acquired Immune Deficiency Syndrome
AIS	All India Services
AP	Andhra Pradesh
ASHA	Accredited Social Health Activist
ATET	Average Treatment Effect on Treated
AYUSH	Ayurveda, Yoga and Naturopathy, Unani, Siddha and Homoeopathy
BAIF	BAIF Development Research Foundation
BCC	Behavioural Change Communication
BDS	Bachelor of Dental Surgery
BPL	Below Poverty Line
BRGF	Backward Regions Grant Fund
BSc	Bachelor of Science
CAT	Computerized Axial Tomography
CBHI	Community-Based Health Insurance
CBI	Community-Based Insurance
CCU	Coronary Care Unit
CDDEP	Center for Disease Dynamics, Economics and Policy
CGHS	Central Government Health Scheme
CHI	Compulsory Health Insurance
CMR	Child Mortality Rate
CT	Computed Tomography
CWTT	Contractual Whole Time Teachers

DID	Difference-in-Difference
DLHS	District Level Household Surveys
DOTS	Directly Observed Treatment, Short-Course
ECG	Electrocardiogram
ESI	Employees' State Insurance
ESIC	Employees' State Insurance Corporation
ESIS	Employees' State Insurance Scheme
FDC	Fixed Dose Combination
FGD	Focus Group Discussions
FM	Frequency Modulation
GDP	Gross Domestic Product
HHW	Honorary Health Worker
HIV	Human Immunodeficiency Virus
HSPH	Harvard School of Public Health
ICDS	Integrated Child Development Services
ICU	Intensive Care Unit
IEC	Information Education Communication
IIPS	International Institute for Population Sciences
IMR	Infant Mortality Rate
IOL	Intraocular Lens
IPFPR	India Public Finance and Policy Report
IRDA	Insurance Regulatory and Development Authority
ISB	Indian School of Business
ISGPP	Institutional Strengthening of Gram Panchayats Project
IT	Information Technology
ITT	Intention to Treat
IUD	Intrauterine Contraceptive Device
IV	Instrumental Variable
LA	Local Anaesthesia
LUCS	Lower Uterine Segment Cesarean Section
MA	Mukhyamantri Amrutam
MBBS	Medicinae Baccalaureus, Baccalaureus Chirurgiae
MCE	Monthly Consumption Expenditure
MIA	Micro Insurance Academy
MICU	Medical Intensive Care Unit
MIS	Management Information System
MN	Multinomial
MNREGA	Mahatma Gandhi National Rural Employment Guarantee Act
MRI	Magnetic Resonance Imaging
MRP	Maximum Retail Price
MSK	Madhyamik Siksha Kendra
MSME	Micro, Small and Medium Enterprises
NABH	National Accreditation Board for Hospitals
NABL	National Accreditation Board for Testing and Calibration Laboratories (India)
NCMS	New Cooperative Medical Scheme (China)
NFHS	National Family Health Survey

NGO	Non-governmental Organization
NHIS	National Health Insurance Scheme
NICU	Neonatal Intensive Care Unit
NLEM	National List of Essential Medicines
NMR	Neonatal Mortality Rate
NPPA	National Pharmaceutical Pricing Authority of India
NSS	National Sample Survey
NSSO	National Sample Survey Office
NVF	National Voluntary Force
OLS	Ordinary Least Squares
OOP	Out-of-Pocket
OPD	Outpatient Department
OXFAM	Oxford Committee for Famine Relief
PAR	Personnel and Administrative Reforms
PBSSM	Paschim Banga Shishu Siksha Mission
PCA	Primary Census Abstract
PHC	Primary Health Centre
PICU	Paediatric Intensive Care Unit
PMAY	Pradhan Mantri Abash Yojna
PMGSY	Pradhan Mantri Gram Sarak Yojana
POP	Plaster of Paris
PPIUD	Postpartum Intrauterine Contraceptive Device
PPP	Public–Private Partnership
PRIs	Panchayati Raj Institutions
PSM	Propensity Score Matching
PTI	Press Trust of India
PTT	Part-Time Teachers
PWD	Public Works Department
RCMS	Rural Co-operative Medical Scheme
RMP	Rural Medical Practitioner
ROI	Return on Investment
RSBY	Rashtriya Swasthya Bima Yojana
SARTHAC	Systemized Administration & Regulation of Tendering and Handling All Court Cases
SAS	Sahibzada Ajit Singh (Nagar)
SDG	Sustainable Development Goals
SEWA	Self Employed Women's Association
SHG	Self-Help Group
SHI	Social Health Insurance Scheme
SKY	Insurance for Our Families
SP	Seguro Popular
SRD	Strengthening Rural Decentralization
SSK	Shishu Siksha Kendra
STARPARD	Society for Training & Research on Panchayats and Rural Development
TAT	Turnaround Time
TMT	Treadmill Test

TPA	Third Party Administrator
TSH	Thyroid Stimulating Hormone
UHC	Universal Health Coverage
UHIS	Universal Health Insurance Scheme
ULB	Urban Local Body
US	United States
VDRL	Venereal Disease Research Laboratory
VHI	Voluntary Health Insurance
WBCADC	West Bengal Comprehensive Area Development Corporation
WBHS	West Bengal Health Scheme
WBSRLM	West Bengal State Rural Livelihood Mission
WHO	World Health Organization

Overview

Twenty years ago, Heera and his family were among the more prosperous households within this village…But things changed for the worse…[they] are among the poorest people [in their village]…Heera recounted the following sequence of events.

My father fell ill about 18 years ago. We must have spent close to 25,000 rupees on his treatment, but to no avail. When my father died, we performed the customary death feast, spending another 10,000 rupees. We sold our cattle, and we also had to take out some loans. We worked hard to repay the debts. Then about 10 years ago my wife fell seriously ill and still has not recovered. We borrowed more money to pay for her medical treatment. More than 20,000 rupees were spent for this purpose. It became hard to keep up with these debts. Somehow we could make do for another two or three years. Then the rains failed for three years in row and that was the end of the road for us. We sold our land. Now my sons and I work as casual labor, earning whatever we can from one day to [the] next.

—Anirudh Krishna, *One Illness Away: Why People Become Poor and How They Escape Poverty*
(New York: Oxford University Press, 2011, p. 12)

Incidents like the above occur frequently not only in poor villages of low- and middle-income countries like Thailand, Vietnam, and India, but also in rich economies like the United States (US). In the US, 18.5 per cent of the non-elderly population is not covered by health insurance, of which 70 per cent are poor or near-poor (Simon 2013).

While health shocks are not necessarily the sole reason for households to fall into poverty or remain poor for long periods, anecdotal evidence and detailed case studies suggest that unanticipated and/or chronic health shocks are by far the most compelling reason why people become poor and remain poor. The Center for Disease Dynamics, Economics and Policy (CDDEP) reports: 'The number of Indians falling below the poverty line

(BPL) due to health spending may run as high as 63 million people: almost 7% of the nation's population.'[1] This is corroborated by the Indian Ministry of Health in its *National Health Policy 2015* draft report, where it states that 'incidence of catastrophic expenditure due to health care costs is growing and is now being estimated to be one of the major contributors to poverty. The drain on family incomes due to health care costs can neutralize the gains of income increases and every Government

[1] Press Information Bureau, Government of India, Vice President's Secretariat published on 18-April-2018, 'Health coverage schemes must provide widest coverage: Vice President: Efforts are needed to arrest the growing incidence of non communicable diseases; Launches Atal Amrit Abhiyan'.

scheme aimed to reduce poverty.'[2] This segment of the population is likely to abstain from preventive healthcare, and seek medical help only when illnesses become severe. Households that are not poor and have the means to better guard themselves against events like chronic or repeated illnesses by taking effective preventive measures are less likely to be vulnerable to negative shocks, and live healthier lives.

The starting point of this *India Public Finance and Policy Report* (*IPFPR*) is that vulnerability to poverty for large sections of populations living in poor and not-so-poor countries is largely due to chronic and/or repeated illnesses. Health crises plague most economies irrespective of their average per capita income levels. Given this paradigm, this report attempts to examine specific alternatives that are available for policy-makers to provide *affordable*, *reliable*, and *effective* care to the population. In this report, we examine the importance of access to affordable, effective, and reliable healthcare, but also recognize that material factors like unhealthy housing, unemployment, and food insecurity—not covered in the report—could be equally important contributory factors for poor health.

In providing reliable and effective healthcare to the vulnerable, one instrument that immediately comes to mind is health insurance. However, the problem of moral hazard may arise where the insured may resort to an unhealthy lifestyle and/or visit a medical facility more frequently than otherwise; or when the provider of medical care may recommend unnecessary medical treatment to get greater reimbursements from the insurance company. Also, those with higher medical risks may precisely be the ones to opt for health insurance (adverse selection). The question is, can government-mandated social health insurance schemes (SHIs) succeed in reducing households' vulnerability to health shocks? Are these schemes financially viable in the long-run? In Chapter 1 in this volume, we analyse three SHIs in India—the *Swasthya Sathi Scheme*[3] implemented by the Government of West Bengal for contractual workers employed by the state, the *Aarogyasri Community Insurance Scheme*[4] for BPL households in Andhra Pradesh, and a *community-based health insurance scheme* (CBHI)[5] implemented in some districts of Uttar Pradesh and Bihar.

Existing social insurance schemes typically target the more vulnerable households in the population. Yet, there is still a large percentage of the population that continues to be hard-hit by health shocks that impose severe economic costs on them, and who are often ineligible under social insurance schemes put in place by the government. In Chapter 2 in this volume,[6] using qualitative surveys of different medical facilities in the state of West Bengal, we make a heuristic comparison of costs of standard health services provided by *Swasthya Sathi*—a scheme set up by the West Bengal government—a semi-private facility like *Ramkrishna Mission Seva Pratishthan*, and a private hospital in the metro city of Kolkata. Using a theoretical model, we show that private hospitals manipulate health package deals in a way that the patient party ends up paying more than the amount prescribed by the package deal.[7] Casual empiricism suggests that the new regulatory act by the Government of West Bengal (The West Bengal Clinical Establishments Bill, 2017) that compels hospitals to provide full cost information to patients before they commence unanticipated treatment beyond the contracted deal may reduce the incentives of private hospitals to indulge in overcharging the patient party. This chapter concludes with a survey that highlights some issues regarding the availability and pricing of generic and branded pharmaceutical drugs in pharmacies and medical retail shops outside the hospital.

---

[2] '*National Health Policy 2015* Draft' published by Ministry of Health & Family Welfare December (2014).

[3] Background material collected from the *Swasthya Sathi* portal of the Government of West Bengal.

[4] Background paper, Sisir Debnath, Tarun Jain, and Revathy Suryanarayana, 'The *Aarogyasri* Health Insurance Program' (2018). Mimeo CTRPFP.

[5] Background paper, A.S. Bedi, A.D. Mebratie, G. Alemu, R. Sparrow, P. Panda, W. Raza, A. Chakraborty, Z. Shigute, E. van de Poel, and F. Rutten, 'Community-Based Health Insurance Schemes: A Review: Experiences from Ethiopia and India and Lessons for Other Initiatives'. Mimeo CTRPFP.

[6] Background paper, Kalyan Khan and K.K. Hati, 'Cost Divergence across Health Sectors and the Paradox of Preference' (2018). Mimeo CTRPFP.

[7] Background paper, Sugata Marjit and Biswajit Mandal, 'The Rise and Fall of "Package Deals" Offered by Private Hospitals' (2018). Mimeo CTRPFP.

In the process of providing affordable, reliable, and effective healthcare, variations in the quality thereof can arise due to differences in endowments of health infrastructure, personnel, and consumables (such as pharmaceutical drugs and assists) as well as from relative efficiency in the utilization of inputs. Chapter 3[8] in this volume uses District Level Health Survey (Round 4), National Family Health Survey (NFHS) (Round 4) for multiple outcome indicators of health attainment at the district level, and District Level Facility Survey (Round 3) to get information on the various quantitative and qualitative aspects of healthcare personnel and health infrastructure at the district level. Collating the above data, the analytical framework uses a multi-output stochastic frontier approach to estimate the inefficiencies at both the state and district levels with respect to an endogenously estimated optimum health frontier. Moreover, the estimated inefficiencies are deconstructed into components corresponding to each outcome to evaluate the relative standings of the districts and the states as regards the respective health outcomes.

Next we present a Statistical Appendix at the end of the report. The first part of the appendix reports the estimated inefficiencies from the statistical exercise of the previous chapter (Chapter 3 in this volume). A second set of statistics computed from data provided by the National Sample Survey Office (NSSO) for the 60th (2004) and 71st (2014) Rounds is provided next. Lastly, a set of statistics compiled from the NFHS, Round 4 (2014–15) is reported.

Each one of us has, sometime during their lifetime, had some good and some bad experiences while accessing healthcare. As the concluding part of the report, we present a Blogspeak, that serves a smorgasbord of unstructured qualitative interviews of different stakeholders in the health sector—patients, doctors, nurses, medical administration, medical representatives—a wide array of opinions held by various individuals connected with the health sector.

REFERENCES

'*National Health Policy 2015* Draft', published by Ministry of Health & Family Welfare December, 2014

Press Information Bureau, Government of India, Vice President's Secretariat, 'Health Coverage Schemes Must Provide Widest Coverage: Vice President—Efforts Are Needed to Arrest the Growing Incidence of Non Communicable Diseases; Launches Atal Amrit Abhiyan'. Retrieved from http://pib.nic.in/newsite/PrintRelease.aspx?relid=178758; 2 May 2019.

Simon, Dan. 2013. 'Poverty Fact Sheet: Poor and in Poor Health', Institute for Research on Poverty, University of Wisconsin, Madison.

---

[8] Background paper, Sattwik Santra, Jyotsna Jalan, and Sandip Sarkar, 'Health Status in India' (2018). Mimeo CTRPFP.

1

Social Health Insurance Schemes

Arjun S. Bedi, Arpita Chakraborty, Sisir Debnath, Tarun Jain, Anagaw Derseh Mebratie,
Pradeep Panda, E. van de Poel, Wameq Raza, Frans Rutten, Zemzem Shigute, Robert
Sparrow, Revathy Suryanarayana, and Getnet Alemu Zewdu

A STUDY OF THREE SCHEMES IN INDIA

Health catastrophes can impoverish all households—rich or poor—or make them vulnerable to poverty in the future. Under such circumstances, most people want to insure themselves against health risks. Insurance, especially voluntary insurance, attracts the twin problems of adverse selection and inability to pay insurance premiums among poor or low-income households.

Social health insurance schemes (SHIs) are a form of financing and management of healthcare that pool low- and high-risk people. Such schemes require 'responsibility for paying contributions with proper organizational arrangement to collect the regular income-related contributions from individuals and to allocate these funds [that is, the payment of contributions for healthcare according to economic means (non-risk related payments) and the choice of healthcare according to the need], and rendering social assistance to cover vulnerable populations' (WHO 2003).

In India, initially SHIs were available only to government bureaucrats (Central Government Health Scheme [CGHS]) and certain segments of the organized sector (Employee's State Insurance Scheme). A public sector insurance company together with its four subsidiaries offered voluntary health insurance schemes that covered in-hospitalization cases. Yet, a large part of the population does not have any insurance cover, and out-of-pocket (OOP) expenses on health continue to be one of the highest in the world. Most SHIs in India provide financial risk cover for in-hospitalization hospital care. This is also true for the several new initiatives undertaken by different state governments in individual states. Another aspect of the newer state-level SHI initiatives is the concern about inadequate resources for long-term financial viability and sustainability. These schemes, targeted towards the poorer sections of society, have no co-payments or deductibles.

However, empirical data suggest that in-hospitalization costs constitute only a proportion of other costs such as transportation, and so on. Furthermore, outpatient costs are also substantial, and can lead to significant vulnerability to financial risk, especially among the poorer segments of society. There is a therefore an urgent need to devise SHIs that cover such risks.

Over the last decade and a half, through several national-level as well as state-level initiatives, SHIs are now offered to the poor and needy segments of the population. Examples of some of these initiatives include *Janaraksha* (2002–3) and several community-based health insurance schemes (CBHI) like those of the Self Employed Women's Association (SEWA) in Gujarat, and Action for Community Organization, Rehabilitation and Development (ACCORD) in Tamil Nadu, among others. Community-based health insurance schemes are non-profit initiatives built upon the principles of social solidarity, and designed to provide financial protection against the impoverishing effects of health expenditure for low-income households in the informal urban sector and in rural areas. A community is defined in terms of the target population which a particular scheme is trying to reach, and the community is involved in some or all aspects of the scheme.

In this chapter, we analyse some health insurance schemes that offer financial protection for people facing health shocks—the SHI, *Swasthya Sathi*, a scheme offered to contractual or part-time employees of the Government of West Bengal and the *Aarogyasri* scheme offered to BPL households in Andhra Pradesh (AP). The insured party does not pay any premium to receive the benefits under both these schemes. We also review CBHIs, and specifically look at two new CBHI initiatives in Bihar and Uttar Pradesh. Under these schemes, poorer households can or must enrol through some formal mechanism at a rate much below the actuarial cost of the package or even free of charge, and in return, receive a defined package of healthcare benefits.

To assess such schemes, we need to ask whether such schemes:

(1) have led to increased enrolment that ensures greater use of healthcare services for treatment,
(2) have encouraged preventive care measures,
(3) have provided financial cover against health shocks, reducing OOP expenses,
(4) have led to an improvement in health, and
(5) in the long-run, with increase of population coverage, are financially sustainable?

The analysis presented in this chapter assesses whether the aforementioned public insurance schemes have reduced vulnerabilities to health shocks, especially for the poor. With the available data sets and analysis, we have provided some adequate insights on points (c) and (e) as stated above while we fully recognize the necessity for future research to address the concerns raised in points (a), (b), and (d).

SWASTHYA SATHI YOJANA[1]

Public health insurance schemes implemented by the Central Government or the different state governments cover several sections of the population. The CGHS provides comprehensive medical care to Central Government employees (legislature, judiciary, executive) and pensioners. Similarly, different schemes implemented by various state governments provide comprehensive health insurance to state government employees. For example, the West Bengal Health Scheme (WBHS) provides cashless medical facilities to employees, officers, and pensioners of the state government (not excepting family pensioners), All India Service (AIS) officers and their family members across empanelled hospitals in West Bengal. Other state governments like AP (*Aarogyasri* Community Health Insurance Scheme), Gujarat (Mukhyamantri Amrutum [MA] Yojana), and Tamil Nadu (Chief Minister's Comprehensive Health Insurance Scheme), among others, have implemented comparable schemes for BPL households. Similarly, the Employees State Insurance Scheme (ESIS) aims to cover individuals employed in non-seasonal factories with 10 or more employees. The scheme covers hotels, shops, cinemas and preview theatres, restaurants, newspaper establishments, road–motor transport undertakings, and private educational and medical institutions that employ 10 or more people. Likewise, the Rashtriya Swasthya Bima Yojana (RSBY) merged with the Ayushman Bharat Scheme provides health insurance coverage to individuals/ families belonging to the BPL category. Currently, this scheme also provides health insurance cover to workers belonging to unorganized categories such as construction and building workers who are registered under welfare

[1] This section is based on information obtained from the official website of the *Swasthya Sathi* Scheme. https://swasthyasathi.gov.in.

boards, street vendors, licensed porters (railway), beedi workers, Mahatma Gandhi National Rural Employment Guarantee Act (MNREGA) workers, sanitation workers, domestic workers, mine workers, rag pickers, rickshaw pullers, and taxi/auto drivers.

Yet a section of state government employees cannot avail of any health insurance cover under any of the schemes mentioned above. These are contractual government workers, civic volunteers, and self-help group (SHG) members. The *Swasthya Sathi* group health scheme announced by the Government of West Bengal on 30 December 2016 is an attempt to cover the population hitherto 'left out' from existing SHIs. The Department of Health and Family Welfare in consultation with the Finance Department of the Government of West Bengal implements the scheme. The scheme covers all twenty-three districts of the state.

The target population of the *Swasthya Sathi* Scheme are the diverse low-earning workers and volunteers associated with various schemes, projects, or programmes administered by various departments of the state government, identified and approved by the Finance Department from time to time. As of now, the scheme covers secondary and tertiary

medical care expenses of almost 45.84 lakh families, accounting for nearly 2.5 crore people in the state spread across 19 departments. Over time, the scheme's objective is to provide healthcare coverage for larger sections of society in the state with an aim to provide health protection for every resident. Table 1.1 gives details of the categories along with the respective administrative departments. Box 1.1 lists the main features of the scheme.

The focal point of the *Swasthya Sathi* Scheme is to provide health cover for secondary and tertiary care. There are more than 1,900 *Swasthya Sathi* packages in insurance and assurance modes for different medical conditions. The scheme provides a cover of up to INR 1,50,000 under the insurance mode for standard illnesses. For critical illnesses like cancer, neurological surgeries, cardiothoracic surgeries, liver diseases, and blood disorders, among others, the scheme provides a cover of up to INR 5,00,000 per annum per family under the assurance mode. The premium payable under the two modes is borne by the state government. Initially, only those insurance companies that belonged to the public sector participated in the *Swasthya Sathi* Scheme, but in recent times, even private insurance companies have joined in.

TABLE 1.1 Categories of Beneficiaries Enrolled in *Swasthya Sathi*

Department	Category	Enrolment (%)
Civil Defence and National Voluntary Force (NVF) department	Civil defence volunteers, disaster management workers, NVF, home guards	0.54
Finance	Contractual/casual workers in government departments covered under Finance Department	0.04
Health & Family Welfare	ASHA (accredited social health activist) workers, Rogi Sahayaks, auxiliary nurse midwife of the National Health Mission, other contractual staff of the National Rural Health Mission and National Urban Health Mission including ASHA supervisors and Rashtriya Bal Swasthya Karyakram doctors, contractual staff of the RSBY and *Swasthya Sathi*, contractual staff of the West Bengal Health & Family Welfare Society, contractual homeopathic, AYUSH, Unani doctors, and compounders at gram-panchayat level	1.14
Higher Education	Government approved contractual whole time teachers (CWTTs), government approved part-time teachers (PTTs), daily rated/casual non-teaching employees, non-teaching permanent staff of government-aided colleges and state-aided universities	0.079
Home Department	Civic Volunteers Force, Green Volunteers Force, village volunteers	1.87

Labour & Employment	Unorganized workers of any category as may be agreed	0.01
Municipal Affairs	SHGs in municipal areas, honorary health workers (HHW)/ASHA workers, contractual/casual workers in urban local bodies (ULBs) covered under the Finance Department	7.76
PWD	Computer operator	0.0037
Women & Child Department	Integrated Child Development Services (ICDS) workers, ICDS helpers	3.49
School Education	Para teachers, Siksha Bandhu, special educators, contractual staff of Sarba Siksha Mission including Circle Level Resource Centre, teachers and non-teaching employees of primary and secondary schools	0.66
Urban Development & Municipal Affairs	Elected representatives of municipalities, employees of development authorities not covered under the WBHS, employees of ULBs not covered under the WBHS, sanitary workers and workers engaged under the West Bengal Urban Employment Scheme in ULBs	0.129
Industry, Commerce, and Enterprise	Contractual staff of Stationery Office	0.0002
Panchayat & Rural Development	Elected panchayat functionaries, contractual/casual workers in panchayati raj institutions (PRIs) covered under Finance Department, members of SHGs, contractual staff of MNREGA, contractual staff of the West Bengal State Rural Livelihood Mission (WBSRLM), contractual staff of Mission Nirmal Bangla, contractual staff of the Pradhan Mantri Abash Yojna (PMAY), contractual staff of health cell, contractual staff of Paschim Banga Shishu Siksha Mission (PBSSM) (Shishu Siksha Kendra (SSK)/Madhyamik Siksha Kendra (MSK)), contractual staff of the Pradhan Mantri Gram Sarak Yojana (PMGSY), contractual staff of the West Bengal Comprehensive Area Development Corporation (WBCADC), contractual staff of the Society for Training & Research on Panchayats and Rural Development (STARPARD), contractual staff of the Strengthening Rural Decentralization (SRD) Cell, contractual staff of computerization cell, contractual staff of e-governance cell, contractual staff of the Institutional Strengthening of Gram Panchayats Project (ISGPP), contractual staff of the Backward Regions Grant Fund (Erstwhile BRGF), Samprasarak/ Samprasarika of SSKs, Samprasarak/ Samprasarika of MSKs, contractual homeopathic doctors/compounders at gram-panchayat level	84.07
Minority Affairs & Madrasah Education	Samprasarak/Samprasarika of Madrasah Siksha Kendras, SSKs, and MSKs, teachers and non-teaching employees of recognized aided Madrasahs	0.023
Animal Husbandry	Pranibandhu	0.015
Fire & Emergency Services	Fire and auxiliary workers	0.014
Self Help Group & Self Employment	Prakalpa sahayaks and supervisors	0.105
PAR and e-Governance	Contractual staff of the West Bengal Information Commission	0.00006
Law	Contractual staff of Systemized Administration & Regulation of Tendering and Handling All Court Cases (SARTHAC)	0.00006

Source: Data compiled from *Swasthya Sathi* Reports May and June 2017.

Beneficiaries can avail of the services through paperless and cashless transactions using a smart card that contains digitally encrypted information. Beneficiaries receive their smart cards at the time of enrolment. This makes the entire process transparent and accelerates programme uptake by beneficiaries.

Both private as well as government hospitals can apply to provide health services under the *Swasthya Sathi* scheme. Empanelled hospitals are grouped into three categories—Grade A, Grade B, and Grade C—based on parameters like healthcare infrastructure, services, facilities, and so on. An expert committee recommends the gradation of empanelled healthcare providers. A beneficiary under *Swasthya Sathi* can get cashless treatment in any of the empanelled hospitals under the scheme. Empanelled hospitals have to display the *Swasthya Sathi* logo in their facilities.

Prior to the rolling out of the scheme, information education communication (IEC) and behavioural change communication (BCC) campaigns were conducted in all the districts of West Bengal to make people aware of the entitlements under the scheme, and to reach out to potential beneficiaries. These were in the form of tableaus, hoardings, folk programmes, advertisements in the local print and audio media, jingles on frequency modulation (FM) channels, flex banners, and house-to-house distribution of leaflets and hospital booklets.

Furthermore, insurance companies, third party administrators (TPA), or healthcare providers conduct health camps in different districts of West Bengal with proper approval of district authorities. The insurance companies along with the state nodal agency jointly design and develop training, workshops, and orientation

---

BOX 1.1   Features of the *Swasthya Sathi* Scheme

Pre-existing diseases: All pre-existing diseases and conditions are covered in the scheme, eliminating preset conditions.

Family size: There is no cap on family size, and parents of both the spouses are covered under this scheme. Cards are issued preferably in the name of the eldest woman family member as head of the family. This goes a long way in women's empowerment.

Beneficiary contribution: No contribution is made towards the insurance premium or card cost on the part of the beneficiary as the entire premium including the cost of smart cards is borne by the Government of West Bengal. The government pays INR 590 per annum per family as the premium to insurance companies.

IT platform: The entire system of the scheme is paperless, and based on a hassle-free cloud-based information technology (IT) platform. Online monitoring of the scheme saves valuable time and resources, apart from ensuring speedy delivery of the services.

Pre-authorization of the treatment: All the medical procedures/treatments of *Swasthya Sathi* beneficiaries are 100 per cent pre-authorized within a 24-hour turnaround time (TAT).

Hospital gradation: The hospitals are graded based on marks obtained on the facilities and services available, physically verified by the insurance company/third party administrator (IC/TPA). The Empanelment Committee approves the grade and empanels hospitals under *Swasthya Sathi*.

Hospitalization: Beneficiaries receive expenses incurred for consultation, diagnostic tests, and medicines up to one day before the admission of the patient, cost of diagnostic tests but not of food during hospitalization, and medicine up to five days after discharge from the hospital for the same ailment/surgery.

SMS alerts: SMS triggers are sent to the beneficiaries during hospitalization and after discharge from the hospital.

Swasthya Sathi *mobile app*: This app is freely downloadable from the Google play store, and information is available regarding enrolment, empanelled hospitals with address, phone numbers, doctor's availability, facilities provided, and so on. Beneficiary details are available at the fingertips, and queries can be raised for information, grievances, and so on. This also includes a one-touch feature that directly connects to the 24x7 help line.

Outreach: The number for the 24x7 toll free call centre (18003455384) for assistance is available on the back of the smart cards. The beneficiaries can also reach out through social media platforms such as Facebook, Twitter, and WhatsApp or can even mail the Nodal Agency. Details are available on the *Swasthya Sathi* web portal. Individuals can lodge grievances through the *Swasthya Sathi* mobile app that can be freely downloaded from the Google play store.

Transport allowance: The package includes the cost of transportation (charges of INR 200) payable to the patient at the time of discharge. Claims data are sent by the hospital to the IC/TPA electronically.

Empanelled hospitals: Beneficiaries can opt for services under the *Swasthya Sathi* scheme in more than 900 empanelled public and private hospitals spread across the state.

Claims settlement: Claims of the healthcare providers are monitored and settled online within 30 days or else interest would have to be paid by the insurance company as per the agreement. This is essential to encourage the healthcare providers.

E-HR (E-Health Record): The e-health records of the patient are stored in the cloud, which eases the process of maintaining medical records, and can be shared across different hospitals as and when required by the physicians concerned. The E-HR system stores data accurately, and captures the state of a patient over time. The huge database of medical records can provide various health determinants to conduct population-based studies that may further support the government in making future policy decisions. Moreover, with real time monitoring, disease outbreaks can be identified promptly that can lead to prevention of major epidemics.

Care of senior citizens vis–à–vis change in family definition: The scheme's objective is to reduce the OOP expenditure of the low-income-group population, which includes women after their marriage who are not able to care for their parents who are too poor to look after themselves. The *Swasthya Sathi* scheme has tried to address this issue by extending the scheme to enroll both parents and in-laws. Further, the smart card is issued with the photograph of the eldest woman member as part of the women's empowerment drive.

programmes for the different stakeholders as a part of capacity-building interventions.

Since the launch of *Swasthya Sathi*, around 2,30,079 people have benefitted from the scheme, resulting in claims totalling to INR 218.57 crore.

Status of the Scheme

1. *Healthcare providers*: Healthcare providers, both government and private, have enthusiastically participated in this scheme. Currently, in about 900 hospitals, cardholders can avail benefits under the *Swasthya Sathi* scheme. Based on their existing infrastructure, health facilities, services, and so on, the empanelled facilities are grouped as Grade A, B, or C facilities. Empanelment is a continual process, whereby facilities may be upgraded or downgraded as and when necessary.

At the start of the programme in May 2017, government healthcare providers accounted for a larger percentage of the total empanelled healthcare providers. However, within a year, this trend showed a complete reversal. By May 2018, the number of private healthcare providers exceeded the public healthcare providers. The remarkable increases in empanelled private healthcare providers ultimately led

to an increase in their share by 10.82 per cent, while the share of government healthcare providers declined by the same percentage (Figure 1.1). This is because most of the government hospitals were empanelled earlier itself owing to an administrative decree while private hospitals continue to apply for empanelment even today. Nevertheless, the number of empanelled hospitals increased in both the government and private sectors by 11.22 per cent and 71.92 per cent, respectively.

If we look at the distribution of hospitals across Grades A, B, and C in both the public and the

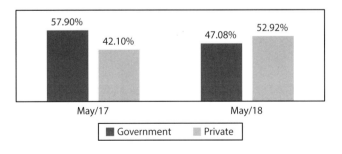

FIGURE 1.1 Distribution of Hospitals between Public and Private Sector

Source: *Swasthya Sathi* Monthly Reports, May 2017 and 2018.

private sector, Grade C facilities account for the largest percentage of empanelled facilities. However, between May 2017 and May 2018, we observe a slight shift away from Grade C facilities towards Grade B facilities. There is an increase in the share of Grade B hospitals among the government healthcare providers by 4.16 percentage points, and by 7.84 percentage points among private healthcare providers. The share of Grade C providers decreased by 3.82 percentage points in the government sector, and by 8.47 percentage points in the private sector. However, in both the government and private sectors, empanelment of Grade A hospitals—with the 'best' infrastructure, facilities, and services—continues to be low suggesting that these hospitals are reluctant to provide services to cardholders at government-prescribed package prices (Figure 1.2).

The criteria on the basis of which public and private hospitals are empanelled as Grade B facilities vary between the two sectors. A private health facility can get Grade B recognition only if it scores 80 per cent or more as per the selection criteria mentioned in the *Swasthya Sathi* agreement. However, all district, general, special, and sub-divisional hospitals that have a critical care unit, a unit for unwell newborns, and modern diagnostics get recognition as Grade B

facilities. If empanelled hospitals fail to get either a Grade A or Grade B tag, they are designated as Grade C facilities.

Higher graded hospitals have the infrastructure to treat diseases that offer higher package rates. This provides an incentive to health facilities in lower grades to improve their infrastructure so that they can also block higher package rates. For instance, one criterion through which hospitals can augment their score is by increasing their bed strength. This has resulted in approximately 71 new beds being added in private hospitals since the launch of the scheme in May 2018. There have also been 23 upgrades in various other facilities. Such steps could possibly be some reasons why we observe a shift towards Grade B hospitals, and a decrease in Grade C hospitals.

2. *Utilization of* Swasthya Sathi: A measure of the usefulness of the scheme is the extent of usage of health facilities by *Swasthya Sathi* cardholders. Figure 1.3 shows the number of hospitalizations per 1,000 cardholders. It is not surprising that urban centres like Kolkata and Paschim Burdwan have a relatively higher uptake of the scheme compared to other districts (Figure 1.3). Most of the beneficiaries have been one-time admits, although there are quite a few who have taken admission twice (12.77 per cent) as well.

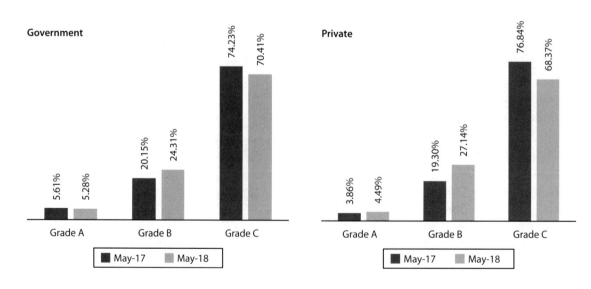

FIGURE 1.2   Composition of Healthcare Providers

Source: *Swasthya Sathi* Monthly Reports, May 2017 and 2018.

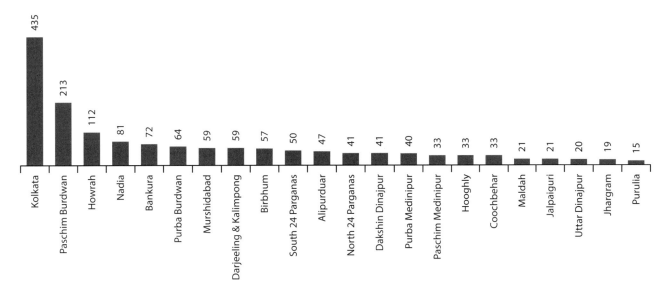

FIGURE 1.3 Hospitalizations per 1,000 Enrolled

Source: Swasthya Sathi Monthly Report, May 2018.

There are two possible reasons for higher hospitalizations in Kolkata. First, two of the top 10 hospitals (by number of cases) are located in Kolkata. Second, many patients migrate to Kolkata for treatment from the adjoining districts of North and South 24 Parganas with the hope of availing better healthcare facilities. The more urbanized district of Paschim Burdwan also displays high hospitalization rates. The number of migrants to Kolkata from Paschim Burdwan is very meagre. On the other end of the spectrum, in districts like Maldah, Jalpaiguri, Uttar Dinajpur, Jhargram, and Purulia, both utilization of the scheme (in terms of hospitalizations) and enrolment into the scheme are low. A possible reason for fewer hospitalizations in these poorer districts may be that many patients requiring more intensive care or specialized treatments are referred to bigger and more equipped hospitals in larger districts.

Kolkata and Paschim Burdwan also record higher mortality rates per 1,000 admissions compared to other districts. A possible reason could be that patients admitted in these facilities suffer from critical or severe diseases.

Districts such as Bankura, Birbhum, South 24 Parganas, and Murshidabad that have low hospitalization rates surprisingly account for a higher percentage of the total amount blocked (Figure 1.4 depicts the percentage of total amount blocked in each district). This is because hospitals in these districts have a larger share of total beneficiaries admitted for packages that cost above INR 30,000; the shares being 8.14 per cent, 12.41 per cent, 12.79 per cent, and 10.23 per cent, respectively.

General surgery, ophthalmology, obstetrics and gynaecology, urology and nephrology, and orthopaedics constitute the major departments utilized under the scheme (Figure 1.5). A large percentage of hospital treatments are used by the age groups 40–9 and 50–9 years. People in these categories account for 21.38 per cent and 30.99 per cent, respectively, of the total packages blocked for haemo-dialysis (repeated use of dialyser). For haemo-dialysis (single use of dialyser) the figures are 24.87 and 27.94 per cent, respectively.

Impact of the *Swasthya Sathi* Scheme

1. **Increase in SHG formation:** The state government has taken a policy decision to set up SHGs as a major poverty alleviation initiative, which is expected to eventually translate into robust economic growth that would be labour intensive and equitable, leading to

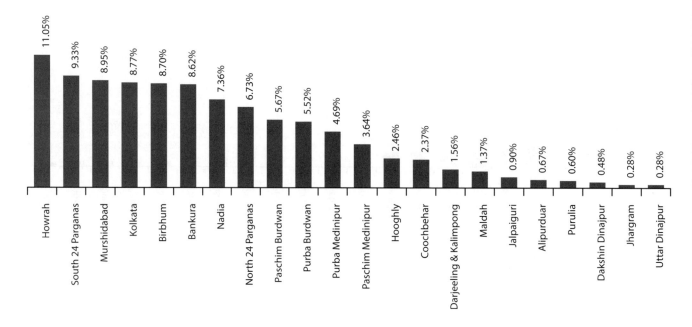

FIGURE 1.4 Percentage of Total Amount Blocked in Each District

Source: *Swasthya Sathi* Monthly Report, May 2018.

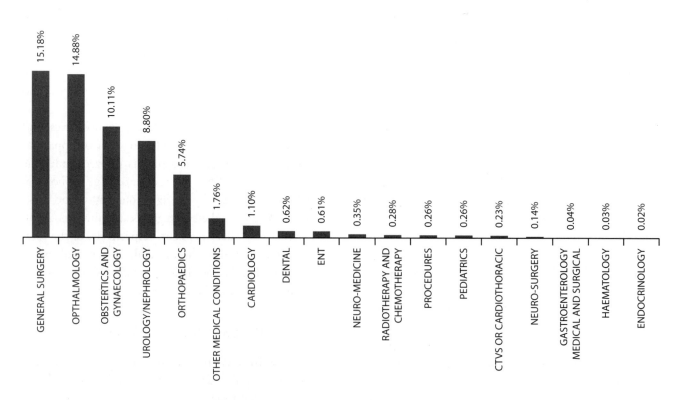

FIGURE 1.5 Departments Most Utilized under *Swasthya Sathi* (as per cent of total admissions)

Source: *Swasthya Sathi* Monthly Report, May 2018.

the development of the social sector. The Government of West Bengal has started an initiative to support micro, small, and medium enterprises (MSME) called 'Muktidhara'. Muktidhara is targetted towards the overall development of SHGs in the state. The objective was to ensure steady earnings, alleviate poverty, and bring about financial improvement among the stakeholders. The introduction of the *Swasthya Sathi* Scheme has acted as a catalyst for new group formations in rural and municipal areas as it allows them to access the SHI as a group. Approximately 1.5 lakh new groups have been formed since the launch of the *Swasthya Sathi* Scheme in May 2018. With these groups registering under the Scheme, the government is in a position to bring under its purview a part of the informal sector and thus, engage in closer monitoring of the same. The rural sector continues to add a substantially larger share of SHGs even today.

2. **Upgrading infrastructure of private hospitals:** Empanelment under the scheme requires healthcare providers to meet certain basic requirements as specified in the *Swasthya Sathi* agreement. For instance, every empanelled private hospital must have a bed strength of at least 30 (changed to 10 in August 2018), provision of safe drinking water, kitchen facility for patients, intensive care unit (ICU), and other such facilities. This provides an incentive for many hospitals to upgrade their infrastructure so that they are eligible to enrol. The need to be associated with the scheme, especially among private health facilities, is mainly political in nature. However, the increase in infrastructure spending cannot entirely negate the gains from services demand that empanelment brings along with it.

3. **Transparency:** As uploading of electronic health records is mandatory for *Swasthya Sathi*, all hospitals, including government hospitals, have been uploading them for all admitted patients, without a single exception till date. The scheme has been entirely on an IT platform from the start, which makes it possible for the managers to monitor the same. Monthly reports are updated on the *Swasthya Sathi* website. These are also shared with the hospitals empanelled under the scheme. Providers are required to make claims electronically by swiping the smart card presented by the beneficiaries at the time of registration, admission, and discharge. They are discouraged from making claims manually. All these steps help reduce, if not completely eliminate, fraud and/or misuse on part of the respective stakeholders.

4. **Distribution of patient load:** A large number of patients use their *Swasthya Sathi* smart card facility to avail services like dialysis from private hospitals. Government hospitals in West Bengal accommodate more than 80 per cent of the total patient load. The same is true for some complicated diagnostic services like computerized axial tomography (CAT) scans, magnetic resonance imaging (MRI), and so on, where the poor have to wait for long periods for their turn. Now, all *Swasthya Sathi* cardholders have the option to move to private hospitals. This widens the choice set available to beneficiaries who many a times are under the belief that services provided by private entities are of a higher quality; at other times, capacity constraints of public hospitals act as a natural push factor towards availing private healthcare. Such push factors coupled with pull factors like the public's general perception about private hospitals, and the infrastructural gap between public and private hospitals, work toward shifting the demand from public to private hospitals. Hence, the adoption of a public–private partnership (PPP) model has proved to be beneficial for the healthcare system in the state. Furthermore, some *Swasthya Sathi* patients using the private sector for treatment reduces to an extent the pressure on the public healthcare system. In the long run, this mitigation of pressure may facilitate the revival of the public healthcare system that seems to be crumbling under the patient load.

Policy Recommendations

1. **Monitoring of empanelled hospitals**: Monitoring is required at regular intervals to ensure that all guidelines mentioned in the agreement are followed, particularly with respect to prominent display of the affiliation of the hospital to the scheme. This will help avoid the malpractice of turning patients away under the pretense that the hospital is not a *Swasthya Sathi* empanelled facility. Though a comprehensive list of empanelled hospitals is available on the *Swasthya Sathi* website, there are two reasons why problems may continue. First, most of the beneficiaries may

not be well equipped or computer literate so as to access the details on the website. Second, the harsh and unwelcoming attitude of hospital workers at the very onset will push seekers away. Moreover, time and financial constraints faced by potential beneficiaries will not allow them to take up this issue formally with a complaints committee.

2. **Further strengthening of the scheme:** There is a pressing need to increase awareness about the scheme not only among potential beneficiaries, but also among personnel in a registered or empanelled hospital under it. Many officers at different levels of command are unaware of the fact that their hospital is associated with the *Swasthya Sathi* Scheme. If any progress is to be made in increasing the popularity and effectiveness of the scheme, all stakeholders must first be clearly informed about their roles, and hence about the fact that they are enlisted under the scheme.

3. **Conduct surprise checks:** Frequent surprise checks on facilities to keep a tab on the quality of services provided to smart cardholders are imperative. In this regard, performance of registered doctors for the project can be sent to the medical council for evaluation. What is important is that the scheme focuses on increasing not only the quantity but also the quality of services. Hence, the scheme must be evaluated on a quality–quantity–price paradigm instead of a simple quantity–price framework.

4. **Ensuring non-transference of monetary burden:** Rules must be established to prevent transfer of monetary burden in the form of increased costs to non-beneficiaries in order to recoup losses arising under the scheme. Checks also need to be carried out to ensure that beneficiaries themselves are not coerced to expend money from their pockets for non-generic medicines or fees for doctors.

5. **Co-payment:** To guarantee continuity of the scheme in the future, it is necessary to devise alternative pricing policies. One such measure can be to divide the burden of the services between the government and the beneficiary in a pre-determined ratio with the majority of the burden falling on the former.

6. **Inclusion of outpatient treatment:** Implementing the above recommendation may also free resources that in turn can be used to include under the scheme, provision of preventive care treatments.

THE *AAROGYASRI* HEALTH INSURANCE SCHEME[2]

Tertiary care plays several crucial roles in a healthcare system. It supports the referral cases from primary[3] and secondary[4] care facilities that require specialized intensive care supported by advanced diagnostic services. Medical research and teaching also take place within the tertiary care setting. Among the three tiers of the healthcare system, tertiary care is the most resource intensive consisting of large hospitals, technology-intensive medical investigations, and specialized medical practitioners. In India, public healthcare has primarily focused on providing primary, preventive, maternal and child, and family-planning healthcare facilities. Publicly provided tertiary care at sub-district, district, and medical-college levels are inadequately funded, poorly monitored, and lack standardization. Due to the dearth of direct public investments in tertiary care, the government extended active support in the form of subsidized land and tax breaks to the private sector as an incentive to invest in tertiary healthcare. The result is a proliferation of private tertiary care in urban and semi-urban India.

In tandem with the burgeoning private tertiary medical care facilities, the demand for tertiary care has grown over time. Decades of policy with a focus on communicable diseases[5] such as malaria, tuberculosis,

[2] This section is based on the background paper by Sisir Debnath, Tarun Jain, and Revathy Suryanarayana, 'The *Aarogyasri* Health Insurance Program' (2018). Mimeo CTRPFP.

[3] Primary healthcare refers to the first line of health intervention provided by health professionals to the patients opting for such services. General practitioners or family physicians, dentists, physiotherapists, or non-physician primary care providers such as physician's assistants or nurse practitioners, community nurses, pharmacists, and midwives, among others usually provide such services.

[4] Secondary care provides necessary treatment for a short period for a brief but serious illness, injury, or other health condition. Often such care is provided in a hospital emergency department, and includes skilled attendance during childbirth, intensive care, and medical imaging services.

[5] Communicable diseases are ailments caused by infectious agents that can be transmitted to susceptible individuals from an infected person, or from animals, objects, or the environment. Infectious agents include helminths, protozoa, fungi, bacteria, and viruses.

diarrhoea, and other infectious diseases have led to a sharp reduction in their incidence. The number of deaths from communicable diseases has decreased from 2.6 million in 2000 to 1.9 million in 2012. Meanwhile, non-communicable tertiary diseases have increased disproportionately in India. In 2016, 61.8 per cent of all deaths were due to non-communicable diseases compared to 37.9 per cent in 1990 (Gething and Hay 2017).

The treatment of tertiary diseases such as cancer, and cardiovascular and respiratory conditions is expensive, and can increase poverty. Out-of-Pocket payments, which are the most inefficient way of financing healthcare, are the primary source of healthcare financing in India (Ghosh 2011; Nagulapalli 2014). In 2015, 62.4 per cent of the total health expenditure was financed by OOP payments by individuals (World Health Organization Global Health Expenditure database 2015). Out-of-Pocket expenditures are deemed 'catastrophic' when they reduce household expenditure on other necessary items. The proportion of households incurring catastrophic health expenditure is a commonly used indicator for measuring the efficiency of a healthcare system. The primary goal of healthcare systems is to offer protection from catastrophic health expenditures. Increasing health insurance coverage is a potential tool for the purpose.

Insurance against catastrophic health expenditures may increase the ability of economically weaker households to withstand the incidence of adverse health shocks. It directly affects the financial access of the poor to treatment, recovery, and restoration of productivity when they fall sick. Uninsured households are more vulnerable to financial shocks, and more likely to slip into poverty when forced to incur OOP expenses for healthcare.

The Insurance Regulatory and Development Authority (IRDA) legislation in 2000 was a milestone that opened the healthcare insurance market to private players. Since then, private health insurers have expanded rapidly in cities with product innovations such as 'inpatient reimbursements' and 'cashless payments' in financial healthcare insurance plans. Most health insurance products offered by private entities are indemnity-based and similar to the government-defined product, Mediclaim. Given high premiums, it is not surprising that holders of these policies often hail from the upper middle class.

There are several reasons as to why the private market fails to provide adequate health insurance coverage. One reason is that only the chronically unhealthy try to enrol, so the premiums quickly spiral beyond affordability. Another reason might be that poor households are not fully aware of the benefits of health insurance. Finally, given the poor past performance of private firms in processing and paying claims, households may not trust insurance providers to reimburse them. Indeed, commenting on the participation of the poor in financial inclusion schemes, N.C. Saxena, a member of the erstwhile National Advisory Council, said 'Typically, people in that strata of society are circumspect about any scheme which needs them to put in money—simply because they do not trust that they will get this money back' (Nair 2016).

Only about 20 per cent of India's population is covered under health insurance schemes (NSS 71st Round and NFHS 2014–15). Moreover, most insurance schemes cover government employees. The introduction of the Universal Health Insurance Scheme (UHIS) in 2003 was one of the first attempts to provide affordable health insurance to economically weaker sections. The scheme guaranteed coverage of annual healthcare expenditures up to INR 30,000. Eligibility was restricted to BPL households, and premiums varied by family size falling between INR 165 and 330. Despite being implemented by the four subsidiaries of the General Insurance Corporation of India (Choudhury and Srinivasan 2011), the scheme failed to appeal to the rural poor. Subsequently, the RSBY was launched in 2008 to provide insurance coverage to BPL households. Over time, eligibility has been extended to unorganized sector workers. The insurance premium is publicly financed while the beneficiaries pay an annual registration fee of INR 30. The insurance covers annual hospitalization bills up to INR 30,000 on family floater[6] basis for a comprehensive list of diseases. Exclusion on the basis of pre-existing conditions or age is prohibited under the scheme. Other novel features

---

[6] A family floater health insurance plan is tailor-made for families. It is similar to individual health plans, but covers the entire family.

of the programme include empanelment of private hospitals, use of portable biometric enabled smart cards for beneficiaries, and cash and paperless transactions. Around the same time, a few other states introduced health insurance programmes covering tertiary care. The *Rajiv Aarogyasri*, *Vajpayee Aarogyasri*, and *Kalaignar* Insurance Schemes introduced in the states of AP, Karnataka, and Tamil Nadu, respectively, have been the most ambitious among them. As a consequence, health insurance coverage in India increased from 75 million in 2007 to 302 million in 2010 (Reddy et al. 2011).

The empirical evidence on the coverage and effectiveness of the RSBY as regards OOP expenditure, is not encouraging. Only 12.7 per cent of households in the poorest quintiles are covered under the programme whereas 36.52 per cent of the households enrolled in the programme are from the richest 40 per cent of sampled households across 18 states of India (Ghosh and Gupta 2017). Rathi, Mukherji, and Sen (2012) find that utilization of the RSBY is between 11 and 55 per cent in the district of Amravati in Maharashtra, while according to Rajasekhar et al. (2011), it is 'virtually zero' in the state of Karnataka. Recent studies have confirmed that the introduction of the RSBY did not lead to a significant decrease in OOP expenditures. On the contrary, Selvaraj and Karan (2012) utilize the phased roll out of central- or state-sponsored health insurance programmes to find that households in the poorer sections with access to public health insurance (in districts with intervention) experienced a rise in real per capita healthcare expenditure, particularly on hospitalization. The programme suffers from mismanagement, low enrolment, and inadequate insurance cover for several medical procedures and out-patient costs. At the same time, public health facilities implementing the programme routinely suffer from non-availability of medicines and diagnostic facilities, and absenteeism of doctors.

In this section, we discuss *Aarogyasri*, the flagship health insurance programme of the states of AP and Telangana, and analyse the factors that affect utilization. *Aarogyasri* has the widest coverage among all state-sponsored health insurance programmes. Existing literature has suggested factors such as social connections in driving utilization of public health insurance programmes in India (Debnath and Jain 2017). Using a large database comprising the universe of the claims filed under the health insurance programme and village-level data from the Census, we are able to establish correlations between village characteristics and utilization of tertiary healthcare. We perform this exercise by the gender and age of patients, and find substantial heterogeneity in the factors behind utilization. Understanding the drivers of utilization could help optimize the locations for healthcare camps to screen patients for non-communicable diseases, leading to further improvements in the utilization of *Aarogyasri* and other similar programmes.

A Discussion on the *Aarogyasri Health Insurance Programme* in Andhra Pradesh

The Government of AP introduced *Aarogyasri* in April 2007 as a cashless health insurance scheme for BPL households. The scheme provided medical assistance to BPL families for the treatment of serious ailments requiring hospitalization and surgery or therapy, such as cancer, kidney failure, heart and neurological diseases, and so on. Under the scheme, BPL households in AP were eligible and covered for medical expenditures up to INR 2,00,000 towards 938 listed treatments. The fraction of households in AP which are classified as BPL is more than 90 per cent, which makes eligibility for the scheme nearly universal. Of the total coverage, 75 per cent is on family floater basis, and the remaining coverage of INR 50,000 is available on the basis of the recommendations of a technical committee. The insurance does not have any deductible or co-payment. All transactions are cashless, where a beneficiary can go to any empanelled hospital and receive care without paying for the procedures covered under the scheme. As of May 2014, 663 public and private hospitals were empanelled under *Aarogyasri* in AP. The *Aarogyasri* Trust pays healthcare providers on a case-by-case basis at a predefined rate. Hospitals must conduct free health camps for patients. Ambulances and help desks facilitate patient access at all primary health centres (PHCs), area/district hospitals, and network hospitals.

A notable feature of the *Aarogyasri* scheme is high adoption among the target population, compared both with public and privately financed health insurance. Figure 1.6 shows the geographical spread of *Aarogyasri* claims across AP between 2007 and 2015.

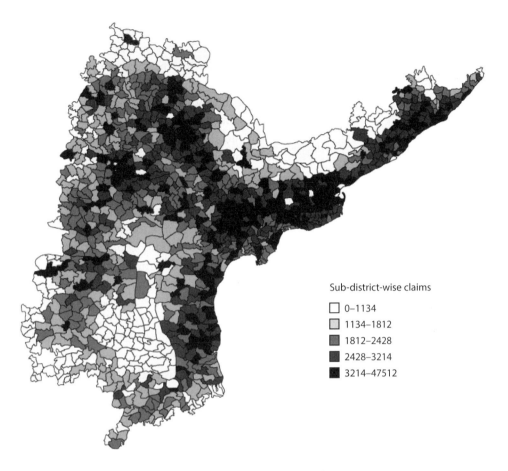

FIGURE 1.6 Sub-district-wise Claims under *Aarogyasri*

Note: This map is not to scale and does not represent authentic national boundaries. Since Telangana was separated from AP towards the end of the study period, for comparison with earlier years, the figure depicts the map of undivided AP.
Source: *Aarogyasri* claims data 2007–15.

Not surprisingly, a large number of claims are from urban areas, and few from the sparsely populated districts of Rayalseema and Telangana. Figures 1.7 and 1.8 show the number of surgeries performed under *Aarogyasri* over time, and the corresponding claims paid out by the Trust (in million Rupees). As of December 2015, about 32 lakh procedures had been performed under the scheme with INR 8,104 crores claimed cumulatively by the beneficiaries.

Empirical Analysis

The objective of the empirical analysis is to uncover village-level factors that are correlated with greater *Aarogyasri* utilization. Though the analysis is not causal in nature, the correlations point to factors that could either

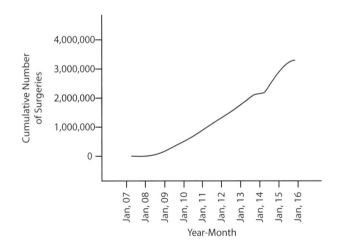

FIGURE 1.7 Cumulative Surgeries from 2007 to 2015

Source: *Aarogyasri* claims data 2007–15.

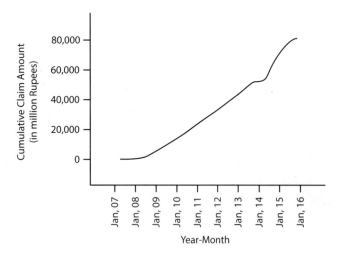

FIGURE 1.8   Cumulative Claim Amount from 2007 to 2015

Source: *Aarogyasri* claims data 2007–15.

promote or be binding constraints for the utilization of publicly financed healthcare.

Data Description

Data used in the analysis is obtained from two primary sources. Claims data from the *Aarogyasri* Trust is combined with village amenities data and the Primary Census Abstract (PCA) from the Census of India (2011) to produce the final data set.

First, we obtain all individual-level claims filed under *Aarogyasri* in the states of Telangana and AP between 2008 and 2015. We collapse these claims at the village level to get the number of claims from each village in those eight years. Village-level claims are further classified by age and gender, for example, claims filed by the elderly, women, and children.

Next, we use village amenities data from Census 2011 which consists of information on village-level facilities for education, health, sanitation, infrastructure, and transportation for villages in AP and Telangana. The binary variables, private tertiary facility and public tertiary facility indicate whether the village had a private (including private medical colleges) or public tertiary healthcare facility (including medical colleges and community health centres) within 10 kilometres. The binary variable 'primary health centre' is 1 if the village has a primary

healthcare centre or sub-centre within 10 kilometres. Meanwhile, the variable 'primary clinics' is an indicator variable for the presence of auxiliary medical facilities like maternity and child welfare centres, tuberculosis clinics, allopathic clinics, dispensaries, and mobile health clinics in the village. Village characteristics such as the presence of a major district road, ASHA worker,[7] SHGs, public and private bus service, and percentage of irrigated area (in hectares) are controls in our analysis (summary statistics are presented in Table 1.2).

Finally, drawing on the PCA (2011), we incorporate the total population (per thousands) of the village and literacy rate, and construct variables to represent the proportion of agricultural and industrial workers in the village.

The claims data are merged with the village amenities and PCA data using village names as identifiers.[8] The district of Hyderabad is excluded from our analysis because both the PCA as well as town amenities data do not cover many sub-districts of Hyderabad. Moreover, a large number of *Aarogyasri* hospitals are located in Hyderabad and a large number of patients migrate to the capital for treatment, which implies that patient characteristics may not match exactly with the city's characteristics. Note that claims from Hyderabad constitute about 6 per cent of the total claims in *Aarogyasri*. Our final data set consists of 23,361 villages from both states.

Specification

The aim of the empirical exercise is to understand the role of village-level characteristics in individual utilization

---

[7] Accredited social health activists are community health workers instituted by the Government of India's Ministry of Health and Family Welfare. Initiated in 2005 by the National Rural Health Mission, the programme aims to build a force of health educators and promoters by training local women from villages.

[8] Due to inconsistency between village names in both the data sets, observations with a string matching score (measure of similarity of village names from both the data sets) of less than 90 per cent were dropped from the data set. Thus, we drop 3,195 villages (out of 29,339) where village codes do not match between the village amenities data set and the PCA, and 2,783 villages where the village names from the claims data do not match entirely with the census village names.

TABLE 1.2 Summary Statistics

	Observations	Mean	Standard Deviation
Private tertiary facility	23,304	0.0187	0.135
Public tertiary facility	23,304	0.241	0.428
Primary health centre	23,304	0.964	0.185
Primary clinics	23,304	0.522	0.5
Road	23,304	0.293	0.455
ASHA worker	23,304	0.784	0.411
Bus service	23,304	0.747	0.435
Self-help groups	23,304	0.999	0.027
Percent area irrigated	23,304	25.31	24.67
Total population	23,304	2.36	2.768
Percent literacy rate	23,304	50.96	11.04
Percentage of agri. workers	23,304	22.79	14.09
Percentage of industrial workers	23,304	1.096	2.553

Source: Census 2011 Village Amenities Data, PCA Census 2011.

of *Aarogyasri*. To do so, we find the linear association between the number of claims filed under *Aarogyasri* and private and public tertiary facilities, PHCs, primary clinics, ASHA workers, SHGs, the amount of irrigated land, presence of bus services, district roads, total population, literacy rate, proportion of agricultural workers, and proportion of industrial workers.

The first set of variables that we include in the model are private tertiary facility and public tertiary facility that are the respective indicators of private and public tertiary health centres in a village. We hypothesize that the presence of these tertiary health centres is positively correlated with *Aarogyasri* claims as these institutions help provide information about the scheme to the patients along with acting as referral points for them.

Meanwhile, the variable primary health centre that includes PHCs and sub-centres constitutes the basis of public healthcare in India, providing preventive as well as curative primary health treatment to rural residents. Both these facilities also act as referral points for patients to community health centres and district hospitals. Facilities included in primary clinics might also serve as a screening point for patients for referral to tertiary facilities. The nature of these facilities is preventive rather than curative, and a majority of them do not have in-patient facilities unlike PHCs and sub-centres. Therefore, the relationship between subsidiary health centres and *Aarogyasri* utilization is uncertain.

The empirical model includes two variables that represent informal and formal social agents existing in

We employ the following specification to understand these factors:

$$
\begin{aligned}
y_{vsd} = \beta_0 &+ \beta_1 \, \textit{private tertiary facility}_{vsd} + \beta_2 \, \textit{public tertiary facility}_{vsd} + \beta_3 \, \textit{primary health centre}_{vsd} \\
&+ \beta_4 \, \textit{primary clinics}_{vsd} + \beta_5 \, \textit{asha worker}_{vsd} + \beta_6 \, \textit{irrigated land}_{vsd} + \beta_7 \, \textit{bus service}_{vsd} + \beta_8 \, \textit{self} - \textit{help groups}_{vsd} \\
&+ \beta_9 \, \textit{district road}_{vsd} + \beta_{10} \, \textit{total population}_{vsd} + \beta_{11} \, \textit{literacy rate}_{vsd} + \beta_{12} \, \textit{prop agricultural workers}_{vsd} \\
&+ \beta_{13} \, \textit{prop industrial workers}_{vsd} + \varepsilon_{vsd}
\end{aligned}
\tag{1}
$$

Here, y_{vsd} indicates the log of the total number of claims filed under *Aarogyasri* in district d, sub-district s, and village v over the entire duration of programme operations. The other independent variables are self-explanatory.

the village—SHGs and ASHA workers. Self-help groups are informal voluntary organizations of people who come together to solve their common problems, especially of a financial nature. Meanwhile, as mentioned previously, ASHA workers are health activists paid by the government to increase awareness on health issues and programmes in villages. Both SHGs and ASHA workers are potential sources of information dissemination in villages, and therefore, their presence can have a positive impact on the number of *Aarogyasri* claims (Debnath 2013). However, neither of them are explicitly incentivized to spread information about *Aarogyasri*. Thus, the role of SHGs and ASHA workers in *Aarogyasri* utilization is expected to be unclear.

Apart from these social and health characteristics of villages, analysing the association between income and health insurance utilization is important. *A priori*, the relationship between income and *Aarogyasri* utilization is not obvious. With higher levels of income, awareness about *Aarogyasri* could be greater. Moreover, with high income levels, auxiliary components of tertiary healthcare like post-surgery care, follow-up treatments, and medicines become more affordable. In contrast, if income is not sufficient to cover supplemental procedures, then we would not see a relationship between village income and the number of *Aarogyasri* claims. We test for this relationship by including total irrigated land in the village to proxy for village income.

To assess the relationship between education and utilization of *Aarogyasri*, the specification also includes the literacy level of the village, since awareness of the scheme as well as health consciousness might increase with education. Similarly, occupational structure of a village could influence the demand for *Aarogyasri*. Agricultural workers and farmers might view health insurance as an important component in reducing their business risk. Moreover, agricultural and industrial workers in industrializing countries are the most prone to health hazards from exposure to airborne particles and carcinogens, and to work-related injuries (WHO 2013); hence, regions with a higher proportion of industrial and agricultural workers may report higher demand for *Aarogyasri*.

Finally, we consider the specification controls for transport and physical communication infrastructure such as district roads and bus services. Transportation costs might be an important constraint for health service utilization

(Aggarwal 2018). Most villages in our sample do not have a tertiary healthcare centre within the village. However, non-availability of health services can be mitigated by transportation infrastructure like roads and public buses.

Results

We report the results of the empirical model (formalized in equation (1)) in Table 1.3.

This table reports that a number of village-level characteristics are associated with the demand for health insurance in the state. The goodness of fit (R-squared) values of the model are high for all specifications (59 per cent for the main specification including total claims) indicating that variation in the observed variables explains much of the variation in the outcome variables. We find that the presence of private tertiary health centres in the village significantly increases total *Aarogyasri* claims by 15 per cent, and presence of public healthcare centres increases total claims by 8.9 per cent. This significance is also noticeable in case of claims by the elderly, claims by women, and claims by children aged below 5 years. Meanwhile, PHCs also play a role in increasing demand for *Aarogyasri*. There is a positive association between the presence of a PHC or sub centre and the use of the health insurance scheme with the total claims increasing by 52 per cent ($p<0.01$). However, there is no association between primary health clinics and *Aarogyasri* utilization in villages with at least one subsidiary health clinic. The result indicates that primary healthcare clinics do not play a significant role in patient referrals and information dissemination.

The results also illustrate the key role played by ASHAs in promoting the scheme. We see that the presence of an ASHA worker in the village is positively associated with an increase in total claims by 43 per cent ($p<0.01$), claims by the elderly by 41 per cent, claims by women by 33 per cent, and claims by children aged 0–5 by 23 per cent. Even though ASHA workers are not explicitly paid for promoting *Aarogyasri*, the result suggests that they might be playing a significant role in advertising *Aarogyasri* in the village they operate from. Meanwhile, the presence of a SHG in the village is positively correlated with the total claims, albeit statistically weakly (+0.38, $p<0.10$), indicating the importance of these social organizations in spreading information about the scheme.

TABLE 1.3   Effect of Village Characteristics on Utilization under *Aarogyasri*

Dependent variable	Total claims	Claims by the elderly	Claims by women	Children 0–5
Private tertiary facility	0.15***	0.16***	0.094**	0.23***
Public tertiary facility	0.089***	0.085***	0.044***	0.047***
Primary health centre	0.52***	0.45***	0.38***	0.26***
Primary clinics	0.016	0.026*	0.049***	0.011
Road	0.090***	0.093***	0.081***	0.059***
ASHA worker	0.43***	0.41***	0.33***	0.23***
Bus service	0.46***	0.46***	0.37***	0.22***
Self-help groups	0.38*	0.35	0.20	0.17
Per cent area irrigated	0.0058***	0.0059***	0.0057***	0.0026***
Total population	0.25***	0.25***	0.23***	0.20***
Per cent literacy rate	0.015***	0.014***	0.016***	–0.0015***
Percentage of agri. workers	0.0024***	0.0023***	0.0012***	0.0016***
Percentage of industrial workers	0.019***	0.021***	0.013***	0.0037*
Constant	0.63***	–0.083	–0.57***	0.045
District fixed effects	Yes	Yes	Yes	Yes
No. of observations	23304	23304	23304	23304
R Squared	0.59	0.56	0.55	0.50

Note: ***Significant at 1 per cent; ** Significant at 5 per cent; *Significant at 10 per cent.

Source: Estimation results compiled by the authors using data from the *Aarogyasri* Trust and the Primary Census Abstract (PCA) from the Census of India (2011).

We observe a positive association between literacy rate and utilization of the scheme. The elasticity between the literacy rate and total claims is 0.015 suggesting that a 1 per cent increase in literacy rate increases total utilization of *Aarogyasri* by 1.5 per cent. However, we also see a negative correlation between literacy rate and the percentage of claims by children (–.0015, p<0.01). The result suggests that children of educated or wealthier parents may be healthier than the children of parents with comparatively lower levels of education. This is not surprising as previous literature has found that a high correlation between education and earnings results in improved access to nutrition and health products for children of more educated parents (Alderman and Headey 2017).

The results also indicate that total irrigated land is positively correlated with total claims suggesting that higher income is complementary to health insurance. At the same time, we find that a unit increase in the proportion of agricultural workers increases the total claims in a village by 0.24 per cent (p<0.01). The proportion of industrial workers and total claims is also

positively correlated, increasing utilization by 2 per cent (p<0.01) for every 1 per cent increase in the proportion of industrial workers. Therefore, *Aarogyasri* health insurance might be a complement good for industrial workers who already have insurance coverage provided by the state under the Employees State Insurance Scheme[9]

The total population of the village is positively associated with *Aarogyasri* claims (25 per cent, p<0.01). Infrastructure in the form of a district road and bus service in the village is also positively associated with total claims (9 per cent and 46 per cent, respectively, p<0.01) suggesting that lack of a network of roads and transportation facilities may be binding constraints in the utilization of health insurance programmes. This result is consistent with Aggarwal (2015) who finds that road construction increased access to healthcare facilities, especially for women.

[9] Realizing the importance of health insurance for industrial workers, the Government of India along with the Ministry of Labour and Employment had set up the Employees' State Insurance Corporation (ESIC) in 1948.

Policy Implications

With the devolution of finances suggested by the 14th Finance Commission, state governments are devising their own customized programmes for tertiary care of low-income households. Given the supply-side constraints in government-operated healthcare, states have established publicly financed health insurance programmes. The empirical analysis in this section examines how village-level factors can influence the utilization of one such long-standing programme in AP (and since 2014, in Telangana as well). The quantitative results allow us to suggest policy implications that could inform the operation of these programmes.

The first insight from the empirical analysis is that *Aarogyasri* use occurs where government health workers and facilities already have a presence. So, while the focus of most government health programmes is on primary care, these could also be vehicles for disseminating information on publicly financed tertiary care programmes.[10]

Programmes such as *Aarogyasri* are intended to provide treatment for socially and economically excluded groups, yet our results on literacy, income, and infrastructure indicate that the most marginalized sections of the population are the least likely to avail the scheme's benefits. Given the findings on literacy, programmes should emphasize the use of electronic media and digital tools (Banerjee, La Ferrara, and Orozco 2017; Kearney and Levine 2015) as well as in-person interaction, to spread programme awareness. An implication of the result on infrastructure is that the scheme should include more outreach camps in villages that are difficult to access.

* * *

The *Aarogyasri* health insurance scheme was implemented with the motto of 'Health for all', aiming to provide health insurance coverage to the poor in the state. Using claims data and census 2011 data, we have sought to enumerate village-level characteristics associated with higher utilization of the scheme. The results indicate that prosperous villages indicated by high literacy rates, higher percentage of irrigated land,

and better transportation facilities have benefitted relatively more by the scheme. In other words, the poorer or relatively backward villages that the scheme was originally designed for, may not be enjoying its full benefits.

This result has a number of caveats. The empirical exercise is neither causal nor predictive of increased claims in a village, but simply measures the degree of association between the total claims and a number of village-level correlates. The demand for health insurance primarily depends on the health of an individual that is unobservable in our study. Moreover, results from this study may not be applicable to other state-run health insurance programmes. *Aarogyasri* differs from other programmes in a number of aspects namely eligibility, financial cover, and procedures covered. At the same time, demographic and economic characteristics may differ across different states. Therefore, it is essential to account for these factors while applying our results in other contexts.

Are Fully Subsidized Social Health Insurance Schemes Sustainable? A Re-look at the Aarogyasri *Health Insurance Scheme in Andhra Pradesh*

The Rajiv Gandhi *Aarogyasri* Community Health Insurance Scheme in AP provides medical coverage of up to INR 200,000 per BPL family for tertiary care per annum. With the majority of the population in AP covered under the scheme, it ensures equality for medical treatment among the diverse population, and thus is socially sustainable. However, social sustainability depends on economic sustainability. The premiums are paid by the state government with no requirement for co-payments by the insured party. This raises serious questions about the financial sustainability of the scheme in the long run. In this section, we relook at the economic sustainability of the scheme.

Until 2 June 2014, the scheme had pre-authorized payments totalling to INR 6,383.63 crore. Of this, the government's share was 23.67 per cent while the private sector's share was 76.33 per cent. Between June 2014 and July 2018, the pre-authorized amount was INR 3,058.51 crore with the shares of the government and private sector being 29.57 per cent and 70.42 per cent,

---

[10] Mane and Khandekar (2014) examine the role of ASHA workers in improving public health delivery in rural India.

respectively.[11] As these numbers suggest, the scheme has helped the private sector generate substantial revenue. Only 30.14 per cent of the pre-authorization cases come from the government with the private sector blocking the remaining 69.86 per cent. As a result, flows out of the state budget (expenditure incurred under *Aarogyasri*) are much greater than flows into the budget (revenue generated under *Aarogyasri* by the government network hospitals). This is quite naturally putting a financial strain on the state government.

The rising inequity between the public and the private sector gets reflected in the fact that while investments are being made by the former, most of the returns are

---

A senior healthcare provider in a private hospital revealed that the *Aarogyasri* backlog in Telangana is now more than eight months. 'Payments are made only when there is a call for withdrawal of services or a strike. This has made many wary, and they do not want to be part of any government insurance scheme.'

Source: 'Hyderabad: CGHS, Aarogyasri Payments to Hospitals Not Made on Time', *Deccan Chronicle*, 1 June 2018.

---

being tapped by the latter. In order to lessen the skew towards the private sector, the scheme reserved 133 cases (Bergkvist et al. 2014) for reimbursement exclusively in the government network hospitals in 2011.

This inequitable share of the government sector in generating revenue from the scheme needs further investigation. Limited evidence suggests that this may have also caused delay of reimbursements, thus eroding faith in the government's schemes.

Studies (Reddy June 2013) show that one of the reasons for underutilization of government network hospitals compared to private network hospitals is the lack of necessary skilled manpower to perform surgeries. It appears that the government hospitals are well equipped with machinery, but there is a serious shortage of specialist doctors to use the same. Thus, even with proper financing, in the short-run, sustainability will be doubtful if fully equipped government network hospitals are incapable of providing specialized treatment.

The health sector provides a classic example of inefficiency arising out of asymmetric information.

[11] http://www.*Aarogyasri*.telangana.gov.in/web/guest/data-tables.

Medical experts have all the information regarding treatments, and the patients have no option but to believe them. Demand for certain procedures and surgeries

---

'We do not know exactly whether some of the surgeries were actually needed or not. However, we can definitely say that appropriate cost utilization studies are required to ensure there is optimum utilization of taxpayers' money on *Aarogyasri* scheme', said author Dr Vivekananda Jha, executive director of the George Institute for Global Health.

Source: 'Private Hospitals Pocketed Rs 1,900 cr Aarogyasri Funds', *The Times of India*, 5 May 2015.

---

happen to be derived demand. Thus, malpractice in the form of prescribing high-technology surgeries/treatments by doctors is commonplace. The government has no control over the suggestions made by medical experts with regard to certain 'necessary' procedures. To the extent that this malpractice continues, it creates additional and uncalled for burden on state finances.

The scheme focuses on provision of tertiary care rather than secondary or primary care. This practice increases the expenditure on health. If preventive care is included under the scheme, then in the longer-run, both the government and the patient party are better off. Treatment costs for such preventive measures are likely to be substantially lesser compared to expensive surgeries. This in turn will work towards reducing cost to the government of running the scheme. Moreover, such a mechanism that only covers high-cost procedures biases the medical system towards the urban-centric specialty system while restricting treatment in remote and rural areas. If the demand for most of these specialty hospitals is from amongst the private network of hospitals, chances of the government recouping its investment become minimal.

Rising concerns about the sustainability of the scheme led the state government to approach the Central Government for financial assistance. However, the latter refused to extend any sort of financial support for an exclusively state-run scheme. Therefore, with this channel being closed, it is now up to the AP government to increase the efficiency of the scheme by setting up an expert panel to finalize packages and their cost, ensuring the infrastructure of government hospitals doesn't stay idle, and bringing preventive care under its ambit.

COMMUNITY-BASED HEALTH INSURANCE SCHEMES: A CASE STUDY FROM INDIA[12]

Over the last few decades, community-based healthcare financing has become an important alternative instrument to provide healthcare, especially to the vulnerable (see Defourny and Failon 2008; WHO 2000; Wiesmann and Jütting 2001). Such schemes are non-profit initiatives built on the principles of social solidarity, designed to provide financial protection against the impoverishing effects of health shocks, especially for low-income households in the informal urban sector and in rural areas (Ahuja and Jütting 2004; Carrin, Waelkens, and Criel 2005; Jacobs et al. 2008; Tabor 2005).

Common forms of community health financing schemes are (i) community prepayment health organizations, (ii) provider-based health insurance, and (iii) government-run but community-involved health insurance. Schemes differ in terms of design and the involvement of the community in setting up the scheme, mobilizing resources, management, and supervision. Table 1.4 provides a snapshot of various scheme characteristics.

In most of these schemes, membership is voluntary and members pay a premium to access the health services provided thereunder. There is community involvement but of varying degrees across the schemes. Often the geographical coverage and health services provided under the scheme are limited in scope. These schemes are introduced and initially financially supported by non-governmental organizations (NGOs) or local governments.

Linkage to formal social insurance schemes makes the government CBHIs different from other CBHI schemes. Government CBHIs usually cover both basic curative and inpatient care. The government (national or regional) plays a substantial role in initiating, designing, and implementing such schemes. Unlike other forms of CBHI, government-supported health insurance schemes have the potential to reach a relatively large number of households. Governments in cooperation with donor agencies may provide reductions in premium and fee waivers for the poorest segments of society while retaining a comprehensive benefit package. However, since such programmes are the result of a top–down approach, they may not be sensitive to local needs in their design and implementation features.

The objectives of this section are twin-fold; first, using a systematic review of existing studies (Box 1.2 details the aims and scope of the review) to examine the operation and effectiveness of CBHIs; and second, to provide an assessment of newly introduced CBHIs in the states of Bihar and Uttar Pradesh in India.

Analysis from a Systematic Review of Existing Studies

Two major studies—Jakab and Krishnan (2001) and Ekman (2004)—analyse whether CBHIs have been successful in reducing the burden of OOP expenditures, especially among the vulnerable. The former claim is that there is convincing evidence that community health financing schemes are able to mobilize resources to finance healthcare needs, albeit with substantial variation across schemes. They also argue that the schemes are effective in terms of reaching low-income groups although the ultra-poor are often excluded. But Ekman, on the other hand, using a systematic review of 36 studies spanning the period 1980–2002, finds that while CBHIs do provide financial protection for low-income groups and increase cost recovery for health service providers, the magnitude of the effect is low. However, the papers on which both the above reviews are based have not accounted for several methodological issues like self-selection in to the programme that most likely will overestimate the effect of CBHIs on utilization and underestimate the effects on financial protection. Ekman (2004) himself concludes that 'overall, the evidence base is limited in scope and questionable in quality'.

Revisiting the papers reviewed by Jakab and Krishnan and Ekman yields a number of conclusions pertinent to both health policy-makers and researchers.

Despite their avowed aim of social inclusion, *the review shows that the ultra-poor do not have access to CBHI schemes. Even if they do enrol, the lowest income*

---

[12] This section is based on a background paper, A.S. Bedi, A.D. Mebratie, G. Alemu, R. Sparrow, P. Panda, W. Raza, A. Chakraborty, et al., 'Community-Based Health Insurance Schemes: A Review: Experiences from Ethiopia and India and Lessons for Other Initiatives'.

groups are less likely to use healthcare services perhaps due to their inability to bear other costs (transportation and opportunity) associated with accessing healthcare. There is also considerable evidence that individuals with pre-existing health conditions are more likely to enrol, which leads to concerns about the sustainability of such schemes. The bulk of the studies find that access to CBHIs is associated with increased healthcare utilization, especially the use of relatively cheaper outpatient care services (4 to 10 percentage point increase) as opposed to inpatient care.

In about half the schemes, there is a reduction in OOP expenditures (12 to 35 per cent). In short, there is evidence to back the claim that such schemes are responsible for enhancing access to healthcare services, and providing a degree of financial protection. The more pertinent question is perhaps not whether such schemes work or not but whether there are specific scheme traits that are more conducive to generating desired outcomes.

Assessment of the link between scheme design characteristics and effectiveness showed that top–down government-run schemes appear to be better in terms of ensuring healthcare access and reducing OOP expenditure as compared to community-run schemes. However, community-run schemes seem to be stronger in terms of reaching out to marginalized groups. Schemes that have access to external sources of financing, in addition to premiums, are more effective in providing financial protection and expanding access to healthcare services, but not at reaching out to the ultra-poor. This pattern suggests that subsidies are more likely to flow to the relatively better-off. A clear pattern, regardless of scheme type is that schemes where the community plays a role in scheme design and implementation are better at ensuring access to healthcare and financial protection. This suggests a greater need to bring in the community into scheme design and implementation.

Scheme uptake averages 37 per cent. The consistency of this across various papers at least with regard to healthcare utilization and financial protection suggests that CBHI schemes may play a limited but important role in ensuring greater access to healthcare and providing some measure of financial protection to a subset of workers in the rural and informal sectors in developing countries.

However, from a methodological, and more importantly, from a policy perspective, future work needs to provide a more careful assessment of scheme design characteristics that impinge on scheme success. Further, scheme roll-out and evaluation need to be integrated so that baseline data and repeated follow-up data are available, and may be used to build a more credible database on which to judge whether and what type of design features offer a viable long-term health financing strategy.

Community Prepayment Health Organization Scheme in Uttar Pradesh and Bihar: A Case Study

Keeping in mind the methodological and policy considerations raised above, we now turn to the recent implementation of a Community Prepayment Health Organization CBHI in India where the introduction of the scheme and randomized control trial evaluation proceeded simultaneously. The evaluation used a baseline and several rounds of follow-up data.

With less than 15 per cent of the population covered by health insurance, 94 per cent of healthcare expenditure is paid for OOP (Berman, Ahuja, and Bhandari 2010; WHO 2012). This near complete dependency on self-financing of health expenses exposes many households to financial hardship, or causes them to forego care altogether (Binnendijk, Koren, and Dror 2012; Bonu et al. 2009). Community-based health insurance schemes that involve beneficiaries in scheme design and management are gaining popularity in several Indian states. Here we focus on three recently launched schemes operating in Bihar and Uttar Pradesh.

The Delhi-based Micro Insurance Academy (MIA)—a non-profit organization—in partnership with three local NGOs, introduced CBHI schemes in Kanpur Dehat and Pratapgarh districts in Uttar Pradesh, and in Vaishali district in Bihar. Households could enrol themselves in the scheme provided at least one woman within the household was a member of a SHG by March 2010. All villages in each of the three districts were grouped into 48 clusters (15 in Pratapgarh, 17 in Kanpur Dehat, and 16 in Vaishali), where clusters combined contiguous villages so that they contained roughly an equal number of SHG households (60–80). At each site, clusters were randomized into one of the waves—2011, 2012, and 2013. In each of the waves, all SHG households within

BOX 1.2   Conducting the Review

The total number of studies reported here is 48 (that is, 16 community prepayment health organizations, seven healthcare-provider-initiated insurance schemes, and 25 government-run-and-community-involved health insurance schemes). However, Table 1.5 covers 46 studies. The difference is because the scheme type in one study (Onwujekwe et al. 2009) is unknown, and each of three studies (Desmet, Chowdhury, and Islam 1999; Diop, Sulzbach, and Chankova 2006; Gumber 2001) examines two different types of schemes.

This study applies the basic principles of a systematic review in order to assess the literature on the impact of CBHI schemes. Unlike a narrative approach, systematic reviews attempt to assess the overall message or develop stylized facts based on knowledge emerging from existing studies while at the same time controlling for or commenting on methodological features of the literature that may influence the conclusions. The protocol followed in this review is as follows:

1. The specific research aim is a review that will provide a synthesis of the existing knowledge on community health financing approaches dealing with three issues—access to schemes or social inclusion, and their effect on healthcare utilization and financial protection.
2. Sources of the data: Published and unpublished papers over an 18-year period (1995–2012) located through a search of six databases—Econlit, PubMed, Science Direct, SSRN, JSTOR, and Google scholar. In addition, a search was conducted on the web pages of the World Health Organization (WHO).
3. To identify papers for review, a search was conducted using the key words 'community health financing', 'micro-insurance', 'OOP payment and community insurance', and 'community-based health insurance'. This generated a large number of papers (several hundred), the titles and abstracts of which were examined, and introductions and conclusions perused for suitability of inclusion. Using this approach, 121 potential papers were selected and passed on to the second round for intensive reading.
4. Papers included for detailed review needed to satisfy the following criteria:

    4.1 They should be concerned with an examination of the impact of community health financing schemes on access to healthcare and financial protection. The definition of 'community health financing schemes' was restricted to non-profit-oriented schemes that serve populations in the informal sector (urban or rural) of low- and middle-income countries. This restriction led to the exclusion of 21 of the 121 papers.
    4.2 Studies that use micro data at the household or individual level (led to the exclusion of 12 studies).
    4.3 Studies that evaluate the effect of community health insurance mainly using quantitative and statistical analysis. Studies relying mainly on qualitative data were included provided they used at least some statistical information (16 studies excluded).
    4.4 Studies that arrived at their findings based on value judgement and self-perception without using any data were excluded. Similarly, studies that did not provide clear information on the research methods applied and the schemes studied in their analysis were excluded (7 studies excluded).
    4.5 The outcome measures should include utilization of healthcare (outpatient and inpatient) services, OOP healthcare payments, adverse selection, and social exclusion in enrolment and service utilization (19 studies excluded).

    The imposition of these criteria led to a list of 46 papers (32 published and 14 unpublished) that were retained for the review. Compared to Ekman (2004), 37 of the papers included in the review are different.

5. After paper selection, the papers were read and carefully scrutinized. A data extraction template was developed to collect information from each paper about scheme impact, the characteristics of the scheme (type of scheme, whether the scheme receives external support, whether there are contracts with providers, and extent of community participation), the statistical/research methods applied, and data characteristics (source, level of analysis, data type, and the use of baseline information). A summary of the key features of each of these studies is provided in Table 1.5.
6. The limited number of studies does not support a formal meta-analysis which links outcomes to scheme characteristics and study characteristics. However, to assess the overall message emerging from the studies, univariate and bivariate distributions were constructed. These are used to construct stylized facts.

the selected clusters could enrol in the CBHI schemes. By the end of the project, the entire target population had a chance to join the schemes. Additional details on the design of the experiment are available in Doyle et al. (2011).

Screening of movies and meetings at the SHG level about the scheme were held in early 2010. Between June and December 2010, enrollees had to choose between a set of four to six initial benefit packages designed by MIA.[13] At the first stage, individual SHG members determined the benefit package they preferred. At the second stage, individual members debated their choices, and the SHG group provided a first and a second choice package. At the third stage, all SHG groups debated their choices, and the package that was chosen by most groups was retained in each district (for details, see Dror et al. 2014). Scheme roll-out took place in February 2011 in Vaishali and Pratapgarh, and in March 2011 in Kanpur Dehat. Prior to the scheme roll-out, SHG members were nominated to the claims committees and governing bodies that steered the day-to-day operations of the insurance scheme. The claims committees met about every three weeks to decide on claims and pay-outs that are settled on a cash basis.

Details on the benefit package selected at each site are in Table 1.6. The packages in Pratapgarh and Kanpur Dehat are similar except that in the first year, SHGs in Pratapgarh did not opt for coverage of outpatient services. The SHGs in Vaishali district opted not to include coverage of inpatient care, but opted for outpatient care and coverage of various diagnostic tests. There were caps on the maximum claimant amounts for inpatient care, and for the use of laboratory and imaging services. There was no limit in terms of using outpatient care. However, only empanelled practitioners could provide care at all three sites. During the second year of the project, the scheme in Pratapgarh also offered outpatient services.

In all sites, coverage for outpatient care was restricted to designated practitioners, mainly rural medical

Practitioners (RMPs).[14] While not necessarily licensed, these providers were responsible for a majority of healthcare visits for outpatient care (Gautham et al. 2011; Raza et al. 2016a). Contracted on a yearly capitation basis, with monthly instalments, they are to provide care and medicines free of charge to the insured. For other covered expenses, receipts submitted by beneficiaries, once sanctioned by the claims committees, were reimbursed.

Initially, the intention was that all household members will be enrolled. But, households claimed that paying premiums for all household members was a heavy financial burden on them. Hence, scheme administrators decided that provided the woman linked to the SHG is enrolled, other members of the household had the choice to join (or not join) the programme.

Data and Uptake

Information from three household surveys with data on enrolment, renewal, premium payments, and claims obtained from MIA's management information system (MIS) are used in the analysis. These surveys were conducted between March and May of 2010, 2012, and 2013. The first round covered 3,685 households. Of these, 3,318 were resurveyed in 2012, and 3,307 in 2013. In all, 3,034 households were covered in all three rounds.

Following the cluster randomized control design, during the first phase of implementation in 2011, 7,722 individuals were offered the possibility of joining the CBHI schemes (see Table 1.7). Of these, 23 per cent enrolled. A year later, the schemes were offered to 6,493 individuals. In the second year, 46 per cent renewed their membership, and two years later, 301 individuals of those who had enrolled in 2011 retained their membership (see Table 1.7). There is some variation across the three schemes with renewal rates in 2013 ranging from 13 per cent in Kanpur Dehat to 21 per cent in Pratapgarh. Among those offered the scheme in 2012, the overall enrolment rate was 24 per cent, and a year later, only 37 per cent renewed their membership. While there are variations across the schemes both in terms of initial enrolment and renewal, there is no clear indication that

---

[13] The benefit packages offered to the SHG members were designed based on information available in the baseline data, and take into account local healthcare costs, availability of facilities, and the probability of experiencing different health problems.

[14] By 2013, the Kanpur CBHI scheme had begun offering the services of a qualified doctor who visited the office of the local partner NGO and other designated places on a weekly basis.

one scheme is performing significantly better than the other in terms of uptake and renewal. The low initial uptake and high dropout rates in these three CBHI schemes are similar in pattern to those observed in other CBHI schemes in India. The low and declining renewal rates despite the efforts to involve the community require further investigation into the factors that influence the decision to renew membership in CBHI schemes.

Impact on Healthcare Utilization and Financial Protection

Healthcare utilization

The top panel of Table 1.8 displays the impact of the randomized offer of insurance (intention to treat (ITT)) and the uptake of insurance (average treatment effect on treated (ATET)) on the probability that individuals reporting sickness use outpatient and inpatient care based on the data pooled across the three sites. The ITT estimates show no significant effect of the offer of insurance on any utilization outcome, including care from RMPs who are the main source of outpatient care covered by CBHIs in all three sites. Scheme uptake is about 23 per cent, and so the ATET estimates are about four times larger than the ITT estimates but insignificant.

Site-specific results are reported in Table 1.9 (top panel). In Kanpur Dehat, the offer of insurance is associated with a 4 percentage point increase in the probability of seeking outpatient care from any provider with the entire increase coming from an increase in the probability of using RMPs, but the estimated effects are not statistically significant at conventional levels. In Vaishali, the CBHI has no effect on utilization. In Pratapgarh, an offer of insurance, which did not initially include coverage of outpatient care in this site, led to a statistically significant 7-percentage-point decline in the probability of seeking outpatient care. Actual uptake of CBHI therefore suggests a large decline (51 percentage points) in the probability of using outpatient care.[15] The decline in use of outpatient care is partly, although not significantly, due to a reduction in

---

[15] Outpatient care was only included in the CBHI schemes offered in Pratapgarh in wave 2 but not in wave 1. Restricting the sample to the baseline and endline surveys also yields negative, albeit statistically insignificant estimates of the CBHI scheme on the probability of using outpatient care in Pratapgarh.

the use of RMPs, but the main change is that households in Pratapgarh are less likely to use general practitioners/specialists once insurance, which does not cover care from these providers, is offered (results not shown in table). Substitution away from practitioners outside the scheme coverage is expected. However, this does not explain the negative coefficient on the use of RMPs.

Healthcare spending

The ITT and ATET estimates of the effect of insurance on OOP healthcare expenditure for outpatient and inpatient care, and on the probability of *hardship financing*, are in the lower panel of Table 1.8. Estimates are for the full sample, and for the sample conditional upon the use of care. The point estimates for outpatient expenses are negative. But those for inpatient expenses are positive, and there is no significant evidence that access to the CBHI scheme works towards reducing OOP expenditures. This is counter to what one might expect given that there is no significant impact on utilization.

Site-specific results (Table 1.9) show that the CBHI scheme has no effect on health expenditure or on the probability of *hardship financing* in Kanpur Dehat and in Vaishali. In the case of Pratapgarh, the ITT estimates indicate that, conditional on use, access to CBHI leads to a 16.4 per cent decline in outpatient care expenditure while the ATET effects indicate an 80 per cent decline for those with CBHI cover. Since this follows from the estimated reduction in the use of outpatient care, it should not be interpreted as indicative of a protective influence of the scheme. There is no evidence of any impact on inpatient expenses or hardship financing in Pratapgarh.

Summarizing, the CBHI schemes show declining uptake. In the first year after the introduction of the scheme, enrolment was around 23 per cent, but by the time of the third survey round in 2013, enrolment fell to 17 per cent of those who had originally enrolled or about 4 per cent of the population who were offered insurance. A randomized evaluation of the effect of the programme found a null effect on healthcare use and financial protection.

Premiums charged by the three Indian CBHI schemes amount to about 0.9–1.3 per cent of annual household expenditure. Analysis of enrolment and renewal rates across different socio-economic groups does not display a strong link between economic status and retention. In fact, retention rates seemed to be positively associated with belonging to a scheduled caste/tribe. For those offered insurance in 2012 and renewed in 2013, we did find stronger economic status effects, with those in the richest tertile more likely to renew their membership. However, the overall impression emerging from the estimates was that differences in socio-economic status as captured by caste, education, and consumption tertiles do not have a very large bearing on renewal. This is perhaps not surprising as the premium for the benefit package and its composition were determined in consultation with the target group.

The offer to join the insurance scheme was through local NGOs, and conditional on belonging to a SHG. The expectation was that such an arrangement amongst a group of 'organized households' would make it easier to carry out awareness-raising activities, and to offer and deliver insurance. While the systematic review suggested that linking microfinance to micro-insurance does have a positive effect on reducing social exclusion and on access to healthcare use and financial protection, such benefits did not materialize in the scheme under scrutiny.

Scheme use, defined in terms of whether anyone in a household had claimed benefits in the year prior to renewal, was positively associated with scheme retention. The importance of this effect increased over the duration of the scheme, and amongst those who renewed insurance for a second year, the marginal effect of this variable was 32 percentage points. Our analysis of claims data also illustrates the role of scheme use, speed of processing claims, and the extent to which claims are honoured in determining retention. Households whose claims took longer to process and who received a lower amount of money as compared to the claims they made were less likely to renew their contracts. For instance, based on those who enrolled in 2012, there are marked differences in scheme experience across those who dropped-out and those who renewed. The claim incidence for those who renewed is 18 per cent versus 5 per cent for those who did not renew. For those who renewed, the time taken between submission of the claim and receipt of funds is 19 days while it is 27 days for those who did not renew. The ratio of the amount of money received through the insurance and the amount claimed is 33 per cent for those who renewed, and 23 per cent for those who did not.

Based on a series of questions designed to probe knowledge of insurance in general and CBHI in particular, we found that 66 per cent of the respondents had above

average knowledge of insurance, and 56 per cent had above average knowledge of CBHI. Both insurance knowledge and a greater understanding of the insurance scheme were associated with a higher probability of renewing contracts. For the sample as a whole, those with greater understanding of insurance were 8 percentage points more likely to renew contracts while for CBHI understanding, the effect was about 14 percentage points. Similar to the claims effects discussed above, in the second wave, the importance of knowledge and understanding in determining enrolment is substantially higher. Individuals in both waves are similar in terms of their socio-economic status and have experienced the same set of awareness activities. Hence, it is likely that the changing importance of these variables over time arises from the greater need to comply with scheme regulations as the schemes mature.

Health-related indicators reveal unexpected patterns. For all three illnesses—long-term, short-term, and hospitalization—and for the full sample we find that such events lead to a reduction in the probability of renewing contracts. It is especially intriguing that those who have used inpatient care in the year that they were insured are less to likely to renew. According to the estimates, those who perhaps have had the most need to rely on insurance are 15 percentage points less likely to renew their membership. There could be several reasons for this. First, the quality of care on offer that is accessible through the scheme may be poor. While this may be true in general, the scheme does not restrict the use of hospital care to specific facilities, and so it is unlikely that poor quality of care offered through the scheme affects renewal behaviour. It could be that the caps of INR 4,000 in Pratapgarh and of INR 3,000 in Kanpur Dehat are too low, and potential clients, despite having played a role in determining the package, find that the product on offer is not suitable. The claims data support this argument as the average claim amongst those who drop out is INR 6,538. It is INR 2,998 amongst those who renew. The third possibility is that, by definition, those hospitalized are more likely to have engaged with the scheme administration in terms of attempting to claim benefits. Their experience in terms of the gap between their expectations and the amount they received from the insurance (on average, the receipt-to-claim ratio is 25 per cent) may have spurred their decision to leave the scheme.

Qualitative fieldwork based on interviews with 33 households who had enrolled in the scheme for at least one year, as well as discussions with the organization implementing the scheme, provides additional clues as to the underlying reasons for the disappointing results. Sixteen of the households reported that they had to pay for outpatient services and medicine for conditions that should have been covered by the insurance scheme. Ten of the 33 households dropped out after a year, and the most common reasons for dropping out included poor quality of services, expenditure on premiums, and the need to pay for care from non-designated providers. The insurance scheme offers access to outpatient care at designated providers paid on a capitation basis. The designated providers are chosen in consultation with the community; therefore it is unlikely that the perception of poor quality services is due to those providers falling short of the standards offered by the alternatives. The most likely explanation is that the payment system, which pays a fixed fee per patient per year, provides an incentive to lower the quality of care offered to insured patients compared to that offered to those paying fee-for-service. A RMP was paid INR 40 per insured patient per year while the estimated cost per visit was INR 125 (see Raza et al. 2016a). Problems related to the capitation system have also been mentioned as the main reason for the absence of positive effects of CBHI in Burkina Faso (Fink et al. 2013), and may be compounded by a lack of competition between providers.[16]

[16] On average, there were only 0.28 RMPs per village in Pratapgarh, while it was 0.5 in the other two sites.

TABLE 1.4 Features of Different Community-Based Health Insurance Models

Type of CBHI	Design features	Management features	Organizational and institutional features	Role of government and NGOs	Role of the community	Strengths of the scheme	Weaknesses of the scheme
Community prepayment health organizations	Financed by contribution from members. Small financial contribution mainly to cover primary healthcare services. Membership is on a voluntary basis.	Strong community involvement in decision making and supervision.	The provider is not involved in the administration of the scheme. The schemes may involve signing contractual agreements with local providers to obtain preferential prices and ensure quality of services.	NGOs often provide technical assistance and start-up funds. Governments provide legal recognition and encourage their establishment.	Pay premiums. All round community involvement in design, implementation, and supervision.	Trust and feeling of ownership.	Small size in nature and low ability to pool enough resources. Lack of technical and managerial skills about health insurance administration.
Provider-based health insurance schemes	Designed by local healthcare providers (hospitals) to encourage service utilization. Often cover expensive inpatient care. Membership is on a voluntary basis.	Providers involved in scheme management.	Providers administer the schemes and collect premiums from subscribers. Providers may obtain technical assistance from the government and NGOs.	NGOs and governments may improve the facility of the providers.	Pay premiums. Provide feedback on quality.	Does not require management and technical skills from the community. Scheme management and service provision are integrated.	Limited scale. Relatively low power of the community to influence benefit package and quality of care.

Source: Data obtained from MIA's management information system (MIS).

TABLE 1.5 List of Papers Included in the Review

Author(s)	Country	Scheme	Scheme type[17]	Year of study	Scheme coverage	Outcome variable	Method of analysis	Findings	Remarks
Aggarwal (2010)	India	Yeshasvini	Government	2007–8	3 million individuals	Social exclusion	Logit model	Richer groups more likely to enrol.	The study attempts to reduce selection bias, but baseline differences between treatment and control groups are not controlled.
Atim and Sock (2000)	Ghana	Nkoranza community health insurance scheme	Provider	1999	30 per cent of the population	Adverse selection	Simple descriptive	Adverse selection	The study compares the socio-economic status of insured households.
Carrin et al. (1999)	China	Rural Co-operative Medical Scheme (RCMS)	Government	1993 and 1995	31–100 per cent of the population	OOP	Simple descriptive	Reduction in healthcare costs	The study collects baseline information, but does not use it appropriately. The findings on financial protection effect are based on descriptive analysis.
Chee, Smith, and Kapinga (2002)	Tanzania	Hanang district health fund	Government	2001	2.8 per cent of households	Outpatient care	Simple descriptive	CBHI members more likely to use services	The results are based on healthcare service utilization data obtained from selected providers, and the sample may not be representative.
Criel and Kegels (1997)	Congo	Bwamanda hospital health insurance	Provider	1986–1995	41 per cent of the population	Inpatient care	Descriptive statistics	Sig. pos. effect	Does not control for differences in socio-economic and demographic characteristics between insured and uninsured groups.
Desmet, Chowdhury, and Islam (1999)	Bangladesh	Gonosasthya	Com'ty	1995	27.5 per cent of households	Inpatient care	Simple descriptive	Insured households use more curative care than the uninsured	Data is from healthcare providers. Does not control for differences between the characteristics of uninsured and insured households.
						Outpatient care	Simple descriptive	Insured households use more hospitalization than the uninsured	

(Contd.)

TABLE 1.5 (Contd.)

Author(s)	Country	Scheme	Scheme type	Year of study	Scheme coverage	Outcome variable	Method of analysis	Findings	Remarks
		Grameen	Provider	1994	41 per cent of households	Outpatient care	Simple descriptive	Insured households use more care than uninsured	
Devadasan et al. 2007	India	ACCORD	Provider	2003–4	35 per cent of the population	Incidence of catastrophic OOP	Simple descriptive	Reduced from 8 per cent to 3.5 per cent	The data are obtained from insurance claimants hospitalized during the study period. There is no control group.
		SEWA	Com'ty	2003–4	20 per cent of the population	Incidence of catastrophic OOP	Simple descriptive	Reduced from 49 per cent to 23 per cent	
Diop, Sulzbach, and Chankova (2006)	Ghana	Nkoranza hospital insurance scheme	Provider	2005	n/a	Social exclusion	Logit model	No effect	The study does not control for endogeneity of scheme participation.
						Outpatient	Logit model	Sig. pos. effect	
						Inpatient	Logit model	No effect	
						OOP	Log-linear	No effect	
						Catastrophic OOP	Log-linear	Sig. neg. effect	
	Mali	Bla and Sikasso scheme	Com'ty	2004	3.3–11.4 per cent of the population	Social exclusion	Logit model	Sig. pos. effect	
						Adverse selection	Logit model	Sig. pos. effect	
						Outpatient care	Logit model	Sig. pos. effect	
						OOP	Log-linear	No effect	
	Senegal	26 Mutual health organizations	Com'ty	2004	n/a	Social exclusion	Logit model	Sig. pos. effect	
						Adverse selection	Logit model	Sig. pos. effect	

Study	Country	Scheme	Type	Year	Sample	Outcome	Method	Effect	Comments
						OOP	Log-linear	No effect	
						Catastrophic OOP	Log-linear	Sig. neg. effect	
Dror et al. (2009)	India	UpLift of health	Com'ty	2005	16,356 individuals	Social inclusion	Descriptive statistics	No effect	In addition to the household survey, the study collects and uses information by interviewing managers of the schemes. However, the study does not control for differences in socio-economic and other household characteristics between insured and uninsured persons.
						Inpatient	Descriptive statistics	Sig. pos effect	
		BAIF	Com'ty		600 individuals	Social inclusion	Descriptive statistics	No effect	
						Inpatient	Descriptive statistics	Sig. pos. effect	
		NIDAN[18]	Com'ty		10,189 individuals	Social inclusion	Descriptive statistics	Non-insured were wealthier than the insured	
						Inpatient	Descriptive statistics	Sig. pos. effect	
Dror, Lorenzo, and Sarol (2005)	Philippines	Six micro health insurance schemes	n/a	2002	n/a	Adverse selection	Simple descriptive	No evidence	The data is collected through field surveys. Robustness of results has been checked. There is evidence of selection that has not been controlled for in the analysis
						Inpatient care	Descriptive statistics	Sig. pos. effect	
Ekman (2007)	Zambia	Prepayment scheme	Gov't	1998	n/a	Catastrophic OOP	Logit model	Sig. increase in the risk of catastrophic payments	Several sensitivity tests for alternative definitions of outcomes and model specification.
Franco et al. (2008)	Mali	Four mutual health organizations in Bla and Sikasso	Gov't	2003–4	3.3–11.4 per cent of the population	Social exclusion	Logit model	No effect	Does not control for selection bias.
						Outpatient care	Logit model	Sig. pos. effect	
						OOP	Ordinary least squares (OLS)	Sig. pos. effect	

(Contd.)

[18] A health scheme that targets market vendors in Patna, Bihar.

TABLE 1.5 (*Contd.*)

Author(s)	Country	Scheme	Scheme type	Year of study	Scheme coverage	Outcome variable	Method of analysis	Findings	Remarks
Galárraga et al. (2010)	Mexico	Seguro Popular (SP)	Gov't	2006	44 per cent of households	OOP	Instrumental Variables	Sig. neg. effect	Uses instrumental variables (IVs) to control for endogeneity in enrolment in insurance schemes.
Gnawali et al. (2009)	Burkina Faso	Nouna community-based insurance (CBI)	Com'ty	2006	5.2 per cent of households	Social exclusion	Propensity score matching (PSM)	Sig. pos. effect	Applies PSM; does not correct for observed differences between treatment and control.
						Outpatient	PSM	Sig. pos. effect	
						Inpatient	PSM	No effect	
Gobah and Zhang (2011)	Ghana	Department of Alcohol, Drug, and Mental Health Services (ADMHS)	Gov't	2010	63.5 per cent of households	Utilization	Descriptive statistics	Sig. pos. effect	Quantitative and qualitative data used.
Gumber (2001)	India	SEWA	Com'ty	1998–9	63,000 individuals	Social exclusion	Multinomial (MN) Logit	No effect	Based on non-random sample. Unclear about the usage of MN logit models.
						Adverse selection	MN Logit	Mixed	
						Outpatient care	MN Logit	Sig. pos. effect	
						Inpatient care	MN Logit	No effect	
						OOP	OLS	No effect	
		ESIS	Gov't	1998–9	n/a	Outpatient care	MN Logit	No effect	
						Inpatient care	MN Logit	Sig. pos. effect	
						OOP	OLS	Sig. neg. effect	
		Mediclaim	Com'ty	1998–9	n/a	Outpatient care	MN Logit	No effect	
						Inpatient care	MN Logit	No effect	
						OOP	OLS	Mixed	

Study	Country	Scheme	Provider	Year	Coverage	Focus	Method	Result	Comments
Hamid, Roberts, and Mosley (2011)	Bangladesh	Grameen Bank	Provider	2006	n/a	Utilization	Probit model	Sig. pos. effect	The paper considers endogeniety and spill-over effects of the programme. However, lack of longitudinal data limits the ability of the paper to deal with such issues.
Ito and Kono (2010)	India	Yeshasvini	Gov't	2008	n/a	Adverse selection	Probit model	Mixed[19]	The study does not control for the quality and quantity of healthcare supply
Jowett, Contoyannis, and Vinh (2003)	Vietnam	Vietnam's voluntary insurance	Gov't	1999	20 per cent of individuals	OOP	Heckman, OLS	Sig. neg. effect	The paper addresses scheme self-selection bias using cross-section data.
Jütting (2004)	Senegal	Les mutuelles de santé	Com'ty	2000	37.4–90.3 per cent of households	Social exclusion	Probit model	Sig. pos. effect	The study pays limited attention to potential bias due to unobservable factors that may drive scheme uptake.
Jütting (2004)	Senegal	Les mutuelles de santé	Com'ty	2000	30,000 individuals	OOP	Log-linear	Sig. neg. effect	Emphasis on endogeneity and self-selection.
						Inpatient care	Logit model	Sig. pos. effect	
Lammers and Warmedram (2010)	Nigeria	Health insurance fund	Com'ty	2008	6 per cent of population	Social exclusion	Logit model	Sig. pos. effect	Conducts sensitivity analysis.
						Adverse selection	Logit model	Sig. pos. effect	
Levine, Polimeni, and Ramage (2012)	Cambodia	Sokapheap Krousat Yeugn (SKY) health insurance	Com'ty	2007–8	n/a	Utilization	IV, ITT	Sig pos. effect	Randomized control, panel household data including baseline.
						OOP	IV, ITT	Sig. neg. effect	
Liu et al. (2012)	China	New Cooperative Medical Scheme (NCMS)	Gov't	2006	85–91.3 per cent of the population	Outpatient care	Descriptive statistics	No effect	
						Inpatient care	Descriptive statistics	Sig. pos. effect	
	Vietnam	Compulsory health insurance (CHI), voluntary health insurance (VHI)	Gov't	2006	49.4–52.7 per cent of the population	Outpatient care	Descriptive statistics	Sig. pos. effect	
						Inpatient care	Descriptive statistics	Sig. pos. effect	

[19] Households with a larger share of sick members are significantly more likely to join the scheme, but households with sick household heads are less likely to apply for membership.

(Contd.)

TABLE 1.5 (*Contd.*)

Author(s)	Country	Scheme	Scheme type	Year of study	Scheme coverage	Outcome variable	Method of analysis	Findings	Remarks
Msuya, Jütting, and Asfaw (2007)	Tanzania	Igunga district health insurance fund	Gov't	2000	n/a	Social exclusion	Probit model	Sig. pos. effect	The conclusions are based on one regression per outcome variable. No sensitivity analysis. Does not deal with self-selection issues.
						Utilization	Probit model	Sig. pos. effect	
Nguyen, Rajkotia, and Wang (2011)	Ghana	National Health Insurance Scheme (NHIS)	Gov't	2007	45 per cent of the population	OOP	Probit and log-linear	Sig. neg. effect	No attention is paid to self-selection bias in insurance uptake.
						Catastrophic OOP	Probit model	Sig. neg. effect	
Noterman et al. (1995)	DeCongo	Masisi referral hospital	Provider	1987–90	26.8 per cent of the population	Inpatient care	Simple descriptive	Increase in hospital admission	The study uses an experimental approach. However, the programme was not implemented randomly across eligible households; also there is evidence of adverse selection.
Onwujekwe et al. (2009)	Nigeria	Anambra state CBHIs	Gov't	n/a	n/a	Social exclusion	Descriptive statistics	No effect	The socio-economic status of the respondents is not properly defined.
Parmar et al. (2012)	Burkina Faso	Assurance maladie à base communautaire	Com'ty	2004–7	n/a	Adverse selection	Fixed effects	Mixed	The study uses panel data to examine adverse selection over time.
Ranson (2002)	India	Women's Association's medical insurance fund	Com'ty	1994–2000	23,214 individuals	Catastrophic OOP	Descriptive statistics	Reduced from 35.6 per cent to 15.1 per cent	Paper is based on data from reimbursement claims submitted between 1994 and 2000.
Ranson et al. (2006)	India	SEWA	Com'ty	2003	1,03,000 individuals	Social exclusion	Simple descriptive	The scheme is inclusive	The study uses well-argued measures of socio-economic status in order to examine the impact of the scheme across different income groups. However, it does not deal with self-selection issues.

Study	Country	Scheme	Type	Year	Coverage	Outcome	Method	Effect	Comments
						Outpatient	Simple descriptive	CBHI members use more care	
Rao et al. (2009)	Afghanistan	Parwan and Saripul community health funds	Gov't	2004 and 2006	1–38 per cent of households	OOP	Descriptive statistics	Increase in OOP payment	This study uses longitudinal data with baseline information. However, the paper applies descriptive analysis, and does not use the panel data to control for differences between the control and treatment groups.
Robyn et al. (2011)	Burkina Faso	Nouna district CBHI scheme	Com'ty	2007	8.6 per cent of the population	Utilization	PSM	Sig. pos. effect	Despite the lack of panel data, the paper tries to deal with selection on observables by minimizing differences between treatment and control groups.
Saksena et al. (2011)	Rwanda	Mutuelles	Gov't	2005–6	74 per cent of the population	OOP	Ordered logit model	Sig. neg. effect	The results are based on cross-sectional data, and there is no sensitivity analysis. The paper checks for endogeneity of enrolment using a Durbin–Wu–Hausman test, which is unable to reject exogeneity of enrolment.
						Catastrophic OOP	Simple descriptive	Reduces the risk of catastrophic health expenditure	
Schneider and Diop (2001)	Rwanda	Byumba, Kabgayi, and Kabutare prepayment plan pilot	Gov't	2000	6.1–10.6 per cent of the population	Utilization	Logit model	Sig. pos. effect	The paper does not pay attention to endogeneity of enrolment. A single regression is estimated for each outcome variable.
						OOP payment	Log-linear	Sig. neg. effect	
Sekyi and Domanban (2012)	Ghana	National health insurance scheme (NHIS)	Gov't	2008	More than 42 per cent of the population	Outpatient care	Logit model	Sig pos. effect	Only limited set of number of individual and household-level controls.
Shimeles (2010)	Rwanda	Mutuelles	Gov't	2005–6	85 per cent of the population	Social exclusion	Probit model	Sig. pos. effect	Despite the lack of longitudinal data, a range of methods are applied and the robustness of the findings are tested using alternative parametric regressions and PSM techniques.
						Utilization	PSM, probit model	Sig. pos. effect	
						Catastrophic OOP	PSM, probit model	Sig. neg. effect	

(Contd.)

TABLE 1.5 (*Contd.*)

Author(s)	Country	Scheme	Scheme type	Year of study	Scheme coverage	Outcome variable	Method of analysis	Findings	Remarks
Sun et al. (2009)	China	Shandong province medical scheme	Gov't	2004	94.6 per cent of the population	Catastrophic OOP	Simple descriptive	Decrease in catastrophic OOP payment	The study is based on comparing health expenditure before and after reimbursement of insurance claims without any control group.
Wagstaff et al. (2009)	China	NCMS	Gov't	2003 and 2005	406 million individuals	Outpatient care	Difference-in-difference (DID) with PSM	Sig. pos. effect	The study is based on household surveys before and after the intervention from treatment and control sites (counties). The study also uses health facility data. Exploiting the panel nature of the data, the study uses DID with PSM to control for potential bias from observable covariates and unobservable time-invariant confounders.
						OOP	DID with PSM	No effect	
Wang et al. (2005)	China	Fengshan Township CBI	Gov't	2002	n/a	Social exclusion	Logit model and OLS	Sig. pos. effect	
						Adverse selection	Logit model and OLS	Sig. pos. effect	
Xuemei and Xiao (2011)	China	NCMS	Gov't	1991–2006	n/a	Utilization	Fixed effects, IV, Logit model	No effect	This study uses six years of panel data, before and after NCMS implementation.
Yip, Wang, and Hsiao (2008)	China	Rural mutual health care	Com'ty	2002 and 2005	60,000 individuals	Outpatient care	DID, PSM	Sig. pos. effect	The paper uses appropriate methods and data from longitudinal household surveys of canvassed treatment and control groups.
						Inpatient care	DID, PSM	No effect	
Zhang and Wang (2008)	China	Fengsan township CBHI scheme	Com'ty	2002–6	n/a	Social exclusion	DID	Sig. pos. effect	The results are based on a four-year longitudinal survey. Random effect logit models are used to control for potential sources of bias.

TABLE 1.6 Description of Benefit Packages under the CBHI Schemes (in INR)

Indicators		Year I Pratapgarh	Year I Kanpur Dehat	Year I Vaishali	Year II Pratapgarh	Year II Kanpur Dehat	Year II Vaishali	Year III Pratapgarh	Year III Kanpur Dehat	Year III Vaishali
Annual CBHI premium per person/per year		176	192	197	250	192	197	250	199	197
Coverage for hospitalization (more than 24 hours)										
Fees (cap per person per event)	per event	6,000	3,000	–	4,000	3,000	–	4,000	4,000	–
	per family per year	–	–	–	30,000	25,000	–	30,000	30,000	–
Wage loss (per day)	per event	100	75	100	100	50	100	100	50	100
	per day	3rd–8th day	4th–13th day	4th–9th day	4th–7th day	3rd–6th day	4th–9th day	4th–7th day	3rd–7th day	4th–9th day
Transport (maximum coverage per episode)	per event	100	100	–	100	250	–	100	300	–
Coverage for outpatient care										
Fees	per event	–	Unlimited	Unlimited	Unlimited	Unlimited	Unlimited	Unlimited	Unlimited	Unlimited
Lab tests (per year)*	per event	–	–	200	–	–	200	–	–	400
	per family per year	–	–	–	–	–	–	–	–	2000
Imaging tests (per year)*	per event	–	–	300	–	–	300	–	–	500
	per family per year	–	–	–	–	–	–	–	–	2,000
Injuries (if plaster is required)	per event	–	–	–	–	400	–	–	100	–
	per family per year	–	–	–	–	1,000	–	–	500	–
Coverage for maternity care										
Caesarean (per episode)	per event	5,000	–	–	–	–	–	–	–	–

Note: '–' indicates 'Not included in package'; * Maximum amount, per person per year.

Source: Authors' calculations based on information from three household surveys conducted between March and May of 2010, 2012, and 2013 obtained from MIA's management information system (MIS).

TABLE 1.7   Renewal Rates for Individuals over the Years

Indicators	Pratapgarh	Kanpur Dehat	Vaishali	All
Individuals offered CBHI in 2011				
1st Year of Implementation (2011)				
Offered enrolment in 2011	2,594	2,264	2,864	7,722
Enrolled in 2011	604	334	868	1,806
Percentage of enrolment in 2011	23%	15%	30%	23%
2nd Year of Implementation (2012)				
Resurveyed in 2012 among the enrolled in 2011	547	314	806	1,667
Renewed in 2012	222	110	436	768
Percentage of renewal in 2012	41%	35%	54%	46%
3rd Year of Implementation (2013)				
Resurveyed in 2013 among the renewed in 2012	194	99	381	674
Renewed in 2013	125	45	131	301
Percentage of renewal with respect to 2012	64%	45%	34%	45%
Percentage of renewal with respect to 2011	21%	13%	15%	17%
Individuals offered CBHI in 2012				
2nd Year of Implementation (2012)				
Offered enrolment in 2012	2,593	1,907	1,993	6,493
Enrolled in 2012	491	451	600	1,542
Percentage of enrolment in 2012	19%	24%	30%	24%
3rd Year of Implementation (2013)				
Resurveyed in 2013 among the enrolled in 2012	419	386	534	1,339
Renewed in 2013	110	177	206	493
Percentage of renewal in 2013[*]	26%	46%	39%	37%

Note: *With respect to enrolment in 2011.

Source: Authors' calculations based on information from three household surveys conducted between March and May of 2010, 2012, and 2013 obtained from MIA's management information system (MIS).

TABLE 1.8 Effects of Randomized Offer (ITT) and Uptake of Insurance (ATET) on Healthcare Utilization and Financial Protection (data pooled across three intervention sites)

	ITT		ATET	
	Marginal effect	Standard error	Marginal effect	Standard error
Healthcare utilization				
Outpatient care conditional upon reporting	−0.016	0.021	−0.065	0.082
Outpatient care from a RMP conditional on reporting	0.001	0.017	0.005	0.069
Observations		22,569		
Inpatient care	−0.001	0.004	−0.005	0.017
Observations		38,045		
Healthcare expenditures conditional on use				
Outpatient care expenses	−0.044	0.063	−0.203	0.173
Hardship financing for outpatient care	0.001	0.020	0.002	0.081
Observations		16,665		
Inpatient care expenses	0.102	0.252	0.047	0.135
Hardship financing for inpatient care	0.016	0.33	0.047	0.135
Observations		914		
Healthcare expenditures (full sample)				
Outpatient care expenses	−0.059	0.060	−0.225	0.206
Observations		22,569		
Inpatient care expenses	0.121	0.256	0.882	1.01
Observations		38,045		

Notes: For binary outcomes (healthcare utilization and hardship financing), ITT effects are estimated by OLS, and ATET effects are estimated by two stage least squares (2SLS), with CBHI enrolment instrumented by the randomized offer of insurance. For expenditure outcomes, ITT effects are estimated by Poisson regression, and ATET effects are estimated by Generalized Method of Moments (GMM) of a Poisson model, with CBHI enrolment instrumented. All models include village-level fixed effects, time effects, and control for the covariates. Hardship financing is defined as having to borrow money with interest or to sell assets to pay out-of-pocket healthcare costs. Effects on outpatient care utilization/expenses are estimated using observations from all three sites. Effects on inpatient care utilization/expenses are estimated using observations from Kanpur Dehat and Pratapgarh.

Source: Authors' calculations based on information from three household surveys conducted between March and May of 2010, 2012, and 2013 obtained from MIA's management information system (MIS).

TABLE 1.9 Effects of Randomized Offer (ITT) and Uptake of Insurance (ATET) on Healthcare Utilization and Financial Protection: Site Specific Estimates

	Kanpur Dehat				Pratapgarh				Vaishali			
	ITT		ATET		ITT		ATET		ITT		ATET	
	Marginal effect	Standard error	Marginal effect	Standard error	Marginal effect	Standard error	Marginal effect	Standard error	Marginal effect	Standard error	Marginal effect	Standard error
Outpatient care conditional upon reporting illness	0.041	0.026	0.163	0.113	−0.07**	0.024	−0.51**	0.256	−0.005	0.028	−0.017	0.082
Outpatient care from a RMP conditional upon reporting illness	0.04	0.033	0.162	0.137	−0.028	0.023	−0.215	0.188	−0.008	0.023	−0.024	0.068
Observations	6,506				8,187				7,944			
Inpatient care	0.002	0.004	0.010	0.023	−0.003	0.004	−0.012	0.018				
Observations	16,479				21,566							
Healthcare expenditures (conditional upon use)												
Outpatient care expenses	0.045	0.106	0.316	0.396	−0.16***	0.061	−0.79**	0.349	0.000	0.072	−0.031	0.220
Hardship financing for outpatient care	0.01	0.028	0.041	0.109	−0.007	0.011	−0.05	0.074	0.008	0.024	0.024	0.071
Observations	4,639				6,107				5,919			
Inpatient care expenses	−0.196	0.312	−0.301	0.261	0.542	0.425	0.989	1.136				
Hardship financing for inpatient care	0.093	0.99	0.301	0.261	−0.045	0.82	−0.114	0.125				
Observations	416				498							
Healthcare expenditures (full sample)												
Outpatient care expenses	0.107	0.095	0.507	0.598	−0.24***	0.077	−1.1***	0.385	−0.028	0.072	−0.049	0.264
Inpatient care expenses	−0.093	0.304	−2.840	3.207	0.385	0.402	0.547	1.207				
Observations	16,479				21,566				20,054			

Notes: ** p<0.05; *** p<0.01.

Source: Authors' calculations based on information from three household surveys conducted between March and May of 2010, 2012, and 2013 obtained from MIA's management information system (MIS).

The low initial enrolment rate and low rates of retention in the Indian CBHI schemes explored in this review suggest that such schemes, which are entirely community-financed and community-managed, and which offer limited benefit packages, are unlikely to be able to meet healthcare needs. In short, such schemes are affordable, but not desirable. The current analysis suggests that financial support may be needed to provide more attractive benefit packages, and to finance activities that lead to a greater awareness of scheme entitlements and claims procedures, and enhance the management capacity of scheme administrators. In short, the results of this study demonstrate that community prepayment schemes, at least of the type examined here, which do not receive external financial or technical support, are unlikely to have a large effect on access to healthcare and financial protection.

ARE EXISTING SOCIAL INSURANCE SCHEMES IN INDIA SUFFICIENT TO REDUCE VULNERABILITY TO HEALTH SHOCKS? A LOOK AT NATIONAL SAMPLE SURVEY DATA

An increase in OOP payments on health by households can have catastrophic effects, and may deplete a household's ability to generate current and future income. Such expenses may have inter-generational consequences as households may be compelled to incur debt, sell productive assets, draw down buffer food stocks, or sacrifice children's education. Furthermore, foregoing medical care may lead to long-lasting illness, disability, or even death (De Weerdt and Dercon 2006; Flores et al. 2008; Meghan 2010; O'Donnell et al. 2005). Some protection against health shocks, therefore, become a necessity. The question, therefore, is whether insurance schemes, especially SHIs that are implemented in India, are sufficient to reduce a household's vulnerability to health shocks.

Karan, Yip, and Mahal (2017: 83) show that the RSBY health insurance scheme for the poor launched in 2008:

did not affect the likelihood of inpatient out-of-pocket spending, the level of inpatient out of pocket spending or catastrophic inpatient spending. We do not find any statistically significant effect of RSBY on the level of outpatient out-of-pocket expenditure

and the probability of incurring outpatient expenditure. In contrast, the likelihood of incurring any out of pocket spending (inpatient and outpatient) rose by 30 percent due to RSBY and was statistically significant suggesting that RSBY has been ineffective in reducing the burden of out-of-pocket spending on poor households.

In the analysis below, we do a much simpler exercise. We estimate the vulnerability of households to health shocks using data from the 60th and 71st Rounds of the National Sample Survey (NSS) for India. The data has information on whether the household and the individual members within the household have insurance cover or not. We compare the vulnerability of households with health insurance cover (state, national, or private) to households that are uninsured. We proxy vulnerability by OOP expenses that households have to bear over and above what their insurance has reimbursed. We do this exercise for hospitalization and for outpatient visits.

Most social insurance schemes primarily cover in-hospitalization costs. The issue is whether these schemes indeed cover all expenses, or whether the household still needs to make OOP payments for episodes of in-hospitalization. Furthermore, households incur a significant portion of health expenditure as outpatients raising the question about further vulnerability of households.

The WHO defines health expenditure as catastrophic if the share of a household's total expenditure on healthcare services is more than 40 per cent of the household's capacity to pay (Ke Xu et al. 2003). A household's capacity to pay is measured by its total non-food expenditure (for details, see Karami, Najafi, and Karami 2009).

Figure 1.9 shows the estimates of OOP expenses borne by patients who are hospitalized. The estimates are for insured and uninsured households separately as well as vulnerability of households on account of in-hospitalization health shocks irrespective of whether they have insurance cover or not. The estimates are for the years 2004–5 (NSS 60th Round) and for 2014 (NSS 71st Round). The estimates show that irrespective of where households reside—the urban or the rural sector—they face financial risks associated with in-hospitalization health episodes. The vulnerability of uninsured households, as expected, is higher. The one

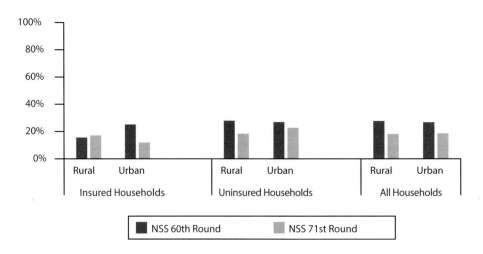

FIGURE 1.9 Inpatient Out-of-Pocket Expenses (per cent of usual consumption expenditure as defined by NSSO)

heartening trend observed in the figure is the lower estimate of vulnerability for the 71st Round NSS data, perhaps indicating that SHIs are making an impact, albeit in a limited way.

The picture changes in case of outpatients (Figure 1.10). First, no longer can we claim that households are better off in terms of financial risks related to health shocks in 2014 as compared to 2004–5. In both the urban and rural sectors, households' vulnerability to health shocks due to payments for outpatient health services show an increase. In the rural sector, OOP expenses are very close to the 'catastrophic expenses' threshold of 40 per cent

of non-food expenditure of the household as defined by the WHO. Recognize that the usual consumption expenditure defined by the NSSO includes food expenditure suggesting that our estimates are a lower bound on the actual OOP payments on outpatient services made by households.

In estimates of OOP expenses across the consumption quartiles (Figure 1.11), as expected, the poorest section of society (bottom quartile) exhibits the highest vulnerability, and has 'catastrophic health expenses' as defined by the WHO. At least for the bottom quartile, health expenses—whether for the insured or

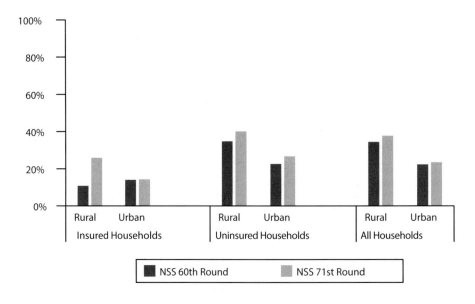

FIGURE 1.10 Outpatient Out-of-Pocket Expenses (per cent of usual consumption expenditure as defined by NSSO)

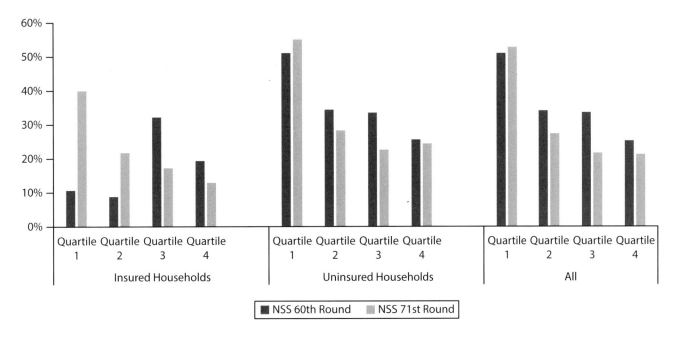

FIGURE 1.11   Total Out-of-Pocket Expenses across Consumption Wealth Quartiles (per cent of usual consumption expenditure as defined by NSSO)

the uninsured household—have risen between the two rounds of NSS data suggesting an increase in their financial vulnerability to health shocks over time. Since government health insurance schemes target the poorest sections of society, SHIs need to play a greater role in alleviating the vulnerability of this group to health shocks by increasing uptake of the schemes.

Social health insurance schemes are a step in the right direction but before they can provide a reasonable cushion to households, especially the poor and vulnerable, against adverse health shocks, they require significant changes in their design. A serious thought to bringing preventive healthcare under its ambit to reduce high OOP expenses on outpatient health services through optimal insurance design is imperative. This will reduce the extent of vulnerability of households to health shocks, and possibly reduce costs to the government and insurance companies in the long run.

REFERENCES

Aggarwal, A. 2010. 'Impact Evaluation of India's "Yeshasvini" Community-Based Health Insurance', *Health Economics*, 19(S1): 5–35.

Aggarwal, S. 2015. 'Paving the Way to a Better Health: Quantity and Quality Evidence from India'. Working Paper, Indian School of Business.

———. 2018. 'The Long Road to Health: Healthcare Utilization Impacts of a Road Pavement Policy in Rural India'. Working paper, Indian School of Business, www.iimb.ac.in/sites/default/files/inline-files/Shilpa%20Aggarwal.pdf; 12 April 2017.

Ahuja, R. and J. Jütting. 2004. 'Are the Poor Too Poor to Demand Health Insurance?', *Journal of Microfinance, ESR Review*, 6(1): 1–20.

Alderman, H. and D. Headey. 2017. 'How Important Is Parental Education for Child Nutrition?', *World Development*, 94: 448–64.

Atim, C. and M. Sock. 2000. *An External Evaluation of the Nkoranza Community Financing Health Insurance Scheme, Ghana.* Bethesda, Maryland: Partnerships for Health Reform, Abt Associates.

Banerjee, A., E. La Ferrara, and V. Orozco. 2017. 'The Entertaining Way to Behavioral Change', https://economics.yale.edu/sites/default/files/banerjeelaferraraorozco_29sept2017.pdf; 5 March 2018.

Bergkvist, S., A. Wagstaff, A. Katyal, P.V. Singh, A. Samarth, and M. Rao. 2014. 'What a Difference a State Makes: Health Reform in Andhra Pradesh'. Policy Research Working Paper, The World Bank, Development Research Group, Human Development and Public Services Team.

Berman, P.A., R. Ahuja, and L. Bhandari. 2010. 'The Impoverishing Effect of Healthcare Payments in India: New Methodology and Findings', *Economic & Political Weekly*, XLV(16): 65–71.

Binnendijk, E., R. Koren, and D. Dror. 2012. 'Can the Rural Poor in India Afford to Treat Non-communicable Diseases', *Tropical Medicine and International Health*, 17(11):1376–85.

Bonu, S., I. Bhushan, M. Rani, and I. Anderson. 2009. 'Incidence and Correlates of "Catastrophic" Maternal Health Care Expenditure in India', *Health Policy and Planning*, 24(6): 445–56.

Carrin, G., A. Ron, Y. Hui, W. Hong, Z. Tuohong, Z. Licheng, Z. Shuo, et al. 1999. 'The Reform of the Rural Cooperative Medical System in the People's Republic of China: Interim Experience in 14 Pilot Counties', *Social Science & Medicine*, 48(7): 961–72.

Carrin, G., M. Waelkens, and B. Criel. 2005. 'Community-based Health Insurance in Developing Countries: A Study of its Contribution to the Performance of Health Financing Systems', *Tropical Medicine and International Health*, 10(8): 799–811.

Chee, G., K. Smith, and A. Kapinga. 2002. *Assessment of Community Health Fund in Hanang District, Tanzania*. Bethesda, MD: The Partners for Health Reformplus Project, Abt Associates Inc.

Choudhury, M. and R. Srinivasan. 2011. *A Study on Insurance Schemes of Government of India*. National Institute of Public Finance and Policy.

Criel, B. and G. Kegels. 1997. 'A Health Insurance Scheme for Hospital Care in Bwamanda District, Zaire: Lessons and Questions after 10 Years of Functioning', *Tropical Medicine and International Health*, 2(7): 654–72.

De Weerdt, J. and S. Dercon. 2006. 'Risk-sharing Networks and Insurance against Illness', *Journal of Development Economics*, 81(2): 337–56.

Debnath, S. 2013. 'Improving Maternal Health with Incentives to Mothers vs. Health Workers: Evidence from India'. Working paper, Indian School of Business.

Debnath, S. and T. Jain. 2017. 'Social Connections and Public Healthcare Utilization'. Working paper, Indian School of Business.

Defourny, J. and J. Failon. 2008. 'Community-Based Health Insurance Schemes in Africa: Which Factors Really Induce Membership?'. *8th International Conference for Third Sector Research*. Barcelona: University of Barcelona.

Desmet, M., A. Chowdhury, and M. Islam. 1999. 'The Potential for Social Mobilisation in Bangladesh: The Organisation and Functioning of Two Health Insurance Schemes', *Social Science & Medicine*, 48(7): 925–38.

Devadasan, N., B. Criel, W. Van Damme, K. Ranson, and P. Van der Stuyft. 2007. 'Indian Community Health Insurance Schemes Provide Partial Protection against Catastrophic Health Expenditure', *BMC Health Services Research*, 7(1): 1–11.

Diop, F., S. Sulzbach, and S. Chankova. 2006. *The Impact of Mutual Health Organizations on Social Inclusion, Access to Health Care, and Household Income Protection: Evidence from Ghana, Senegal, and Mali*. Bethesda: PHRplus, Abt Associates Inc.

Doyle, C., P. Panda, E. Van de Poel, R. Radermacher, and D. Dror. 2011. 'Reconciling Research and Implementation in Micro Health Insurance Experiments in India: Study Protocol for a Randomized Controlled Trial', *Trials*, 12(1), Article No. 224.

Dror, D.M., M. Lorenzo, and J. Sarol. 2005. 'Field Based Evidence of Enhanced Healthcare Utilization among Persons Insured by Micro Health Insurance Units in Philippines', *Health Policy*, 73(3): 263–71.

Dror, D.M., P. Panda, C. May, A. Majumdar, and R. Koren. 2014. 'One for All and All for One: Consensus-building within Communities in Rural India on their Health Microinsurance Package', *Risk Management and Healthcare Policy*, 7: 139–53.

Dror, D.M., R. Radermacher, S. Khadilkar, P. Schout, F. Hay, A. Singh, and R. Koren. 2009. 'Microinsurance: Innovations in Low-cost Health Insurance', *Health Affairs*, 28(6): 1788–98.

Ekman, B. 2004. 'Community-Based Health Insurance in Low-income Countries: A Systematic Review of the Evidence', *Health Policy and Planning*, 19(5): 249–70.

———. 2007. 'Catastrophic Health Payments and Health Insurance: Some Counterintuitive Evidence from One Low-income Country', *Health Policy*, 83(2–3): 304–13.

Fink, G., P. Robyn, A. Sié, and R. Sauerborn. 2013. 'Does Health Insurance Improve Health? Evidence from a Randomized Community-Based Insurance Rollout in Rural Burkina Faso', *Journal of Health Economics*, 32(6): 1043–56.

Flores, G., J. Krishnakumar, O. O'Donnell, and E. Van Doorslaer. 2008. 'Coping with Healthcare Costs: Implications for the Measurement of Catastrophic Expenditures and Poverty', *Health Economics*, 17(12): 1393–412.

Franco, L., F. Diop, C. Burgert, A. Kelley, M. Makinen, and C. Simpara. 2008. 'Effects of Mutual Health Organizations on use of Priority Health-Care Services in Urban and Rural Mali: A Case-control Study', *Bulletin of the World Health Organization*, 86(11): 830–8.

Galárraga, O., S. Sosa-Rubí, A. Salinas-Rodríguez, and S. Sesma-Vázquez. 2010. 'Health Insurance for the Poor: Impact on Catastrophic and Out-of-Pocket Health Expenditures in Mexico', *The European Journal of Health Economics*, 11(5): 437–47.

Gautham, M., E. Binnendijk, R. Koren, and D. Dror. 2011. 'First We Go to the Small Doctor: First Contact for Curative Health Care Sought by Rural Communities in Andhra Pradesh and Orissa, India', *Indian Journal of Medical Research*, 134(5): 627–38.

Gething, P. and S. Hay. 2017. 'Nations within a Nation: Variations in Epidemiological Transition across the States of India, 1990–2016 in the Global Burden of Disease Study', *The Lancet*, 390(10111): 2437–60.

Ghosh, S. 2011. 'Catastrophic Payments and Impoverishment Due to Out-of-Pocket Health Spending', *Economic & Political Weekly*, XLVI(47): 63–70.

Ghosh, S. and N. Gupta. 2017. 'Targeting and Effects of Rashtriya Swasthya Bima Yojana on Access to Care and Financial Protection', *Economic & Political Weekly*, LII(4): 61–70.

Gnawali, D., S. Pokhrel, A. Sié, M. Sanon, M. De Allegri, A. Souares, H. Dong, and R. Sauerborn. 2009. 'The Effect of Community-Based Health Insurance on the Utilization of Modern Health Care Services: Evidence from Burkina Faso', *Health Policy*, 90(2–3): 214–22.

Gobah, F. and L. Zhang. 2011. 'The National Health Insurance Scheme in Ghana: Prospects and Challenges: A Cross-sectional Evidence', *Global Journal of Health Science*, 3(2): 90–101.

Gumber, A. 2001. 'Hedging the Health of the Poor: The Case for Community Financing in India'. Health, Nutrition and Population Discussion Paper. Washington, DC: The World Bank.

Hamid, S., J. Roberts, and P. Mosley. 2011. 'Can Micro Health Insurance Reduce Poverty? Evidence from Bangladesh', *Journal of Risk and Insurance*, 78 (1): 57–82.

Ito, S. and H. Kono. 2010. 'Why is the Take-up of Microinsurance So Low? Evidence from a Health Insurance Scheme in India', *The Developing Economies*, 48(1): 74–101.

Jacobs, Bart, Maryam Bigdeli, Maurits van Pelt, Por Ir, Cedric Salze, and Bart Criel. 2008. 'Bridging Community-Based Health Insurance and Social Protection for Health Care: A Step in the Direction of Universal Coverage?', *Tropical Medicine & International Health*, 13(2): 140–3.

Jakab, M. and C. Krishnan. 2001. 'Community Involvement in Health Care Financing: Impact, Strengths and Weaknesses: A Synthesis of Literature'. Discussion paper for WHO Commission on Macroeconomics and Health. Washington, DC: The World Bank.

Jowett, M., P. Contoyannis, and N. Vinh. 2003. 'The Impact of Public Voluntary Health Insurance on Private Health Expenditures in Vietnam', *Social Science & Medicine*, 56(2): 333–42.

Jütting, J. 2004. 'Do Community-Based Health Insurance Schemes Improve Poor People's Access to Health Care? Evidence from Rural Senegal', *World Development*, 32(2): 273–88.

Karami, M., F. Najafi, and M. Karami. 2009. 'Catastrophic Health Expenditures in Kermanshah, West of Iran: Magnitude and Distribution', *Journal of Research in Health Sciences*, 9(2): 36–40.

Karan, A., W. Yip, and A. Mahal. 2017. 'Extending Health Insurance to the Poor in India: An Impact Evaluation of Rashtriya Swasthya Bima Yojana on Out of Pocket Spending for Healthcare', *Social Science & Medicine*, 181: 83–92.

Kearney, M. and P. Levine. 2015. 'Media Influences on Social Outcomes: The Impact of MTV's 16 and Pregnant on Teen Childbearing', *American Economic Review*, 105(12): 3597–632.

Ke Xu, David B. Evans, Kei Kawabata, Riadh Zeramdini, Jan Klavus, and C.J. Murray. 2003. 'Household Catastrophic Health Expenditure: A Multicountry Analysis', *The Lancet*, 362(9378): 111–17.

Lammers, J. and S. Warmerdam. 2010. *Adverse Selection in Voluntary Micro Health Insurance in Nigeria*. Amesterdam: Amsterdam Institute for International Research Series 10-06.

Levine, D., R. Polimeni, and I. Ramage. 2012. *Insuring Health or Insuring Wealth? An Experimental Evaluation of Health Insurance in Rural Cambodia*. Paris: Agence Française de Développement Impact Analysis Series no. 08.

Liu, X., S. Tang, B. Yu, N. Phuong, F. Yan, D. Thien, and R. Tolhurst. 2012. 'Can Rural Health Insurance Improve Equity in Health Care Utilization? A Comparison between China and Vietnam', *International Journal for Equity in Health*, 11(1): 3–9.

Mane, A. and S. Khandekar. 2014. 'Strengthening Primary Health Care through ASHA Workers: A Novel Approach in India', *Primary Health Care*, 4(1): 149.

Mebratie, A., R. Sparrow, G. Alemu, and A. Bedi. 2013. 'Community-Based Health Insurance Schemes: A Systematic Review'. ISS Working Paper No. 568.

Mebratie, A., R. Sparrow, Z. Yilma, D. Abebaw, G. Alemu, and A. Bedi. 2013. 'Impact of Ethiopian Pilot Community-based Health Insurance Scheme on Health-Care Utilisation: A Household Panel Data Analysis', *The Lancet*, 381 (Supplement 2): S92.

———. 2014. 'The Impact of Ethiopia's Pilot Community Based Health Insurance Scheme on Healthcare Utilization and Cost of Care'. ISS Working Paper No. 593.

Mebratie, A., R. Sparrow, Z. Yilma, G. Alemu, and A. Bedi. 2015a. 'Dropping Out of Ethiopia's Community Based Health Insurance Scheme', *Health Policy and Planning*, 30(10): 1296–306.

———. 2015b. 'Enrolment in Ethiopia's Community Based Health Insurance Scheme', *World Development*, 74: 58–76.

Meghan, S. 2010. 'Micro-finance Health Insurance in Developing Countries'. Wharton Research Scholars Working Paper. Philadelphia: University of Pennsylvania.

Msuya, J., J. Jütting, and A. Asfaw. 2007. 'Impact of Community Health Funds on the Access to Health Care: Empirical Evidence from Rural Tanzania', *International Journal of Public Administration*, 30(8–9): 813–33.

Nagulapalli, S. 2014. 'Burden of Out-of-Pocket Health Payments in Andhra Pradesh', *Economic & Political Weekly*, XLIX(42): 64–72.

Nair, R. 2016. 'Flagship Government Schemes Set for a Revamp', *Mint*, 25 January.

Nguyen, H., Y. Rajkotia, and H. Wang. 2011. 'The Financial Protection Effect of Ghana National Health Insurance Scheme: Evidence from a Study in Two Rural Districts', *International Journal for Equity in Health*, 10(1): 1–12.

Noterman, J., B. Criel, G. Kegels, and K. Isu. 1995. 'A Prepayment Scheme for Hospital Care in the Masisi District in Zaire: A Critical Evaluation', *Social Science & Medicine*, 40(7): 919–30.

O'Donnell, O., E.V. Doorslaer, R.P. Rannan-Eliya, A. Somanathan, C.C. Garg, P. Hanvoravongchai, M.N. Hug et al. 2005. *Explaining the Incidence of Catastrophic Expenditures on Health Care: Comparative Evidence from Asia.* Manila: Equity in Asia-Pacific Health Systems: EQUITAP Working Paper 05.

Onwujekwe, O., C. Onoka, B. Uzichukwu, C. Okoli, E. Obikeze, and S. Eze. 2009. 'Is Community-Based Health Insurance an Equitable Strategy for Paying for Healthcare? Experience from Southeast Nigeria', *Health Policy*, 92(1): 96–102.

Panda, P., A. Chakraborty, W. Raza, and A.S. Bedi. 2016. 'Renewing Membership in Three Community-Based Health Insurance Schemes in Rural India', *Health Policy and Planning*, 31(10): 1433–44.

Parmar, D., A. Souares, M. Allegri, G. Savadogo, and R. Sauerborn. 2012. 'Adverse Selection in a Community-Based Health Insurance Scheme in Rural Africa: Implications for Introducing Targeted Subsidies', *BMC Health Services Research*, 12(1): 1–27.

Rajasekhar, D., E. Berg, M. Ghatak, R. Manjula, and S. Roy. 2011. 'Implementing Health Insurance for the Poor: The Rollout of RSBY in Karnataka'. Research Paper, The Suntory and Toyota International Centres for Economics and Related Disciplines, London School of Economics and Political Science.

Ranson, M.K. 2002. 'Reduction of Catastrophic Health Care Expenditures by a Community-Based Health Insurance Scheme in Gujarat, India: Current Experiences and Challenges', *Bulletin of the World Health Organization*, 80(8): 613–21.

Ranson, M.K, T. Sinha, M. Chatterjee, A. Acharya, A. Bhavsar, S. Morris, and A.J. Mills. 2006. 'Making Health Insurance Work for the Poor: Learning from the Self-Employed Women's Association's (SEWA) Community-Based Health Insurance Scheme in India', *Social Science & Medicine*, 62(3): 707–20.

Rao, K., H. Waters, L. Steinhardt, S. Alam, P. Hansen, and A. Naeem. 2009. 'An Experiment with Community Health Funds in Afghanistan', *Health Policy and Planning*, 24(4): 301–11.

Rathi, P., A. Mukherji, and G. Sen. 2012. 'Rashtriya Swasthya Bima Yojana: Evaluating Utilisation, Roll-out and Perceptions in Amaravati District, Maharashtra', *Economic & Political Weekly*, XLVII(39): 57–64.

Raza, W., E.V. Poel, A.S. Bedi, and F. Rutten. 2016a. 'Impact of Community Based Health Insurance on Access to Care and Financial Protection: Evidence from Three Randomized Control Trials in Rural India', *Health Economics*, 25(6): 675–87.

Raza, W., E. Van de Poel, D. Dror, P. Panda, and A. Bedi. 2016b. 'Healthcare Seeking Behavior among Self-help Group Households in Rural Bihar and Uttar Pradesh, India', *BMC Health Services Research*, 16(1), doi: 10.1186/s12913-015-1254-9.

Reddy, K.S., S. Selvaraj, K. Rao, M. Chokshi, P. Kumar, V. Arora, S. Bhokare, and I. Ganguly. 2011. *A Critical Assessment of the Existing Health Insurance Models in India*, Public Health Foundation of India, 1–115.

Robyn, P., A. Hill, Y. Liu, A. Souares, G. Savadogo, A. Sié, and R. Sauerborn. 2011. 'Econometric Analysis to Evaluate the Effect of Community-Based Health Insurance on Reducing Informal Self-care in Burkina Faso', *Health Policy and Planning*, 11(1): 1–10.

Saksena, P., A. Antunes, K. Xu, L. Musango, and G. Carrin. 2011. 'Mutual Health Insurance in Rwanda: Evidence on Access to Care and Financial Risk Protection', *Health Policy*, 99(3): 203–9.

Schneider, P. and F. Diop. 2001. 'Synopsis of Results on the Impact of Community-Based Health Insurance on Financial Accessibility to Health Care in Rwanda'. Health, Nutrition and Population (HNP) Discussion Paper. Washington, DC: The World Bank

Sekyi, S. and P. Domanban. 2012. 'The Effects of Health Insurance on Outpatient Utilization and Health Care Expenditure in Ghana', *International Journal of Humanities and Social Science*, 2(10): 40–9.

Selvaraj, S. and A. Karan. 2012. 'Why Publicly-Financed Health Insurance Schemes are Ineffective in Providing Financial Risk Protection', *Economic & Political Weekly*, XLVII(11): 61–8.

Shigute, Z., A. Mebratie, R. Sparrow, Z. Yilma, G. Alemu, and A. Bedi. 2017. 'Uptake of Health Insurance and the Productive Safety Net Program in Rural Ethiopia', *Social Science & Medicine*, 176: 133–41.

Shimeles, A. 2010. 'Community Based Health Insurance Schemes in Africa: The Case of Rwanda'. GU Working Papers in Economics 463. Göteborg: Göteborg University.

Sun, X., S. Jackson, G. Carmichael, and A. Sleigh. 2009. 'Catastrophic Medical Payment and Financial Protection in Rural China: Evidence from the New Cooperative Medical Scheme in Shandong Province', *Health Economics*, 18(1): 103–19.

Swasthya Sathi. 2017. *Swasthya Sathi Report May 2017*, 1(3). Kolkata: Data Analysis Department, State Nodal Agency, Swasthya Sathi, Government of West Bengal.

———. 2018. *Swasthya Sathi Report May 2018*, 2(4). Kolkata: Data Analysis Department, State Nodal Agency, Swasthya Sathi, Government of West Bengal.

Tabor, S. 2005. 'Community-Based Health Insurance and Social Protection Policy'. World Bank Social Protection Discussion Paper Series No. 0503. Washington, DC: The World Bank.

Wagstaff, A., M. Lindelow, G. Jun, X. Ling, and J. Qian. 2009. 'Extending Health Insurance to the Rural Population: An

Impact Evaluation of China's New Cooperative Medical Scheme', *Journal of Health Economics*, 28(1): 1–19.

Wang, H., W. Yip, L. Zhang, L. Wang, and W. Hsiao 2005. 'Community-Based Health Insurance in Poor Rural China: The Distribution of Net Benefits', *Health Policy and Planning*, 20(6): 366–74.

Wiesmann, D., and J. Jütting. 2001. 'Determinants of Viable Health Insurance Schemes in Rural Sub-Saharan Africa', *Quarterly Journal of International Agriculture*, 40(4): 361–78.

World Bank. 2011. *The World Bank Data: How We Classify Countries*. Washington, DC: The World Bank.

World Health Organization (WHO). 2000. *The World Health Report 2000: Health Systems: Improving Performance*. Geneva: World Health Organization.

————. 2003. *Social Health Insurance Report of a Regional Expert Group Meeting*. India: New Delhi, 13–15 March.

————. 2012. *World Health Statistics 2012*, http://goo.gl/RHlNk; 2 July 2018.

————. 2013. *The World Health Report 2013: Research for Universal Health Coverage*. Geneva: World Health Organization.

World Health Organization Global Health Expenditure database. 2015. Accessed from http://apps.who.int/nha/database on 4/7/2018, World Health Organization, Geneva, Switzerland.

Xuemei, L. and H. Xiao. 2011. 'Statistical Analysis of the Effectiveness of the New Cooperative Medical Scheme in Rural China', *Canadian Social Science*, 7(3): 21–6.

Yip, W., H. Wang, and W. Hsiao. 2008. 'The Impact of Rural Mutual Health Care on Access to Care: Evaluation of a Social Experiment in Rural China'. HSPH Working Paper. Harvard School of Public Health, Cambridge, MA.

Zhang, L. and H. Wang. 2008. 'Dynamic Process of Adverse Selection: Evidence from a Subsidized Community-Based Health Insurance in Rural China', *Social Science & Medicine*, 67(7): 1173–82.

2

Inexpensive and Effective Healthcare?

Koushik Kumar Hati, Kalyan Khan, and Biswajit Mandal

A LOOK AT HEALTH PRICING POLICIES IN INDIA

Social insurance schemes in India, whether implemented by the Central or state governments, primarily cover the poor in society (below poverty line [BPL] households, contractual government workers, and so on). Yet, there is a vast population not covered by government-sponsored health insurance schemes which requires affordable quality healthcare. A large proportion of this segment of the population goes to private sector health facilities for their healthcare needs.

India's public expenditure on health, at less than 1.5 per cent of the gross domestic product (GDP), is among the lowest in the world, lower than the average among low-income countries. Sri Lanka spends four times more than India in terms of per capita public health expenditure, and Indonesia twice as much. 'Yet India ranks among the top 20 of the world's countries in its private spending, at 4.2% of GDP. Employers pay for 9% of spending on private care, health insurance 5–10%, and 82% is from personal funds' (Sengupta and Nandy 2005).

The above trend is despite rumblings about oft-unchecked corrupt practices—overbilling, unnecessary diagnostic testing and surgical procedures—by private healthcare providers.

This is because the public alternative is so much worse, with interminable waits in dirty surroundings with hordes of other patients. Many medicines and tests are not available in the public sector, so patients have to go to private shops and laboratories. Each harassed doctor may have to see more than 100 patients in a single outpatient session. Some of these doctors advise patients, legally or illegally, to 'meet them privately' if they want more personalised care. In a recent survey carried out by Transparency International, 30% of patients in government hospitals claimed that they had had to pay bribes or use influence to jump queues for treatment and for outpatient appointments with senior doctors, and to get clean bed sheets and better food in hospital' (Sengupta and Nandy 2005, p. 1158).

The growth of the private health sector has had tacit support of governments by way of subsidized land for building hospitals, tax concessions on imported drugs and machines, and so on. There is a clause about treating a certain percentage of patients free of cost—a rarely met nor monitored requirement. Given that the private health sector is an integral part of health provisioning in India, it becomes imperative on part of governments to 'introduce reforms and build protocols and systems of price-fixation… [to] achieve [the] goal of reducing impoverishment and out-of-pocket expenditures' (Rao 2018b).

Pricing, rather, overpricing of health services provided by the private sector, has been in the news of late. Headlines such as 'India Costlier for Heart Operations than Richer Nations' (Nagarajan 2018a), 'Why India's Private Hospitals Can Get Away with Over-charging' (Rao 2018b), and 'Health Panel Walks Pricing Tightrope' (Mandal 2018) are but a few examples of such media reports.

In this chapter, we look at three aspects of pricing policies related to health in India. In the first section,[1] we compare average pricing of different procedures in government, for-profit private, and not-for-profit private health facilities. We do this using information gathered through a primary survey of health facilities in West Bengal. In the second section,[2] using a theoretical model backed by some anecdotal evidence, we question the usefulness of 'health packages' that are sold to consumers by private sector health facilities. Finally, in the third section,[3] we look at an important component of providing affordable care to all—the pricing policy for medicinal drugs. Through anecdotal evidence, we trace the nexus between the pharmaceutical company, the medical representative, and the doctor.

Health Panel Walks Pricing Tightrope
Sanjay Mandal, *The Times of India*, 8 March 2018

GIVE-AND-TAKE FORMULA
- Proposal to have between 30 and 40 per cent of beds in every private hospital under fixed package pricing
- Hospitals could be allowed to fix tariff for single and twin-sharing cabins to remain economically viable
- Proposed rates for medical procedures to be higher than that of *Swasthya Sathi* scheme but less than existing packages
- Availability of beds under the new scheme to be displayed prominently by each hospital

---

[1] Based on a background paper, K. Khan and K.K. Hati, 'Cost Divergence across Health Sectors and the Paradox of Preference' (2018). Mimeo CTRPFP.

[2] Based on a background paper, Sugata Marjit and Biswajit Mandal, 'The Rise and Fall of "Package Deals" offered by Private Hospitals' (2018), Mimeo CTRPFP.

[3] Based on a background paper, Sattwik Santra, 'Medicines' (2018), Mimeo CTRPFP.

PARADOX OF PREFERENCES[4]

Despite high medical costs in the private sector, more and more Indians are using private healthcare services to fulfil their health needs. The 71st Round (2014) data of the National Sample Survey (NSS) on health shows that on average, it is four times costlier to get treated in a private health facility per hospitalization case when compared to a government health facility (NSS 2015). Yet, in India's most populous state—Uttar Pradesh—more than 80 per cent of the population uses a private healthcare facility when they fall ill (IIPS 2017). This pattern is true even across the wealth quintiles. While in the top quintile, two-thirds prefer using a private healthcare facility, in the first four quintiles, usage of a private facility ranges between 48 to 52 per cent of households (IIPS 2017).

'I prefer visiting the doctor's chamber for check-ups and visit hospitals only in instances of admission because visiting the hospital for check-ups would imply forgoing an entire day's wage which is unaffordable.'

— *Casual factory worker*

'The reason for this seems to do with the pitiable quality and accessibility of public healthcare systems across rural and urban areas—which remain dismally funded, poorly monitored, and inadequately standardised' (Bhattacharjee and Mohan 2017).

Healthcare is provided by the government, and private sector through 'for-profit' hospitals and self-employed practitioners, and 'not-for-profit' non-government providers, including faith-based organizations.

In this section, using data from the 71st Round of the NSS (2014), we analyse the differences in costs for similar health procedures in government and private sector health facilities. We also gather cost information for different medical procedures from 'for-profit' private hospitals and 'not-for-profit' private hospitals in West Bengal. We compare these costs to the rates under the Central Government Health Scheme (CGHS) and *Swasthya Sathi*—a recent social health insurance scheme (SHI) introduced by the Government of West Bengal

---

[4] This section is based on a background paper, K. Khan and K.K. Hati, 'Cost Divergence across Health Sectors and Paradox of Preference'.

for its contractual employees and civic volunteers. We also try to put forth reasons regarding the choice of consumers to go to the private sector despite the higher cost charged in these facilities compared to government sector units.

Use and Cost of Private Healthcare in India

From the latest round of NSS data, we estimate that an average Indian spends approximately INR 15,000 towards inpatient expenses per year to treat his/her illnesses. There is a fourfold increase in treatment costs if the person opts for a private hospital instead of a government hospital. The difference in costs between private and public health facilities is larger in urban areas as compared to rural areas. Table 2.1 summarizes component-wise health expenditures across sectors, and public and private healthcare facilities in India.

'My sister was diagnosed with sleep apnea and suspected pulmonary hypertension. As her saturation levels plummeted to less than 60%, she was admitted into the intensive care unit for two days and then kept in a private room for observation for another two days before being discharged. The major interventions required were intubation for about six hours till she stabilized and five arterial blood gas tests to check her carbon dioxide levels. I was curious to see how the prices charged by the hospital compared with those of *Aarogyasri*—the health scheme of the Telangana and Andhra Pradesh governments that aims

to provide quality healthcare to the poor. A comparison showed a price difference of 30% to 40% for most items, leading to the question: were the *Aarogyasri* prices too low or the hospital billing too high? Some of the hospital's prices were over the top: it charged Rs 19,080 for a CT scan of the lungs and Rs 880 for four tablets of thyroxin against *Aarogyasri* rates of Rs 2,500 and Rs 3.4. And though only the pulmonologist and the internist in the intensive care unit had examined my sister, eight other doctors were remunerated. In fact, the doctors' fee alone accounted for 15.4% of the bill.'

Source: K. Sujatha Rao, Quartz India: Real Talk: 'Why India's Private Hospitals Can Get Away with Overcharging Patients', 26 March 2018.

The NSS data show that in India, two components, namely, medicines and expenditures for the overall package, are the leading contributors to health expenditures. A rural Indian pays nearly seven times the fee to a doctor/surgeon if s/he prefers to visit a private hospital located in an urban area rather than visiting a doctor/surgeon in a government hospital closer to their residence. Similarly, the cost of the package component reduces to about a quarter whereas the costs of medicines and diagnostic tests fall to one third if s/he opts for inpatient hospitalization in a rural government hospital. Note that if a patient is hospitalized, then this is normally preceded or followed by non-hospitalization, and there is a cost associated with that.

TABLE 2.1   Component-Specific (in-hospitalization) Average Health Expense in India (INR)

Components	Government Facility		Private Facility	
	Rural	Urban	Rural	Urban
Package component	5,269.68	11,598.48	21,873.57	37,765.17
Doctor's/Surgeon's fee	1,147.35	2,430.86	5,079.88	7,833.97
Medicines	2,397.20	2,999.23	5,857.98	7,347.63
Diagnostic tests	1,233.82	1,622.86	2,473.59	3,533.34
Bed charges	603.41	962.44	3,154.59	4,279.50
Other medical charges	829.60	2,960.03	2,422.37	3,384.71
Transport charge for patient	566.32	437.38	813.69	715.90
Other non-medical expenditure	1,012.82	1,077.19	1,557.75	1,725.77
Average total expenditure (INR)	**13,060.20**	**24,088.47**	**43,233.42**	**66,585.99**

Source: Authors' own calculations based on NSS 71st Round data.

Similar to in-hospitalization, substantial cost differences across sectors and facilities exist for cases of non-hospitalization as well (Table 2.2). Overall, at the country level, medicines and diagnostic tests are the most expensive components of health services in case of non-hospitalization.

If we focus on average health expenses for West Bengal, we find that in-hospitalization health services in the state are relatively at par when compared to the country average (Table 2.3). The package component in the urban private sector, however, costs roughly 5.7 times more than that in a government facility in the urban sector, and doctors' fees are double the rates in urban public hospitals.

However, in recent times, the Government of West Bengal has taken initiatives to provide different types of health services in government hospitals at no cost.[5] This step is likely to widen the existing gap between private and public health expenditures in the state.

The picture is similar with respect to non-hospitalization expenses (Table 2.4). The average non-hospitalization expenditure in a private hospital in West Bengal is INR 1,240.67, whereas in a government hospital, it is INR 991.76. Non-hospitalization costs are higher in urban areas compared to rural areas.

[5] Government of West Bengal, Department of Health, Memorandum No. HF/O/TDE/29/M-08/13.

TABLE 2.2 Component-Specific (non-hospitalization) Average Health Expense in India (INR)

Particulars	Government Facility			Private Facility		
	Rural	Urban	Total	Rural	Urban	Total
Doctor's/Surgeon's fee	61.84	351.30	139.21	157.56	205.65	175.89
Medicines: AYUSH	114.82	132.69	119.05	157.83	228.10	185.61
Medicines: excluding AYUSH	480.66	490.82	483.71	479.29	577.93	519.91
Diagnostic tests	277.58	307.04	285.43	295.15	379.48	330.92
Other medical expenses	99.10	102.49	99.95	123.40	256.57	174.55
Transport for patient	96.26	95.40	96.01	88.07	115.98	97.76
Other non-medical expenses	116.24	112.15	115.25	100.13	139.69	112.32
Average expenditure	**1,246.51**	**1,591.90**	**1,338.60**	**1,401.44**	**1,903.41**	**1,596.95**

Source: Authors' own calculations based on NSS 71st Round data.

TABLE 2.3 Component-Specific (in-hospitalization) Average Health Expense in West Bengal (INR)

Components	Government Facility			Private Facility		
	Rural	Urban	Total	Rural	Urban	Total
Package component	5,964.93	7,054.33	6,230.15	23,236.68	40,772.31	32,457.41
Doctor's/Surgeon's fee	2,534.55	5,440.12	3,192.69	5,967.50	11,661.59	8,535.38
Medicines	2,496.80	2,656.36	2,536.47	5,792.77	6,965.19	6,311.80
Diagnostic tests	1,944.30	1,630.51	1,871.64	3,285.35	5,132.99	4,120.41
Bed charges	681.56	383.36	615.68	2,951.59	4,354.98	3,602.52
Other medical charges	876.96	1,826.67	1,125.31	1,363.51	4,344.12	2,696.21
Transport charge for patient	632.18	446.53	584.81	1,017.14	1,100.50	1,056.22
Other non-medical expenditure	661.79	764.50	686.34	1,281.64	2,819.14	1,978.81
Average expenditure	**15,793.08**	**20,202.39**	**16,843.09**	**44,896.18**	**77,150.81**	**60,758.75**

Source: Authors' own calculations based on NSS 71st Round data.

TABLE 2.4 Component-Specific (non-hospitalization) Average Health Expense in West Bengal (INR)

Particulars	Government Facility			Private Facility		
	Rural	Urban	Total	Rural	Urban	Total
Doctor's/Surgeon's fee	27.74	83.20	36.65	153.65	183.30	163.59
Medicines: AYUSH	24.50	89.94	33.81	66.46	57.72	63.00
Medicines: excluding AYUSH	345.44	418.00	364.16	467.91	497.04	479.71
Diagnostic tests	312.65	591.04	352.14	296.79	330.33	309.92
Other medical expenses	7.37	104.49	16.40	39.21	149.90	84.92
Transport for patient	96.63	60.97	89.41	86.10	65.14	79.83
Other non-medical expense	108.68	59.51	99.20	67.88	31.01	59.71
Average expenditure	**923.00**	**1,407.16**	**991.76**	**1,178.01**	**1,314.45**	**1,240.67**

Source: Authors' own calculations based on NSS 71st Round data.

TABLE 2.5 Health Expenditure as Percentage of Household Consumption Expenditure (per capita terms)

State	Rural	Urban	Combined
Andhra Pradesh	23.38	21.82	22.69
Bihar	30.87	30.51	30.85
Gujarat	12.50	6.23	8.57
Haryana	9.76	29.60	25.30
Jharkhand	14.75	40.10	25.03
Karnataka	34.61	19.04	27.92
Kerala	17.23	14.89	15.93
Madhya Pradesh	18.24	45.50	30.24
Maharashtra	33.15	19.84	28.58
Orissa	49.05	28.06	46.47
Punjab	37.73	27.40	34.47
Rajasthan	20.78	13.58	18.80
Tamil Nadu	21.55	27.60	25.69
Uttar Pradesh	25.35	21.21	24.58
West Bengal	41.61	24.19	37.59
INDIA	**33.15**	**24.24**	**30.48**

Source: Authors' own calculation based on NSS 71st Round data.

To estimate the extent of vulnerability of households to health shocks, we compute out-of-pocket (OOP) health expense as a per cent of usual consumption expenditure (Table 2.5). We find that on an average, OOP expense is as much as 30.48 per cent of the usual consumption expenditure with considerable variation between states. Orissa is found to have the highest OOP expense as a per cent of usual consumption expenditure while Gujarat has the lowest.

Table 2.6 highlights the facility preferred by patients to seek treatment for different diseases in West Bengal. It is seen that in rural West Bengal, people prefer government hospitals over private facilities for most diseases. The scenario seems to change in urban areas. Here, for critical conditions relating to cancers, blood, endocrinal, metabolic and nutrition, eye, ear, gastrointestinal, skin, musculo-skeletal, and genito-urinary illnesses (as shown in Table 2.6), patients prefer to visit private facilities. Accessibility and affordability could be a possible explanation for the difference observed in the use of government and private facilities across rural and urban areas. Controlling for family income and distance to the health facility, the pattern may change in favour of private hospitals, especially for critical diseases.

Around 80 per cent of the patients did not have any health insurance in India. In urban India, 24.56 per cent of patients were covered by health insurance while roughly 19.45 per cent patients were covered by health insurance in rural areas. Roughly equal percentage of patients had insurance coverage in rural and urban areas in the state of Kerala (Table 2.7).

The Paradox Explained

Despite significant differences in costs and large expenses borne by patients, as reported in Tables 2.3 and 2.4, patients prefer to use the private health sector for their health needs. Estimates suggest that the Indian healthcare sector has grown at a compound annual rate of 16.5 per cent, and is likely to be worth USD 280 billion by 2020

TABLE 2.6 Percentage of Patients Using Private/Public Facilities in Rural/Urban Centres for Different Prognosis in West Bengal (in-hospitalization)

Disease	Rural		Urban	
	Government Facility	Private Facility	Government Facility	Private Facility
Infection	89.79	10.21	73.28	26.72
Cancers	69.44	30.56	35.53	64.47
Blood diseases	68.26	31.74	47.43	52.57
Endocrine, metabolic, and nutritional	83.53	16.47	34.91	65.09
Neurological and psychiatric	85.71	14.29	71.36	28.64
Eye	68.22	31.78	13.62	86.38
Ear	73.87	26.13	44.74	55.26
Cardiovascular	87.61	12.39	60.15	39.85
Respiratory	86.23	13.77	63.32	36.68
Gastrointestinal	52.14	47.86	41.63	58.37
Skin	93.33	6.67	45.52	54.48
Musculo-skeletal	73.68	26.32	49.48	50.52
Genito-urinary	49.02	50.98	43.20	56.80
Obstetric	80.59	19.41	67.82	32.18
Injuries	79.74	20.26	54.29	45.71
Child birth	78.38	21.62	65.52	34.48

Source: Authors' own calculations based on NSS 71st Round data.

TABLE 2.7 Percentage of Patients with Health Insurance

State	Rural	Urban	Aggregate
Punjab	4.40	16.53	9.02
Haryana	0.90	16.30	7.00
Rajasthan	23.55	33.10	26.58
Uttar Pradesh	4.09	9.36	5.50
Bihar	7.68	3.96	7.29
West Bengal	18.99	26.69	21.39
Jharkhand	2.01	11.13	4.89
Orissa	26.74	17.43	25.32
Chhattisgarh	45.05	40.96	44.20
Madhya Pradesh	0.68	9.42	3.34
Gujarat	16.98	20.78	18.64
Maharashtra	1.72	14.34	6.72
Andhra Pradesh	71.05	51.59	64.32
Karnataka	8.66	18.73	12.57
Kerala	43.23	40.22	41.77
Tamil Nadu	23.68	25.59	24.72
ALL INDIA	**19.45**	**24.56**	**21.20**

Source: Authors' own calculation based on NSS 71st Round data.

(Ahmed, Halim, and Ahmad 2018). This significant growth within the Indian healthcare industry is often ascribed to the rapid privatization of healthcare (particularly of secondary and tertiary healthcare services). Under these circumstances, it becomes imperative for the government to enforce strong regulatory reforms in the health sector, and rationalize pricing, particularly in private health facilities. In this context, we collected pricing data for similar treatments from public, private, and not-for-profit health facilities.

We collected price data from three types of healthcare facilities—public, private, and semi-private—for different procedures. Common diagnostic and therapeutic, surgical and non-surgical, as well as cold and emergency procedures were selected randomly for comparison. For the sake of comparison, information on only those procedures was collected that were available in all three categories of hospitals. The reimbursement costs of procedures in the Central-Government-sponsored Group Health Protection Scheme (CGHS), and the Government of West Bengal's *Swasthya Sathi* for its contractual employees were collated to proxy for pricing in the public health sector. Under the *Swasthya Sathi* scheme, hospitals have been divided into three grades, A, B, and C based on the following criteria apart from bed strength and National Accreditation Board for Hospitals (NABH) accreditation:

1. General environment including air-conditioning, and so on.
2. Facilities such as ambulance, blood bank, coronary care unit (CCU), dialysis unit, medical intensive care unit (MICU), neonatal intensive care unit (NICU), paediatric intensive care unit (PICU), nursery, and pharmacy.
3. Separate specialized wards, burn unit, trauma centre, interventional and vascular radiology, organ transplant, and joint replacement facilities.

The cost of selected common procedures was collected from all three grades of private hospitals. From the list of hospitals of similar grade determined by the *Swasthya Sathi* Scheme, one metro (Kolkata) and another non-metro hospital were selected randomly. Hence, costs of six groups of hospitals were considered and compared against the reimbursement rates of *Swasthya Sathi* and CGHS. One metro (Kolkata)-based semi-private, not-for-profit hospital was also selected through convenience sampling based on perception among patients and doctors regarding quality of service delivery by that particular hospital. Difference of costs ranged from 17 to 440 per cent between public and private, and from 10 to 133 per cent between public and semi-private hospitals (Table 2.8).

The appropriate role and balance of the public and private sector in providing healthcare services to the population is a much-debated issue in our country since long, and views of most stakeholders as well as experts regarding this issue are variably polarized (Basu et al. 2012). Globally and nationally, it is argued that to achieve universal and equitable access to healthcare, the public sector must be made to work as the majority provider (Berendes et al. 2011). To achieve this goal, public sector healthcare services have been made more accessible and affordable to the common man in the past few years. Infrastructure development has seen a change during the decade of 2008–18 at all levels of service delivery including super speciality areas. In

spite of this, the low- and middle-income groups are still showing a definite preference to access private healthcare services in comparison to government-provided services.

Multiple household surveys conducted both in rural and urban areas of different states of India showed a significant prevalence of, and also preference for, private healthcare delivery. The 71st NSS conducted in early 2014 concluded that out of the total number of hospitalization cases, even in rural areas, 42 per cent were in government hospitals and 58 per cent in private. The corresponding admissions in urban areas were 32 per cent in public and 68 per cent in private hospitals. Hence, the NSS findings over the last two decades clearly show a decline in the share of public hospitals in treating both rural and urban patients. This has created an asymmetric healthcare distributive network across states in India, which is disproportionately divided between the public and private healthcare sectors.

Published studies document that in India, more than 90 per cent of children affected by diarrhoea are still taken to private healthcare providers, with households even incurring substantial OOP expenditure (Bustreo, Harding, and Axelsson 2003). Current data from developing countries do not support claims that the private sector has been more efficient, accountable, or medically effective than the public sector (OXFAM International 2009).

However, this comparison between private and public sector providers is not so straightforward primarily because of two reasons. First, there is considerable overlap between the two sectors as far as manpower and resources are concerned, and second, the private sector is inherently heterogeneous and consists of for-profit multinational and national corporations, formal and informal for-profit individual providers, and not-for-profit providers like non-governmental, civil society, or charitable organizations. Public–private partnership (PPP) projects also exist.

Advocates of universal state-based healthcare and the proponents of a private healthcare system, both seem to have significant conflict of interest, and criticize one another as ideologically biased (Berendes et al. 2011; Montague et al. 2009; Rosenthal and Newbrander 1996; Smith et al. 2009; and Stocking 2009). They usually selectively point towards case studies and published

TABLE 2.8 Cost Comparison of Common Surgical and Non-surgical Procedures (in INR)

Surgical Procedures	Swasthya Sathi			Semi-private (incl. paying bed charge wherever applicable)	Private Corporate Hospital						Central Government Health Scheme	
	Grade A	Grade B	Grade C		Grade A		Grade B		Grade C		Non-NABH/Non-NABL rates	NABH/NABL rates
					Metro	Non-Metro	Metro	Non-Metro	Metro	Non-Metro		
Heart failure medical treatment	20,000	18,000	16,000	25,000	120,000	100,000	110,000	90,000	100,000	85,000		
Excision of dental cyst under local anaesthesia (LA)	1,500	1,350	1,250	2,000	7,000	6,000	6,500	6,000	6,000	5,500		
Hernioplasty with orchidectomy	18,000	16,200	14,580	20,000	35,000	32,000	30,000	27,000	25,000	21,000	25,399.33	29,209.44
Appendectomy with ovarian cystectomy	15,000	13,500	12,150	18,000	28,000	21,000	25,000	21,000	20,000	18,500	18,565.83	21,350.94
Diabetic ketoacidosis	3,000	2,000	1,500	3,500	5,500	4,500	4,500	4,000	3,500	3,000		
Cholecystectomy with abdominal hysterectomy	27,600	24,840	21,500	30,000	38,000	28,000	35,000	30,000	33,000	32,000	26,579.28	30,566.67
Excision of venereal warts	840	756	680	1,000	2,000	1,850	1,800	1,500	1,500	1,200	157.33	181.00
Breast lump excision	9,600	8,200	7,776	10,000	13,000	12,500	12,000	11,800	11,500	11,000	6,659.22	7,658.00
Cervical polypectomy	5,000	4,000	3,000	5,500							1,475.78*	1,697.39*
Comprehensive mother package (Three antenatal care (ANC) visits to delivery—normal/lower uterine segment caesarian section (LUCS))	15,000	13,500	12,000	15,000	18,000	16,500	16,500	15,800	16,000	15,500	7,785.83**	8,953.72**
Laparoscopic sterilization	5,000	4,500	3,000	6,000	8,500	8,000	7,800	7,200	7,500	7,000	3,422.50	3,936.33
Below elbow plaster of paris (POP) cast	8,000	7,200	4,455	9,000	12,000	10,000	9,800	9,400	9,500	9,200		
Phacoemulsification with foldable hydrophilic lens	6,000	5,400	3,000	7,500	9,500	9,000	8,500	8,200	8,000	7,800	10,481.56***	12,053.56***
Excision of mole	850	756	567	900	1,350	1,250	1,200	1,100	1,200	1,000	337.44	388.28

Source: Field data collected from private hospitals, *Swasthya Sathi* and CGHS portals, and Ramkrishna Mission Seva Pratisthan.

Notes: *Polypectomy; ** Normal delivery with or without Episiotomy and P. repair, *** Phacoemulsification with foldable intraocular (IOL) lens.

reports to uphold their viewpoint (Harding 2009; OXFAM International 2009).

However, researchers have also attempted a systematic, structured review of the performance of various healthcare sectors against six health systems themes used by the World Health Organization (WHO), adapted from the 2000 World Health Report. The six themes or categories are: accessibility and responsiveness; quality; outcomes; accountability, transparency, and regulation; fairness and equity; and efficiency. Evaluation of several subcategories like timeliness of service, distributive justice, public health functions; reform capacity, management standards, and so on, was also conducted. Published studies dealing with data from middle- and low-income countries including India revealed that private sector healthcare systems tended to lack published data by which to evaluate their performance, had greater risks of low-quality care, and served higher socio-economic groups, whereas the public sector tended to be less responsive to patients and lacked supplies. Both public and private sector systems have poor accountability and transparency. Contrary to prevailing assumptions, the private sector appears to have lower efficiency than the public sector, resulting from higher drug costs, perverse incentives for unnecessary testing and treatment, greater risks of complications, and weak regulation (Basu et al. 2012; Bustreo, Harding, and Axelsson 2003; and Rosenthal and Newbrander 1996). Thus, the preference of people for private healthcare seems apparently paradoxical. Added to that is the impact of dual (simultaneous private and public) practice by healthcare providers. Although there is scarcity of hard evidence regarding the extent of dual practice by physicians, it is documented in published literature that the practice is ubiquitous in all countries, and unregulated in most of them (Antunes et al. 2002; Banda and Simukonda 1994; Chen and Hiebert 1994; Ferrinho et al. 2003; Fresta et al. 2001; Hipólito 2001, 2002; Nittayaramphong and Tangcharoensathien 1994; Thomason 1994; Uplekar, Pathania, and Raviglione 2000; Volmink et al. 1993). In most states of India including West Bengal, the present legalization of dual practice has led to an increase in its extent. In a broad-based study, physicians mentioned early departure (N = 13, 41.9 per cent), late arrival (N = 8, 25.8 per cent), reduced attention to their public hospital job (N = 7, 22.6 per cent), taking long breaks due to tiredness (N = 5, 16.1 per cent), and

absenteeism (N = 3, 9.7 per cent) as some of the negative consequences of dual practice on public sector services (Abera, Alemayehu, and Henry 2017).

During focus group discussions (FGD) in this study, it was unequivocally accepted by hospital administrators that the principle positive impact of the current dual practice policy is retention of senior specialist clinicians in public healthcare facilities. However, dual practice also affects the public sector adversely, and in multiple ways. It leads to competition for physicians' time in each sector, and transfer of resources from the public to the private sector, both perceptible and imperceptible, in the form of diagnostic and therapeutic resource pilferage which has been reported to account for between 10 per cent median drug leakage in Venezuela to 78 per cent in Uganda (Asiimwe et al. 1997; Harding 2009; Jaén and Paravisini 2001; McPake et al. 2000; Montague et al. 2009; Smith et al. 2009; Stocking 2009). These are worsened by the fact that the best-trained and most competent healthcare providers are also the most likely to divert their time to other private activities outside the public health sector which amounts to a de facto brain drain. Increased extent of dual practice leads to almost the same set of senior clinical practitioners in both private and public set-ups. Patients prefer to consult the same specialist at private hospitals incurring even substantial OOP expenditure instead of consulting the specialist clinician at a public hospital totally free of cost. However as per the literature, in developing countries, many physicians carrying on dual practice noted that poor organization and management in public hospitals contributes to lack of motivation and absenteeism during public working hours (Abera, Alemayehu, and Henry 2017).

In one study, 64.5 per cent physicians recommended improving the working environment in public hospitals in order to retain physicians. The principal suggestions were increasing availability of necessary medical supplies and instruments, decreasing bureaucracy, and improving hospital management (Abera, Alemayehu, and Henry 2017). Hence, the inadequate performance of the public sector mostly seems to have managerial causes. As per Koontz and O'Donnell (1959), 'management' involves 'the design or creation and maintenance of an internal environment in an enterprise where individuals working together in groups can perform efficiently and effectively towards the attainment of group goals'. Therefore, in other words, public healthcare institutions may have inherent system defects in relation to the environment in which they are operating.

The stakes, as identified in a patient satisfaction survey in the present study, are undoubtedly high because of the fact that the perception of the quality of overall healthcare services across all sectors is based on the performance of the public sector. Even beyond that, an important determinant of demand for a service or product, for example, private healthcare services, is the willingness of patients to pay for it. The aversion towards public healthcare services and facilities is also acting as a negative, and forcing low-income-group patients to attempt to buy private healthcare services. This results in around one fifth of households incurring 'Catastrophic Health Expenditure' (Loganathan, Deshmukh, and Raut 2017).

As per the WHO *Bulletin*, in India, between 1993 and 2014, the proportion of households experiencing catastrophic health expenditure increased more in the poorest than in the richest quintile (Pandey et al. 2018). In the 1993–4 and the 2011–12 expenditure survey, the proportion increased 1.84-fold in the poorest quintile compared with 1.38-fold in the richest. But in the 1995–6 and the 2014 utilization survey, the proportion increased 3.00-fold in the poorest quintile and 1.74-fold in the richest quintile. It is obvious that people from households in the poorest quintile are supposed to seek healthcare services at public hospitals. The developing general trend of preference of these households to seek services in the substantially costlier private sector has led to an increased proportion of catastrophic health expenditure in this subset of population (Pandey et al. 2018). This adds to the urgent need for improving the status of the public healthcare sector as the dominant provider of services to the masses. In a sense, the public sector needs to improve on its return on investment (ROI).

The management process is a way of converting input into output through a logical sequence of major managerial functions—planning, organizing, staffing, leading, and controlling (Koontz and O'Donnell 1959). Comparisons between different healthcare sectors were based on the above parameters.

Focus group discussions with relevant experts and a pilot study on this topic led to the decision that questionnaires and discussion need to be based on the above parameters for an effective and structured analysis of the healthcare paradox in the state.

Analysis has been done through:

1. Semi-structured, pre-validated questionnaires for patients, selected stakeholders, and external experts from all three healthcare sectors (public, semi-private, and private).
2. Collection of relevant data regarding infrastructure, performance, and delivery-related aspects from all three sectors.
3. Root cause analysis of different elements.

Evaluation of the modus operandi and pricing structure of successful semi-private organizations was also conducted.

The WHO has defined health as 'a state of complete physical, mental and social well-being and not merely an absence of disease or infirmity' (Constitution of the World Health Organization 1946).

Based on this definition, the types of healthcare services are divided into:

- Primary: deals with health promotion (primordial) and illness prevention,
- Secondary: related to diagnosis and treatment, and
- Tertiary: concerned with rehabilitation and health restoration.

Healthcare services essentially call for multidimensional and inter-sectoral involvement at the government level, especially to deliver primary and tertiary types of care. The recent trend is a shift in focus and priority from primary (preventive) to secondary (curative) healthcare in all three sectors. It is said that most healthcare delivery centres are basically sickness-care delivery centres. Some authors even describe them as 'monuments to disease'. In fact, these institutions in reality will be so, if they continue to provide only curative care, detaching their services from the larger social, economic, cultural, and political context of people's lives, which largely determines their health (Bajpai 2014). In view of this, and also due to the practice of 'evidence-based medicine', and threat of the Consumer Protection Act against doctors, there is extreme dependence on clinical investigations. This has increased the cost of healthcare at all levels. The fine line of demarcation between a necessary healthcare activity or investigation and one added for purposes of overbilling becomes almost obscure at times. The essentially uneven construct of healthcare institutions' and patients' relationships does not allow detection of such irregularities and so-called unethical practices in most cases.

During the last decade (2004–14), government-sponsored health insurance schemes have contributed to a significant increase in the proportion of the general population covered by health insurance in India. A WHO report in 2015 (Forgia and Nagpal 2012) stated that such rapid increment is possibly unseen elsewhere in the world. Most of these schemes give patients the choice to visit any public or private healthcare provider empanelled by the government. The transactions are fully cashless, requiring no payment to be made by the patient to the hospital. These schemes have targeted low-income groups, made impressive use of information and communication technology, and used pre-agreed package rates for payment. Universal coverage of the population under insurance schemes ensures delivery of curative services essentially. Although drawing from international experience, government-sponsored health insurance schemes have suggested augmentation of primary healthcare, channelization of efforts and resources towards effective delivery of preventive healthcare is still not noticeable at the state or national level.

Certain key areas of concern for the public sector healthcare delivery system were identified, which need priority attention. The suggested interventions in these areas, revealed during the study, are summarized as follows:

1. Lack of effective and efficient administrative control, especially at the peripheral level.

Beginning with the Bhore Committee in 1946, several committees have stressed the need for a comprehensive and integrated health manpower policy dealing with health manpower requirement projection, manpower training, recruitment, career development, supportive supervision, skill enhancement, postings in underserved areas, retention and transfers, and so on, which is yet to be implemented in most states (Nandan, Nair, and Datta 2007; Rao et al. 2011).

Indrani Gupta and Mrigesh Bhatia of the London School of Economics and Political Science, in their article 'The Indian Health Care System' commented: 'The Indian health system does not promote efficiencies or control costs (Gupta and Bhatia 2017). Studies have found that most hospital systems across states are inefficient (Sebastian, Jat, and San 2013; Tigga and Mishra 2015). Lack of competition has made the public health infrastructure costly.'

The root cause for the lack of desired performance appears to be the lack of effective administrative and management training for the human resources responsible for driving the system. Other non-training gaps also exist, like the absence of vision and mission statements of the department along with lack of communication of the larger goals to be achieved to the ground-level staff. These gaps exist in both wings of the service at the state level, that is, the medical education service and health service. The medical education service is supposed to train competent medical professionals in government-run medical colleges. Any gap at that level invites further downstream gaps in the entire system. Suggested interventions by various stakeholders were as follows:

a) Introduction of administrative service cadres in the medical education service (principal, medical superintendent, heads of departments, nursing superintendent in medical colleges) with willing and adequately trained existing manpower.

b) To introduce basic management training in the MBBS, BDS, and BSc Nursing curricula. These graduates are expected to act as obvious team leaders. This can be extended to the individual Ayurveda, Yoga and Naturopathy, Unani, Siddha and Homeopathy (AYUSH) curricula also.

c) Decentralization of administrative control by way of empowerment and making operational the health department at peripheral locations like the North Bengal Secretariat, 'Uttorkanya' for both healthcare and medical education purposes.

d) Presently only a single university of healthcare exists at the state level. The university also needs to decentralize its academic control through peripheral offices for the sake of proper functioning of peripheral medical colleges and hospitals.

2. Universal free facility at government hospitals: percolation of benefits to the intended lowest level.

The larger goal of universal healthcare for the basic level of care needs to be targeted by the public sector even beyond just providing all services free of cost to everyone, irrespective of their income level. In the present scenario, free services in many cases are ineffective because of two simple reasons: excessively long waiting times, and disparity between demand and supply of infrastructure or services. For example, a couple, who is about to marry, needed to be screened for Thalassemia. In the public sector, facility for the test as well as pre- and post-test counselling is available. But the turnaround time (TAT) for release of the report in many cases is so long that by the time the report is ready, the couple actually gets married. Intensive care unit beds and operation theatre facilities are far too short of the required numbers. These are the principal reasons for patients seeking private facility care in spite of the costs being unaffordable for many of them. Semi-private facilities fare well as far as the management aspect is concerned. But even in the case of such facilities, infrastructural shortage is an issue.

The suggested interventions and actions are as follows:

a) Adequate indoor beds and infrastructure development is necessary to reduce the waiting time. If lengthy waiting times are given for surgeries or investigations, the sole purpose of making all services free becomes irrelevant. For example, the TAT of a simple investigation like serum thyroid stimulating hormone (TSH) is 4–6 hours in a standard private facility. The TAT for the same investigation can go up to an unbelievable three and half months in a government medical college setup. Much of the delay is due to providing lengthy waiting times, and the root causes for this are operational rather than infrastructural.

b) There is a need for structured and continuous surveys as well as operational research on this issue. Actions should be based on reports and conclusions of such surveys.

c) Tie-up between public and semi-private organizations for better delivery of services should be considered.

3. Untoward violent incidents against healthcare providers within hospital premises hampering vital services and causing loss of precious man-hours.

On 29 April 2017 an article was published in *The Lancet*, the nearly-200-year-old international medical journal, where it was said: 'Health workers in India have reached a breaking point as they face risk of physical attacks while carrying out their work. These incidents are responsible for lack of confidence and trust between the physicians and patients.' According to the *Lancet* article, 'These instances point not just to poor safety of health workers in the workplace, but also to deeper malaise of growing mistrust between doctors and patients and inadequate health infrastructure.'

The *Lancet* report also cited a 2016 study which said that over 40 per cent of resident doctors in a tertiary care hospital in New Delhi faced violence at work in the last one year. It also said that according to the Indian Medical Association, 75 per cent of doctors have faced violence—verbal or physical—during their lifetime (Sharma 2017).

It was also pointed out that junior doctors were more exposed to violence for they are the first responders during emergencies, and also inexperienced in handling the patients' relatives.

Citing various reasons for this situation, the Lancet article also cited one expert who said funding of public healthcare has declined and passive privatization has been encouraged. He said it is important that the government begins to spend more on public healthcare, and regulates private services. It may be mentioned here that exorbitant medical bills often make conflict between patients' relatives and hospital authorities inevitable (Sharma 2017).

Some steps for rectifying this situation can include:

a) Constitution of a state-level team consisting of general and health administration personnel as well as legal experts to investigate each and every untoward incident and suggest remedies.

b) Increasing security of healthcare providers, specially the junior tier, in all facilities.

c) Strengthening of state- and district-level liaisons between the general and health administration. Filling up necessary posts in this regard, for example, the post of 'Secretary' of medical college hospitals (vacant in most hospitals for the last almost 8–10 years causing major inconvenience).

d) Strict vigilance, appropriate and timely legal action, and guideline circulation to curb the menace of touts within government facilities.

e) Mandatory inclusion of formal and informal medical ethics and bioethics teaching at the undergraduate and postgraduate levels. The medical education unit of every medical college should be equipped for this activity.

f) Introduction of mandatory pathological autopsies for determination of cause of death and deficiencies in management of patients in cases of alleged and suspected negligence before the final verdict by investigating authorities. This will substantially increase the transparency of services provided, and at the same time, provide a learning experience for the medical faculty and administration.

g) Improving emergency medical services, which are in tatters in a majority of hospitals, more so in understaffed and overcrowded government hospitals. High priority should be accorded to ensuring 24x7 availability of critical lifesaving medicines in the emergency departments of all government hospitals.

4. Lack of adequate and efficient human resources

The requirement of specialist healthcare providers including doctors, in most cases, is an overestimation. This can be explained as follows. Appointment of a cardiothoracic surgeon in any district hospital where the setup for cardiothoracic operations does not exist is not only underutilization of skilled human resources, but leads to providing private setups operating nearby with facilities for such operations and procedures with the necessary manpower. Hence patients, due to obvious reasons, are forced to receive services from the private hospital, and in most cases, incur OOP expenditure. Interventions suggested were:

a) The existing pool of doctors in PHCs is low. While the government needs to invest in the system to increase the pool in the future, as a stopgap measure, the government can train AYUSH healthcare providers to supplement the existing PHCs. This will also ensure proper utilization of AYUSH manpower.

b) Closely related services, for instance, investigative services like radiology, biochemistry, microbiology, and pathology should be integrated. Surgical and medical services also need base-level integration rather than dissipation, at least up to the secondary level of care.

c) To identify and take administrative action against non-performing staff. These actions are significantly lacking at present. Tangible and measurable performance and quality of performance indicators need to be developed keeping in view the ground reality of public sector functioning.

d) Awards for best service providers, especially appreciating the soft skills of the profession, need to be introduced for all healthcare facilities.

5. Gaps in coordination and communication within and outside the organizations

Most stakeholders perceived these gaps and suggested:

a) Increment of operational coordination and communication among different departments of tertiary and peripheral healthcare facilities like block-level hospitals.

b) To train and recruit a group of volunteers for helping patients and their relatives access public healthcare services, and avoid unscrupulous agents of profit-making organizations.

c) Utilization of the community medicine department of all medical colleges in this regard.

d) Quarterly or at least an annual meeting of all members of the hospital team. In larger hospitals, the key staff members do not know each other properly.

6. Improvement in quality of healthcare and medical education

Providing quality service is the single most important way by which patients can be drawn into a healthcare facility. Third party audits of the quality and competence of the services and staff of all public sector facilities should be made mandatory. Proactive steps can then be taken for improvement of individual hospitals. This assurance of quality can go a long way in making the public sector the majority provider of healthcare in our country once again. In this regard:

a) Concrete steps towards accreditation of hospitals, blood banks, and laboratories by national-level bodies like the NABH, the National Accreditation Board for Testing and Calibration Laboratories, and so on should be initiated. However, it must be ensured that such accreditation schemes do not obstruct the running of small start-up clinics and PHCs.

b) Multidisciplinary research activities can be undertaken for improvement in the quality of management and technical issues.

c) Skill labs should be developed in medical colleges and district hospitals to improve the technical skills of healthcare providers, and minimize the tendency of medical students and junior doctors of experimenting directly on patients.

d) Improving the quality of healthcare in the public sector, which can be expected to halt the setting-up of satellite private healthcare centres that tend to crop up near major government healthcare establishments.

7. **Strengthening primary and tertiary levels of care**

This would require participation of both the Central and state governments and interdepartmental coordination. Although health is a state subject, family welfare, and primary and tertiary healthcare are funded and taken care of by the union government. Biomedical waste management can be carried out in-house in larger hospitals and the elements recycled for generation of revenue and sustainability of projects. International-level cooperation can also be sought.

Vertically running projects for preventive or rehabilitative healthcare should be oriented horizontally and aligned with other curative and routine hospital services.

In India, it is said that the 'private medical sector' has proved to be the proverbial 'camel' that has pushed the Arab (the 'public medical sector') out of the tent (Bajpai 2014).

The business-oriented private healthcare sector takes advantage of this situation. The National Health Policy 2017 points out that nearly 6.3 crore Indians are pushed below the poverty line by OOP expenditure on health, out of which expenditure on drugs is to the tune of 67 per cent. On 13 July 2017 Anand Patel wrote an article in *India Today*

titled 'How Hospitals in Collusion with Pharma Firms are Burning a Hole in Your Pocket' in which he commented that '"India Today" has exclusive access to quotations from pharmaceutical companies of repute to hospitals and stockists that show how pharma firms are hand-in-glove with hospitals to fleece cancer patients. While hospitals receive a particular life-saving drug from pharma firms for a nominal cost, the former charge the patients many times that cost for the same.' In the same article it was said that, 'As per industry figures, the business of pharma companies in the country is well over Rs 1 lakh crore. The All India Drug Action Network alleges that 25 per cent of this amount is earmarked for medical corruption which goes to doctors, bureaucrats and politicians. The central government has asked doctors to prescribe generic drugs, which are relatively cheaper. But even these generic drugs have different prices from patients, stockists and retailers.' Regulation of drug prices may be the single most important intervention to reduce healthcare expenditure both in outpatient and inpatient services. Also, the number of pharmaceutical companies manufacturing the same branded generic medicines should be limited, to reduce cut-throat competition among companies selling 'me too' drugs and resorting to unscrupulous means, including providing freebies to doctors and pharmacists, in order to reach unrealistic sales targets. Strict quality control also needs to be enforced in case of generic medicines.

Addressing cost divergence across different healthcare sectors with the objective of drawing at least a line for ceiling costs can contribute towards making advanced healthcare affordable for majority of the population. In spite of significant cost divergence, apparent preference for costlier services, when studied by experts and stakeholders, provided the platform for unveiling different areas with potential scope for improvement in the public healthcare sector. On an analysis of these gaps and comparison with the other two sectors, most root causes pointed more towards managerial and administrative issues than infrastructure-related deficiencies. Easy to implement, simple suggestions came forth through FGDs among the experts, which need to be tested through subsequent operational research in different phases.

HEALTH PACKAGE DEALS: A PANACEA?[6]

Overbilling by private hospitals and prescribing of unnecessary diagnostics are common complaints made by both the poor and the rich when using health services, especially in the private sector in India. According to data available from the NSS 71st Round (2014), the average cost of treatment in a private hospital is INR 25,850 as compared to INR 6,120 in a public hospital.

India Costlier for Heart Operations than Other Nations					
Cost in PPP $ (2011–14)	India	China	South Korea	Hong Kong	Singapore
Angioplasty (1 stent)	11,477	5,558	**2,581**	5,879	65,580
Bypass surgery	10,137	16,033	**5,810**	10,197	110,058
Angiography	1,067	1,205	**869**	2,072	17,426
Stay in CCU	282	298	**161**	1,999	3,210
Echo-cardiography	**78**	98	241	353	1,652
ECG	9.9	**7.6**	9.9	58.9	130.5

China has a per capita income about two-and-a-half times that of India. South Korea's per capita income is 5.4 times India's. Yet, the cost of most procedures in China is just 13–25 per cent more than in India. In India, the study covered some 50 hospitals—mostly private, but a handful of them were government-run—across major cities. The average cost of a procedure is the figure taken into account.

Source: *The Times of India*, 2 September 2018.

Despite implementing various SHI programmes over decades, pricing of health services in India is still an unresolved issue since there is no universally accepted logical consensus as to fixing prices in the government

---

[6] This section is based on a background paper, Sugata Marjit and Biswajit Mandal, 'The Rise and Fall of Package Deals'.

as well as private sectors. This leads to price and quality distortions. Pricing becomes non-transparent, and often arbitrary and exorbitant.

A private medical institution may overcharge patients in several ways. Some common methods are prescribing and dispensing non-scheduled branded drugs, instead of scheduled drugs from the National List of Essential Medicines (NLEM) that are subject to price control. Indirect pressure on patients to buy medicines only from the hospital's counter at an inflated maximum retail price (MRP) or physicians' unwillingness to prescribe generic medicines is observed. Sometimes industries are forced to print such higher MRPs to get bulk supply orders, and in some places, hospitals charge huge margins on their purchase price during billing.

As K. Sujatha Rao, former Health Secretary, Government of India writes:

There is no reference point that defines a fair price. Comparison with government hospitals is problematic as several cost components are subsidised, such as land or buildings. In the absence of a price range based on acceptable methodology, the cost of, say, a CT scan can vary from hospital to hospital and be dependent on factors like utilisation levels, the source of financing, such as an interest-bearing loan as opposed to a donation, and so on. Likewise, how does one price a specialist's consultation in an imperfect market? (Rao 2018a)

To tackle the problem of overpricing by private healthcare facilities, the Central Government and several state governments have taken various legislative initiatives. In 2017, the Karnataka government instituted laws to deal with medical negligence and overpricing (PTI 2017). The aim of the Karnataka Private Medical Establishments (Amendment) Bill, 2017 was to provide for emergency treatment as needed without insisting on payment of advance from patients or their representatives in specified cases. The bill also empowered the state government to fix uniform package rates for treatment and procedures under its health assurance schemes. Yet, a strike by private doctors forced the government to make the Act applicable to only those patients treated under government schemes, leaving almost 80 per cent of the population outside its scope.

Following frequent and violent unrest among patients availing facilities of private hospitals in Kolkata and in the state of West Bengal at large, the state government passed the West Bengal Clinical Establishments Bill, 2017 that established the 'West Bengal Clinical Regulatory Commission' (Rashshit 2017). The primary purpose of the Commission is to investigate grievances against private health service providers for their undue and exploitative actions. The Commission aims at bringing transparency, ending harassment of patients, and checking medical negligence in private hospitals and nursing homes.

WHAT MAKES UP YOUR BILL

	Amount in ₹ lakh	Share (%)
Non-scheduled formulations	17.8	25.7
Diagnostics	10.8	15.6
Consultation & medical supervision	8.8	12.7
Room rent	8.0	11.6
Procedures	7.9	11.4
Consumables	6.6	9.6
Equipment charges	5.2	7.5
Scheduled formulations	2.8	4.1
Non-scheduled devices	1.1	1.5
Surgery	0.3	0.4
Total	**69.3**	**100.0**

The expenditure on drugs, devices, and diagnostics, constituting almost half the billed amount, is not part of the 'estimate' or 'package' (in case of implants) given by hospitals unlike procedures (about 11 per cent of the bill) or room rent (12 per cent), which are 'the more visible components', stated the National Pharmaceutical Pricing Authority of India (NPPA).

The NPPA's analysis came after complaints of overcharging by families of some patients who died from dengue and other ailments (Jha 2017). Patients in all cases had complained that the initial estimate of expenditure got inflated by three to four times, the NPPA said. It said the hospitals involved had requested anonymity. Sources said the request was honoured since these practices are widely prevalent.

Source: Times of India, February 20, 2018

One common way of fixing prices in health facilities is through health packages, that is, a collection of health services offered for a clinically defined episode of care. Such 'packages' require a single comprehensive payment made for a group of related and often complementary services. The advantages of this system are that hospitals get cost settlements done easily, and at least on paper, patients are aware upfront of charges. Perhaps such deals also help in reducing the significant variation in the cost of a particular procedure in different hospitals.

However, such packages can also trigger distortionary behaviour with most doctors tending to opt for packages with better economic returns. Alternatively, hospitals may charge patients unanticipated additional amounts beyond the initial contracted payments. The *modus operandi* is that once admitted for treatment, patients are informed that the actual ailment was far more complicated than initially hypothesized. Therefore, additional tests and procedures were conducted that required significant additional expenses. Of course, an alternative scenario may occur. Packages may deter doctors from 'fixing' unforeseen problems that may occur during surgery or when new ailments are discovered during the 'package' treatment that were outside the scope of the initial contract. This could increase mortality rates and even put patients at risk (Bhattacharya 2005).

The question is whether such unanticipated costs would decline if patients are informed about treatments beyond the contracted 'package'? Under the new regulatory act by the Government of West Bengal, it is mandatory that hospitals provide prior information to patients before undertaking any unanticipated treatment beyond the contracted deal. Our intuition suggests that this will lead to a reduction in the manipulation of 'package deals'. In this section, we present a simple theoretical model to examine the extent to which information transmission to patients reduces the extent of medical malpractice under 'health package' deals.

Given the assumptions, the model demonstrates that when hospitals are honest in the sense that they charge for treatment for illnesses that really exist, from the patients' point of view, package deals are a better option. Intuitively this stems from the fact that under these conditions, the price of a package deal would reflect the expected opportunity cost for the patient to obtain the treatment at a competitive (lowest) price. On the other hand, dishonest hospitals reap the benefits associated with asymmetric information through excessive charges.

A Formal Model

Let Z be the distribution of ailment in the interval between '0' and '1'; $Z \in [0,1]$. '0' indicates no ailment and '1' denotes severe ailment. And $P(Z)$ is the cost/price of treatment for ailment of degree Z in a private hospital. Therefore, $P(0) = 0$ and $P(1) = Maximum$. For brevity we assume away the existence of government/public hospitals. Let there be some other private hospitals that charge $P_0(Z)$ for the same disease Z such that

$$P_0(Z) < P(Z) \tag{1}$$

But to identify the hospital which charges $P_0(Z)$, patients need to search which would have some search cost, say $s > 1$. So the effective cost (to the patient) of treatment from other hospitals becomes

$$sP_0(Z) > P_0(Z) \tag{2}$$

If $P_0(Z) > P(Z)$, the patient would not search for package treatment. When $sP_0(Z) < P(Z)$, search for other hospitals is beneficial, and the patients would be happy with the arrangement. If $sP_0(Z) > P(Z)$, the hospital can charge at most $sP_0(Z)$ to get the patient with the condition that this will be a price under a 'take it or leave it offer'. At the time of signing the contract for $sP_0(Z)$, the patient cannot guarantee that the degree of ailment won't be higher than what is declared at the time of the contract. In that case, the treatment cost is not fully covered in $sP_0(Z)$. Say the probability of having $Z > \tilde{Z}$ is q, and the cost of treatment for $\tilde{Z}$ is $P(\tilde{Z}) > P(Z)$.

REGIME-1: Honest Hospitals
Case 1: Contracted Package and No Scope for Further Searching:
Total cost required for treatment in this situation is

$$C_{HWS} = sP_0(Z) + q\left[P(\tilde{Z}) - sP_0(Z) \right]$$
$$C_{HWS} = sP_0(Z) + q\left[\Delta(\tilde{Z} - Z) \right] \tag{3}$$

The exact cost for a patient is given by equation (3) if further ailment is detected with probability q, and the hospital gets duly paid for the extra treatment for $\Delta(\tilde{Z} - Z)$ ailment when the exact cost is properly notified to the patient. As long as the package costs no more than (3) the patient should accept the same. However, with q close to zero, the package is likely to cost $sP_0(Z)$.

Case 2: Contracted Package and Scope for Further Searching:
Under Case 2, the cost to the patient becomes

$$C_{HS} = sP_0(Z) + sq\left[P(\tilde{Z}) - sP_0(Z) \right]$$
$$C_{HS} = sP_0(Z) + sq\left[\Delta(\tilde{Z} - Z) \right] \tag{4}$$

Note it is apparent that $C_{HS} = sP_0(Z) + sq\left[\Delta(\tilde{Z} - Z) \right] > C_{HWS} = sP_0(Z) + q\left[\Delta(\tilde{Z} - Z) \right]$ as $s > 1$. So from the patient's point of view, a package with no further searching is a better option. This happens when hospitals are honest and charge extra cost only for the illness that really exists. So as long as $C_{HS} > C_{HWS}$, patients would always prefer to go for no-searching. If the maximum anticipated cost to the patient is given by (4), any package price that is less than or equal to (4) would be acceptable. Hence, the contracted package fee should be as given by (4), s can depend on $\tilde{Z}$, which we ignore for simplicity.

However, this may not be the case for dishonest hospitals, and here lies the main problem of the 'package' system. If a hospital charges an amount equal to $sP_0(Z) + sq\left[\Delta(\tilde{Z} - Z) \right]$, patients are indifferent between package and non-package rates, and searching and non-searching. In case hospitals charge more than $sP_0(Z) + sq\left[\Delta(\tilde{Z} - Z) \right]$, a patient will opt to search for a cheaper alternative. This would depend on $\Delta(\tilde{Z} - Z)$, and the issue of the honesty of hospitals gradually creeps into the scenario. This may happen in both Case 1 and Case 2. We will not talk about Case 1 since if our arguments hold for Case 2, they would automatically hold for Case 1.

REGIME-2: Dishonest Hospitals
Say θ is the probability that the hospital is dishonest. So the maximum cost to the patient is

$$C_{DH} = sP_0(Z) + s\Delta(\tilde{Z} - Z)\left[q + (1-q)\theta \right] \tag{5}$$

It is clear if the hospital is honest ($\theta = 0$) and/or there is guaranteed certainty of post-contract ailment ($q = 1$), it won't matter. Equation (5) actually reveals only one part of the impact of dishonesty reflected in $s\Delta\left(\tilde{Z} - Z\right)\theta\left(1 - q\right)$.

But it is possible as the treatment is completed without patient's approval or her ability to look for alternative at that stage, the hospital may charge a price higher than above as the search option is simply not there anymore. Return to dishonesty is actually greater than the above quantity.

Thus one can classify the strategies of the hospital in the following manner.

(1) Misreport the extent of additional treatment and charge as much as possible once the treatment is done. Patient has no option.
(2) Just misreport the possible treatment before actual treatment is done. In that case the expected cost to the patient will be given by (5). But the patient may try to cross-check the diagnosis in other hospitals. In fact, the new regulatory act provides this opportunity to the patients. However, the patient may not be in a condition to search around but she has an option.

If the patient searches with probability α, and if dishonesty is revealed, there will be actual costs imposed on the hospital to an extent F. Then the net pay-off from dishonesty will be given by

$$\Delta\Pi_{DH} = s\Delta\left(\tilde{Z} - Z\right)\left(1 - q\right)\left(1 - \alpha\right) - \alpha F \tag{6}$$

$$\text{Thus } \Delta\Pi_{DH} \leq 0 \text{ iff } s\Delta\left(\tilde{Z} - Z\right)\left(1 - q\right) \leq \frac{\alpha}{1 - \alpha}F \tag{7}$$

Absent regulations $F = 0$ and (7) does not hold.

Let $\bar{P}\Delta\left(\tilde{Z} - Z\right)$ be the maximum price charged to a hostage patient. Then

$$C_{DH} = sP_0(Z) + \bar{P}\Delta\left(\tilde{Z} - Z\right)\left(q + \left(1 - q\right)\theta\right) \tag{8}$$

$$\Pi_{DH} = sP_0(Z) + \bar{P}\Delta\left(\tilde{Z} - Z\right) \text{ [where } \theta = 1\text{]} \tag{9}$$

To attract patients with the package deal, a dishonest hospital may actually ask for a package price $P(Z) < sP_0(Z)$ as long as

$$P(Z) + \bar{P}\Delta\left(\tilde{Z} - Z\right) > sP_0(Z) + sq\Delta\left(\tilde{Z} - Z\right) > sP_0(Z) \tag{10}$$

$$sP_0(Z) - P(Z)] < \Delta\left(\tilde{Z} - Z\right)\left[\bar{P} - sq\right]$$

The strategy is lower $P(Z)$ relative to $sP_0(Z)$ attracts patients now, and the hospital can earn a premium $\Delta\left(\tilde{Z} - Z\right)\left[\bar{P} - sq\right]$ later when they are hostage.

Note that if the hospitals cannot engage in further treatment without telling the patient and (7) holds, they can at most earn $sP_0(Z) + sq\Delta\left(\tilde{Z} - Z\right)$ which is the same as before. But currently asking for $P(Z) < sP_0(Z)$ may entice patients if they are unaware of the realization of 'θ'. If the hospital cannot charge the combination $\left(P(Z), \bar{P}\right)$, it can at most charge $sP_0(Z) + sq\Delta\left(\tilde{Z} - Z\right)$. Thus a package deal now will be less lucrative for dishonest hospitals. If they charge $P(Z)$, and the regulation binds them, then they would get at most $sq\Delta\left(\tilde{Z} - Z\right)$ and they will lose earnings as $P(Z) < sP_0(Z)$.

If the hospitals are dishonest, they can lower their package prices relative to the competitive price to attract patients, and once the patient is in a 'hostage' situation, earn a premium over and above the initial loss incurred due to their lower prices of the package. In terms of policy implications, this model concludes that both an increase in penalty imposed on hospitals in case any dishonesty is revealed as well as the imposition of a ceiling on the maximum price charged to a patient whose ailment is found to involve more cost than what was initially contracted upon at the time of signing the package deal, would serve as impediments to hospitals engaging in such malpractices. These implications of the model should however be considered with a hint of caution. This model takes recourse to a particular set of arguments to critically evaluate the outcomes of healthcare packages, and in no way reflects a comprehensive analysis of the other avenues through which a package deal may operate in particular circumstances. For example, imposing legal obligations on healthcare providers may lead to the prescription of conservative treatment regimens from doctors to avoid legal complications, and this may instead increase morbidity/mortality rates and be counterproductive for patients.

MEDICINES: AFFORDABLE?[7]

An important complementary input to any healthcare system is the use of drugs to prevent and treat different ailments. Drug therapy or pharmacotherapy uses pharmaceutical drugs as opposed to surgery (surgical therapy), radiation (radiation therapy), movement (physical therapy), and so on. In India, drugs are supplied by pharmaceutical companies, and are dispensed through retail outlets. Therefore, production, access, and pricing of pharmaceutical drugs plays an important role in providing affordable quality healthcare to all—rich or

[7] The section is based on a background paper, Sattwik Santra, 'Medicines' (2018), Mimeo CTRPFP.

poor. In this section, using anecdotal evidence from qualitative surveys carried out over the last few months, we analyse the issues in the pricing of medical drugs in India.

A recent study by the NPPA (Nagarajan 2018b; Porecha 2018) shows that 'private hospitals make a profit of up to 1,737% on drugs, consumables and diagnostics. The profit margins for the hospitals were highest on consumables, ranging from almost 350% to over 1,700%. On drugs that are not under price control, the margins ranged from about 160% to 1,200%. Those on drugs under price control were between 115% and 360%'. The study goes on to note that it was the hospitals rather than the manufacturers who benefitted from the overpricing of drugs. For all hospitalization cases, drugs prescribed by doctors and used by patients are procured from the hospitals' in-house pharmacies. Patients do not have the option to buy the medicines from outside possibly at lower prices. Hospitals often

---

BOX 2.1   Criteria for Inclusion and Deletion of Medicines from the National List of Essential Medicines 2015

The criteria for *inclusion* of a medicine in the NLEM are as follows:

- The medicine should be approved/licensed in India.
- The medicine should be useful for a disease which is a public health problem in India.
- The medicine should have proven efficacy and safety profile based on valid scientific evidence.
- The medicine should be cost effective.
- The medicine should be aligned with the current treatment guidelines for the disease.
- The medicine should be stable under storage conditions in India.
- When more than one medicine is available from the same therapeutic class, preferably one prototype/medically best suited medicine of that class is to be included after due deliberation and careful evaluation of their relative safety, efficacy, and cost effectiveness.
- Price of total treatment to be considered and not the unit price of a medicine.
- Fixed dose combinations (FDCs) are generally not included unless the combination has unequivocally proven advantage over individual ingredients administered separately, in terms of increasing efficacy, reducing adverse effects, and/or improving compliance.
- The listing of a medicine in the NLEM is based on the level of healthcare, that is, primary (P), secondary (S), or tertiary (T), because the treatment facilities, training, experience, and availability of healthcare personnel differ at each of these levels.

The criteria for *deletion* of a medicine from the NLEM is as follows:

- The medicine has been banned in India.
- There are reports of concerns on the safety profile of a medicine.
- A medicine with better efficacy or more favourable safety profile and better cost-effectiveness is now available.
- The disease burden for which a medicine is indicated is no longer a national health concern in India.
- In the case of antimicrobials, if the resistance pattern has rendered a medicine ineffective in the Indian context.

arm-twist manufacturers to print higher MRPs on drugs with an implicit threat to withdraw bulk orders if not adhered to. This makes it easier for them to indulge in 'profiteering on drugs and devices even without the need to violate the MRPs'. The NPPA goes on to state that, '[t]his is a clear case of market distortion where manufacturers after accounting for their profits print inflated MRPs to meet the demands of a distorted trade channel without getting any benefits from this "artificial inflation" and patients have to incur huge out-of-pocket expenditure in hospitalization cases'.

In this section, using evidence from quantitative surveys, we analyse the availability and pricing of generic and branded pharmaceutical drugs in pharmacies and medical retail shops outside the hospital. We surveyed four major private retail pharmacy outlets, four medical representatives who supply to other retail outlets, and two websites (1mg.com and DrugsUpdate.com) in the course of our analysis (Santra 2018a, 2018b). In consultation with physicians, we constructed a list of common medications consumed orally, and widely prescribed by physicians. We obtained data on availability, pricing, and relative sales of a number of these drugs.

In Table 2.9, we report the availability of drugs that are listed in the NLEM. Of a total number of 93 generic medications commonly prescribed, almost half were not sold by any of the pharmacists that we surveyed. The pharmacists informed us that a number of these drugs were either not in supply or could only be procured by placing advance orders. It is noteworthy that of the total number of generics unavailable with any retailers, almost half are listed in the NLEM and are supposed to be available through all retail medical outlets. Box 2.1 details the criteria for the inclusion of drugs in and exclusion of drugs from the NLEM, 2015.

In Tables 2.10 and 2.11, we report the MRPs of selected generics for a number of brands enumerated from the retailers that were surveyed, and from online web resources. Tabulated values are corrected for dosages of the medications that represent the lowest per-unit values applicable for each brand. We find generics that exhibit the maximum variation in brand prices measured by differences in maximum and minimum prices of available brands pertain to the anti-inflamatories, the anti-asthamatics, and the drugs for hypercholesterolemia. These ailments are primarily chronic and non-communicable in nature, and are often treated as diseases of the 'industrial world'.

Average prices of brands commonly sold by retailers show that for the majority of formulations, average prices are greater than the minimum available brand prices. A common explanation for the lowest available brand price not being the most commonly sold brand is that lower prices are often assumed to reflect poor quality of the medicines. In India, for scheduled drugs/new drugs in the NLEM, the price notified by the NPPA is the ceiling/retail price per unit, and the MRP of the pack must not exceed the ceiling price of the pack plus local taxes.

On investigating the retail prices of medicines, we found that most brands follow a common pricing mechanism:

- In retail outlets owned privately by individuals, with the exception of certain brands, most products are sold at a discount of 10–16 per cent on the MRP. The extent of discount varies from one retail shop to another, and may depend on the degree of acquaintance of the shopkeeper with the customer in question.
- In retail outlets owned by companies, the amount of discount varies with the amount of medicines purchased per transaction. Transaction amounts less than a certain threshold (typically between INR 200 and INR 500

TABLE 2.9   Availability of Drugs (percentages in brackets)

	Drugs listed in NLEM 2015	Drugs not listed in NLEM 2015	Drugs deleted from NLEM 2015 or previous NLEMs	Total
Drugs available with at least one retailer	33 (60%)	8 (28%)	6 (67%)	47 (50.5%)
Drugs not available with any retailer	22 (40%)	21 (72%)	3 (33%)	46 (49.5%)
Total	**55**	**29**	**9**	**93**

Source: Primary survey 2018.

TABLE 2.10 Distribution of Maximum Retail Prices (in INR) over Drugs

Ailment	Drug	Mean	Mean of common brands	Median	Minimum	Maximum	Standard deviation
Analgesic, anti-inflammatory, and antipyretic	Aceclofenac	5.07		6.27	2.63	6.30	2.11
	Aspirin	1.84	0.82	1.52	0.82	3.48	1.15
	Diclofenac	3.78	3.17	3.25	2.77	5.88	1.42
	Ibuprofen	0.82	0.73	0.73	0.73	1.00	0.16
	Nimesulide	3.69	5.05	4.21	1.09	5.14	1.48
	Paracetamol	0.67	0.71	0.66	0.25	1.12	0.36
	Tramadol	3.73		4.59	1.00	4.75	1.82
Antacid	Famotidine	1.07	0.45	0.46	0.32	3.70	1.15
	Omeprazole	5.37	5.20	5.08	4.84	7.09	0.86
	Pantoprazole	6.89	9.20	7.75	2.90	11.30	3.18
	Rabeprazole	12.84	6.00	13.90	3.90	19.30	4.68
	Ranitidine	1.97	1.61	1.60	1.44	3.90	0.95
Antibacterial	Amoxycillin	6.92	6.56	6.56	6.19	10.94	1.42
	Azithromycin	21.11	21.65	21.65	17.85	22.39	1.50
	Cefalexin	13.37	14.76	13.13	4.50	19.07	4.10
	Cefixime	7.30	4.19	7.15	2.38	14.00	2.84
	Ciprofloxacin	3.76	3.83	3.71	3.46	4.05	0.16
	Doxycycline	3.64	2.85	2.85	1.02	9.31	3.01
	Erythromycin	6.00	7.68	6.07	3.02	9.00	2.44
	Levofloxacin	8.24	8.48	8.48	6.67	8.48	0.56
	Metronidazole	0.79	0.85	0.82	0.64	0.85	0.08
	Ofloxacin	14.42	11.60	12.15	4.95	28.00	6.83
Anticoagulant	Clopidogrel	9.90	5.19	9.90	1.42	14.00	3.95
Anticonvulsant	Carbamazepine	0.71		0.69	0.68	0.79	0.04
	Clonazepam	8.19	8.40	8.15	5.20	12.58	2.05
	Gabapentin	13.74		14.49	9.00	17.40	2.51
	Phenytoin	1.58	1.63	1.58	1.45	1.65	0.06
Antidepressant	Fluoxetin	5.34	6.86	5.19	3.55	7.28	1.17
Antidiabetic	Metformin	1.71	1.96	1.67	1.52	2.00	0.18
	Pioglitazone	7.21	8.30	7.81	2.55	8.85	1.88
	Voglibose	9.48	10.80	10.34	4.77	11.87	2.21
Antihypertensive	Amlodipine	5.41	4.37	5.33	2.62	10.20	1.79
	Atenolol	3.09	3.66	3.59	1.35	4.15	1.01
	Losartan	4.73	4.64	5.39	1.98	6.01	1.39
	Telmisartan	9.00	6.48	10.39	4.61	10.56	2.26
	Verapamil	1.26	1.40	1.20	0.91	1.74	0.38
Anti-inflammatory (general and gastrointestinal)	Betamethasone	0.78		0.80	0.55	1.02	0.22
	Dexamethasone	9.12	0.89	1.63	0.89	29.26	12.21
	Hydrocortisone	10.81		10.81	5.80	15.82	7.09
	Prednisolone	1.63	2.26	1.48	1.15	2.26	0.57
Antiviral	Acyclovir	12.69	12.94	12.93	9.42	14.55	1.49
Anti-asthmatic	Montelukast	9.78	15.95	8.70	1.52	17.87	6.09
Anti-hypercholesterolemia	Atorvastitin	32.97	32.84	33.18	19.97	48.45	7.36
	Fenofibrate	12.35		12.35	5.60	17.52	3.74
	Rosuvastatin	42.79	40.00	44.98	25.86	56.15	9.50
Hypnotic	Alprazolam	6.92	5.00	6.93	4.07	10.67	2.09
	Diazepam	1.43	1.49	1.42	0.88	1.95	0.34
	Lorazepam	2.46		2.51	2.08	3.00	0.28
	Nitrazepam	3.96		3.92	1.73	9.52	2.20

Source: Primary survey 2018.

TABLE 2.11 Distribution of Prices (in INR) across Diseases

Ailment	Mean	Mean of common brands	Median	Minimum	Maximum	Standard deviation
Antacid	6.10	4.49	4.87	0.32	19.30	5.29
Anticoagulant	9.90	5.19	9.90	1.42	14.00	3.95
Anti-inflammatory	5.07	1.57	1.48	0.55	29.26	8.12
Antiviral	12.69	12.94	12.93	9.42	14.55	1.49
Anti-asthmatic	9.78	15.95	8.70	1.52	17.87	6.09
Analgesic	2.96	1.70	2.95	0.25	6.30	1.91
Antibacterial	9.35	7.93	7.69	0.64	28.00	6.61
Anticonvulsant	6.50	5.02	6.10	0.68	17.40	5.68
Antidepressant	5.34	6.86	5.19	3.55	7.28	1.17
Antidiabetic	6.13	5.75	7.25	1.52	11.87	3.69
Antihypertensive	5.17	4.49	5.15	0.91	10.56	2.86
Anti-hypercholesterolemia	29.37	34.63	32.13	5.60	56.15	14.68
Hypnotic	3.75	3.25	2.59	0.88	10.67	2.57

Source: Primary survey 2018.

across retail outlets of different companies) are sold at MRP. Transactions exceeding the above limit are discounted at 10 per cent. The amount of discount offered rises with the value of the transaction up to a maximum value of 16 per cent. Many retail outlets privately owned by individuals also operate along this principle.

- Some retail outlets operated by private hospitals sell medicines only at MRP. Some of them provide some discounts on the MRP, but such discounts are only available if the buyer is a member of the franchise. Membership entails the deposit of a certain amount with/without maintaining a credit account.
- Public retail outlets and fair price shops often give discounts similar to their private counterparts, but can also provide a discount of up to 50 per cent in some areas.

With a few exceptions, there are differences in prices across brands for any given generic formulation. While these differences may appear insignificant for short-duration treatments, for chronic illnesses that require long-term treatment regimes, even small price differences may be burdensome for patients and their families.

There are also significant differences in prices of medicines across different retail outlets. Moreover, discounts on MRPs are given based on total transaction

Corruption in the Supply Chain

'As medical representatives, we try to identify doctors likely to succumb to their greed. Once identified, we explore his/her wants or demands—whether they want consumer goods (mobile phones), expensive electronics (air conditioners), gift cards for shopping, expensive medical books costing above INR 10,000–15,000, or cash. Doctors who provide significant business to a particular company by prescribing their medicines are "rewarded" for their efforts by receiving fully-paid foreign tours, expensive cars, real estate, and sometimes even payments for escorts. To make sure that the doctors honour their part in the deal, we often visit pharmacies near their chambers to check sales figures of specific medicines that the doctors have promised to prescribe. We also visit the stockists to reconfirm whether there has been an increase in demand for specific medicines. It is only after confirmation that the doctor is indeed prescribing medicines manufactured by our company, in keeping with our end of the deal, we give him the promised "goodies". As medical representatives, we too get a commission in addition to our regular salaries.'

—*Medical Representative*

amounts. This implies that individual customers buying smaller quantities of medicines are forced to pay higher prices.

Fallout of Corruption in the Supply Chain

'To fulfil promised targets, doctors are tempted to overprescribe medicines to patients that are often not required. Doctors belonging to the same locality compete with each other to get the most benefits from medicine companies. As a result, to "win" in this game, doctors try to give more business to specific medicine companies by prescribing more and more medicines. The doctors take advantage of hypochondriac patients who are eager to consume more medicines. Even we medical representatives are involved in this dishonesty. Many a times, we medical representatives also buy medicines from the stockists and sell them in villages together with sample medicines that we get from companies. This nexus in the supply chain between doctors, medical representatives, and pharmaceutical companies suggests that manufacturing costs of medicines are reasonably low. It is the "add-ons" like incentives to doctors, commissions to medical representatives—that lead to the consumer paying exorbitant prices for medicines. Earlier medical representatives followed up with doctors on complaints by patients about potential side effects of new drugs introduced in the market. Nowadays, doctors do not provide even this information.'

—*Medical Representative*

On the Nexus between the Pharmaceutical Company, Stockists, Chemists, and Doctors: Is It Possible to Break This?

'In the current scenario, it is virtually impossible to break the nexus since the problem is deeply entrenched in our medical system. This system has been in place for generations, and at least to my understanding it cannot be broken. Everything works on monetary exchange, and once money is involved, it is nearly impossible to control or change [the system]. Moreover, livelihoods of several "players" depend on the sustenance of this system. My survival as a medical representative depends on the continuance of this nexus. Of course, there are some positives of my profession too—we are able to disseminate information to the doctors about the introduction of new medicines in the market. Else, doctors do not have any other source to learn about the introduction of new medicines in the market.'

—*Medical Representative*

Finally, regulating prices (as formulated by the NPPA) may be the optimal way to supply quality medicines at reasonable prices to consumers. Anecdotal evidence collected by us shows that almost all stakeholders—firms producing medical products, doctors, stockists, medical representatives, retailers, hospitals, and so on—in the supply chain of medical products in general, and pharmaceutical products in particular, engage in collusive behaviour to maximize their own individual profits. This in the long-run may lead to loss of product diversity and quality, hamper competition, and discourage research and development in the pharmaceutical industry. Ultimately, each of these will lead to lowering of the welfare of patients. A robust pricing and price regulatory mechanism for the pharmaceutical industry is the need of the day.

REFERENCES

American Journal of Public Health and the Nation's Health.1946. 'Constitution of the World Health Organization', 36(11): 1315–23.

Abera, G., Y. Alemayehu, and J. Henry. 2017. 'Public-on-private Dual Practice among Physicians in Public Hospitals of Tigray National Regional State, North Ethiopia: Perspectives of Physicians, Patients and Managers', *BMC Health Services Research*, 17(1): 713.

Ahmed, S., H.A. Halim, and N.H. Ahmad. 2018. 'Open and Closed Innovation and Enhanced Performance of SME Hospitals—A Conceptual Model', *Business Perspectives and Research*, 6(1): 1–12.

Antunes, A., A. Biscaia, C. Conceição, I. Fronteira, I. Craveiro, I. Flores, O. Santos, and P. Ferrinho. 2002. *Workplace Violence in the Health Sector: Portuguese Case Studies Final Report*. Lisbon: AGO.

Asiimwe, D., B. McPake, F. Mwesigye, M. Ofoumbi, L. Oertenblad, P. Streefland, and A. Turinde. 1997. 'The Private Sector Activities of Public-sector Health Workers in Uganda', in S. Bennett, B. McPake, and A. Mills (eds), *Private Health Providers in Developing Countries: Serving the Public Interest?*, pp. 140–57. London and New Jersey: Zed Books.

Bajpai, V. 2014. 'The Challenges Confronting Public Hospitals in India, their Origins, and Possible Solutions', *Advances in Public Health*, article ID 898502: doi:10.1155/2014/898502.

Banda, E. and H.P. Simukonda. 1994. 'The Public–Private Mix in the Health Care System in Malawi', *Health Policy and Planning*, 9(1): 63–71.

Basu, S., J. Andrews, S. Kishore, R. Panjabi, and D. Stuckler. 2012. 'Comparative Performance of Private and Public

Healthcare Systems in Low- and Middle-income Countries: A Systematic Review', *PLOS Medicine*, 19 June: doi:https://doi.org/10.1371/journal.pmed.1001244.

Berendes, S., P. Heywood, S. Oliver, and P. Garner. 2011. 'Quality of Private and Public Ambulatory Health Care in Low and Middle Income Countries: Systematic Review of Comparative Studies', *PLOS Medicine*, 12 April: doi:https://doi.org/10.1371/journal.pmed.1000433.

Bhattacharjee, A. and D. Mohan. 2017. 'India's Healthcare System Is Becoming More and More Unequal', *The Wire*, 12 June, https://thewire.in/featured/india-healthcare-system-inequality; 12 April 2018.

Bhattacharya, K. 2005. 'Surgical Procedures for Laparoscopic Surgery', *Journal of Minimal Access Surgery*, 1(2): 74–5.

Bustreo, F., A. Harding, and H. Axelsson. 2003. 'Can Developing Countries Achieve Adequate Improvements in Child Health Outcomes without Engaging the Private Sector?', *Bulletin of the World Health Organization*, 81(12): 886–95.

Chen, L. and L. Hiebert. 1994. *From Socialism to Private Markets: Vietnam's Health in Rapid Transition*. Rockefeller Foundation, Bellagio Study Centre, http://www.hsph.harvard.edu/hcpds/wpweb/94_11.pdf; 12 April 2018.

Ferrinho, P., A. Biscaia, I. Craveiro, A. Antunes, I. Fronteira, C. Conceição, I. Flores, and O. Santos. 2003. 'Patterns of Perceptions of Workplace Violence in the Portuguese Health Care Sector', *Human Resources for Health*, 1:11, doi:10.1186/1478-4491-1-11.

Forgia, G.L., and S. Nagpal. 2012. 'Government-Sponsored Health Insurance in India: Are You Covered?', in *Directions in Development: Human Development*. Washington, DC: The World Bank, http://documents.worldbank.org/curated/en/644241468042840697/Government-sponsored-health-insurance-in-India-are-you-covered; 12 April 2018.

Fresta, E., M. Fresta, W. Van Lerberghe, P. Laise, M. Bugalho, and P. Ferrinho. 2001. *The Health Care Sector in Luanda, Angola: The Unsteered Growth of the Private Sector*. Lisbon: AGO.

Gupta, Indrani and Mrigesh Bhatia. 2017. 'Indian Health Care System'. In *International Profiles of Health Care System*, ed. Elias Mossialos, Ana Djordjevic, Robin Osborn, and Dana Sarnak, pp. 77–84. The Commonwealth Fund.

Harding, A. 2009. *Oxfam: This Is Not How to Help the Poor*. Washington, DC: Center for Global Development.

Hipólito, F. 2001. 'Regime Remuneratório Experimental', in *Dissertação Submetida na Cadeira de Estágio da Licenciatura em Sociologia da Universidade Lusófona de Humanidades e Tecnologias*. Lisboa, Julho de.

Hipólito, Fatima, Cláudia Conceição, Vítor Ramos, Pedro Aguiar, Wim Van Lerberghe, and Paulo Ferrinho. 2002. 'Quem Aderiu ao Regime Remuneratório Experimental e Porquê?', *Revista Portuguesa de Clínica Geral*, 18(2): 89–96.

International Institute for Population Sciences (IIPS) and ICF. 2017. *National Family Health Survey (NFHS-4) 2015–16*. Mumbai, India: IIPS.

Jaén, M. and D. Paravisini. 2001. 'Wages, Capture and Penalties in Venezuela's Public Hospitals', in R. Di Tella and W.D. Savedoff (eds), *Diagnosis Corruption: Fraud in Latin America's Public Hospitals*, pp. 57–94. Washington, DC: Inter-American Development Bank.

Jat, T.R. and M.S. Sebastian. 2013. 'Technical Efficiency of Public District Hospitals in Madhya Pradesh, India: A Data Envelopment Analysis'. *Global Health Action*, 6: Article No. 21742. doi:10.3402/gha.v6i0.21742.

Jha, D.N. 2017. 'Dengue Patient Dies, Parents Billed Rs 16 lakh for 2 Weeks in ICU', *The Times of* India, 21 November, http://timesofindia.indiatimes.com/city/delhi/dengue-patient-dies-parents-billed-16-lakh-for-2-weeks-in-icu/articleshow/61732259.cms (accessed 30 July 2018).

Koontz, H. and C. O'Donnell. 1959. *Principles of Management: An Analysis of Managerial Functions*. London, New York, Toronto: McGraw-Hill Book Company.

Loganathan, K., P. Deshmukh, and A. Raut. 2017. 'Socio-demographic Determinants of Out-of-Pocket Health Expenditure in a Rural Area of Wardha District of Maharashtra, India', *Indian Journal of Medical Research*, 146(5): 654–61, doi:10.4103/ijmr.IJMR_256_15.

Mandal, S. 2018. 'Health Panel Walks Pricing Tightrope', *The Telegraph*, 17 September, https://www.telegraphindia.com/calcutta/health-panel-walks-pricing-tightrope-214033; 12 April 2018.

McPake, B., D. Asiimwe, F. Mwesigye, M. Ofumbi, P. Streefland, A. Turinde, and M. Ofumbi. 2000. 'Coping Strategies of Health Workers in Uganda', in *Providing Health Care under Adverse Circumstances: Health Personnel Performance & Individual Coping Strategies*, ed. P. Ferrinho and W. van Lerberghe, pp. 135–55. Belgium: ITGPress

Montague, D., R. Feachem, N. Feachem, T. Koehlmoos, H. Kinlaw, et al. 2009. 'Oxfam Must Shed its Ideological Bias to be Taken Seriously', *BMJ*, 338:b1202, https://www.bmj.com/rapid-response/2011/11/02/oxfam-must-shed-its-ideological-bias-be-taken-seriously; 12 April 2018.

Nagarajan, R. 2018a. 'India Costlier for Heart Operations than Richer Nations', *The Times of India*, 2 September, Mumbai eEdition, https://epaper.timesgroup.com/Olive/ODN/TimesOfIndia/shared/ShowArticle.aspx?doc=TOIM%2F2018%2F09%2F02&entity=Ar00129&sk=7C0CDC4C&mode=text#; 12 April 2018.

————. 2018b. 'Private Hospitals Making Profits of up to 1,737% on Drugs, Consumables and Diagnostics: Study'. *The Times of India*, 21 February, https://timesofindia.indiatimes.com/india/private-hospitals-making-over-1700-profit-on-drugs-consumables-and-diagnostics-study/articleshow/62997879.cms; 12 April 2018.

Nandan, D., K. Nair, and U. Datta. 2007. 'Human Resources for Public Health in India: Issues and Challenges', *Health and Population: Perspectives and Issues*, 30(4): 230–42.

National Sample Survey Office (NSSO). 2015. NSS 71st Round (January–June 2014): *Key Indicators of Social Consumption in India: Health*. Ministry of Statistics and Programme Implementation.

Nittayaramphong, S. and V. Tangcharoensathien. 1994. 'Thailand: Private Health Care Out of Control?', *Health Policy and Planning*, 9(1): 31–40.

OXFAM International. 2009. *Blind Optimism: Challenging the Myths about Private Health Care in Poor Countries*, https://www.oxfam.org/sites/www.oxfam.org/files/bp125-blind-optimism-0902.pdf (accessed 31 December 2017).

Pandey, A., G. Ploubidis, L. Clarke, and L. Dandona. 2018. 'Trends in Catastrophic Health Expenditure in India: 1993 to 2014', *Bulletin of the World Health Organization*, 96(1): 18–28, doi:10.2471/BLT.17.191759.

Patel, A. 2017. 'How Hospitals in Collusion with Pharma Firms are Burning a Hole in Your Pocket', *India Today*, 13 July.

Porecha, M. 2018. 'Private Hospitals Fleece Patients, Overcharge up to 1737%', *DNA India*, 21 February, http://www.dnaindia.com/delhi/report-private-hospitals-fleece-patients-overcharge-up-to-1737-2586945; 30 July 2018.

PTI. 2017. 'Karnataka Assembly Passes Medical Bill after Dropping Controversial Clauses', *Livemint*, 22 November, https://www.livemint.com/Politics/YfLwqZAnn9OZDpu4YTKJdI/Karnataka-Assembly-passes-medical-bill-after-dropping-contro.html; 30 July 2018.

Rakshit, A. 2017. 'Mamata Introduces Bill to Regulate Private Hospitals', *Business Standard*, 4 March, https://www.business-standard.com/article/economy-policy/mamata-introduces-bill-to-regulate-private-hospitals-117030300936_1.html; 30 July 2018.

Rao, K.S. 2018a. 'Expert View: What Can India Do to Stop Hospitals from Overcharging?', *Scroll.in*, 17 September, https://scroll.in/pulse/872309/expert-view-what-can-india-do-to-stop-hospitals-from-overcharging; 12 April 2018.

———. 2018b. 'Why India's Private Hospitals Can Get Away with Overcharging Patients', *qz.com*, 26 March, https://qz.com/india/1237169/why-indias-private-hospitals-can-get-away-with-overcharging-patients/ (accessed 30 July 2018).

Rao, M., K. Rao, A. Kumar, M. Chatterjee, and T. Sundararaman. 2011. 'Human Resources for Health in India', *The Lancet*, 377(9765): 587–98.

Rosenthal, G. and W. Newbrander. 1996. 'Public Policy and Private Sector Provision of Health Services', *The International Journal of Health Planning and Management*, 11(3): 203–16.

Santra, Sattwik. 2018a. 1mg.com, https://www.1mg.com/ (accessed 2 August 2018).

———. 2018b. *DrugsUpdate.com*, http://www.drugsupdate.com (accessed 2 August 2018).

Sengupta, A. and S. Nandy. 2005. 'The Private Health Sector in India: Is Burgeoning but at the Cost of Public Health Care', *BMJ*, 331(7526): 1157–8.

Sharma, D. 2017. 'Rising Violence against Health Workers in India', *The Lancet*, 389(10080):1685.

Smith, R., R. Feachem, N. Feachem, T. Koehlmoos, and H. Kinlaw. 2009. 'The Fallacy of Impartiality: Competing Interest Bias in Academic Publications', *Journal of the Royal Society of Medicine*, 102(2): 44–5.

Stocking, B. 2009. 'Critique of Oxfam Paper Inaccurate, Unconstructive and Ideologically Biased', *BMJ*, 338: b667, http://www.bmj.com/rapid-response/2011/11/02/critique-oxfam-paper-inaccurate-unconstructive-and-ideologically-biased; 12 April 2018.

Thomason, J. 1994. 'A Cautious Approach to Privatisation in Papua New Guinea', *Health Policy and Planning*, 9(1): 41–9.

Tigga, N.S. and U.S. Mishra. 2015. 'On Measuring Technical Efficiency of the Health System in India: An Application of Data Envelopment Analysis', *Journal of Health Management*, 17(3): 285–98.

Uplekar, Mukund, Vikram Pathania, and Mario Raviglione. 2000. *Involving Private Practitioners in Tuberculosis Control Issues*. I.A. Geneva: World Health Organization.

Volmink, J., C. Metcalf, M. Zwarenstein, S. Heath, and J. Laubscher. 1993. 'Attitudes of Private General Practitioners towards Health Care in South Africa', *South African Medical Journal*, 83(11): 827–33.

3

Health Inefficiencies
A Statistical Profile*

Sandip Sarkar

Nearly 70 years ago, the World Health Organization (WHO) (1946) declared health as a fundamental human right stating, '[t]he extension to all peoples of the benefits of medical, psychological and related knowledge is essential to the fullest attainment of health'. In 2015, all member states of the United-Nations promised to '[e]nsure healthy lives and promote well-being for all at all ages'. Yet, in India, provision of equitable, quality healthcare to all citizens continues to be a pipedream.

According to WHO statistics released recently, India's spending on public health is dismal. The current health expenditure per capita in India stands at USD 63, which is among the lowest for developing countries, with China reporting a per capita spending of USD 426, Thailand USD 217, Malaysia USD 386, Philippines USD 127, Sri Lanka USD 118, and Indonesia USD 112.

Low expenses on health translate into shortage of health personnel at all levels, and poor health indicators with a high risk of morbidity and mortality during the life cycle. Keeping the objective of universal health coverage (UHC) in mind, the WHO constructed a Sustainable

UNHEALTHY NUMBERS

59.3 years Healthy life expectancy at birth	**$63** Current health expenditure per capita	**0.8** Density of physicians per 1,000 population	**2.1** Nursing and midwifery personnel per 1,000 population
3.9% Current health expenditure as percentage of GDP	**174** Maternal mortality ratio per lakh live births	**20.6%** Prevalence of tobacco smoking among males above 15	**88%** DPT vaccine coverage among 1-year-olds
86% Births attended by skilled healthcare professionals	**43** Under-5 mortality rate per 1,000 live births	**184.3** Mortality rate due to air pollution per lakh population	**16.6** Road traffic mortality rate per 100,000 population
56 Universal health coverage index ranking			

Source: *The New Indian Express*, 9 September 2018.
Original Source: World Health Organization Global Health Observatory data for India during 2010–17, as on 6 April 2018.

---

*This chapter is based on a background paper, Sattwik Santra, Jyotsna Jalan, and Sandip Sarkar, 'Health Status in India' (2018), Mimeo CTRPFP.

Development Goals (SDG) healthcare index for over 150 countries. Indicators grouped into four categories are reproductive, maternal, newborn, and child health; infectious diseases; non-communicable diseases; and service capacity and access. Box 3.1 shows the SDG healthcare score for high-income, upper-middle-income, lower-middle-income, and low-income countries. India's

score of less than 60 puts it among the low-achievers in the group of lower-middle-income countries.

Spatial variations in the quality of healthcare influence the extent of interregional health inequalities that in turn serve as impediments to 'health for all'. Differences in health outcomes can arise due to various factors. These include differences in endowments of health

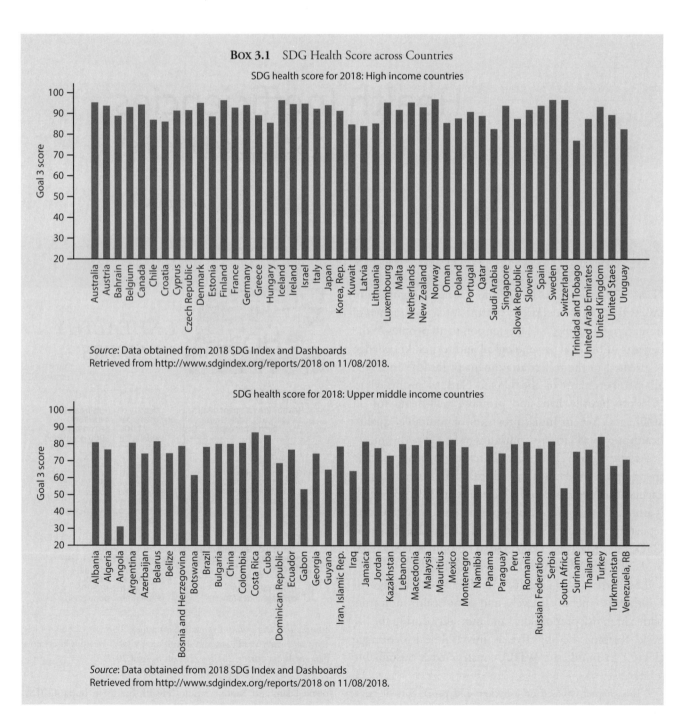

Box 3.1 SDG Health Score across Countries

SDG health score for 2018: High income countries

Source: Data obtained from 2018 SDG Index and Dashboards
Retrieved from http://www.sdgindex.org/reports/2018 on 11/08/2018.

SDG health score for 2018: Upper middle income countries

Source: Data obtained from 2018 SDG Index and Dashboards
Retrieved from http://www.sdgindex.org/reports/2018 on 11/08/2018.

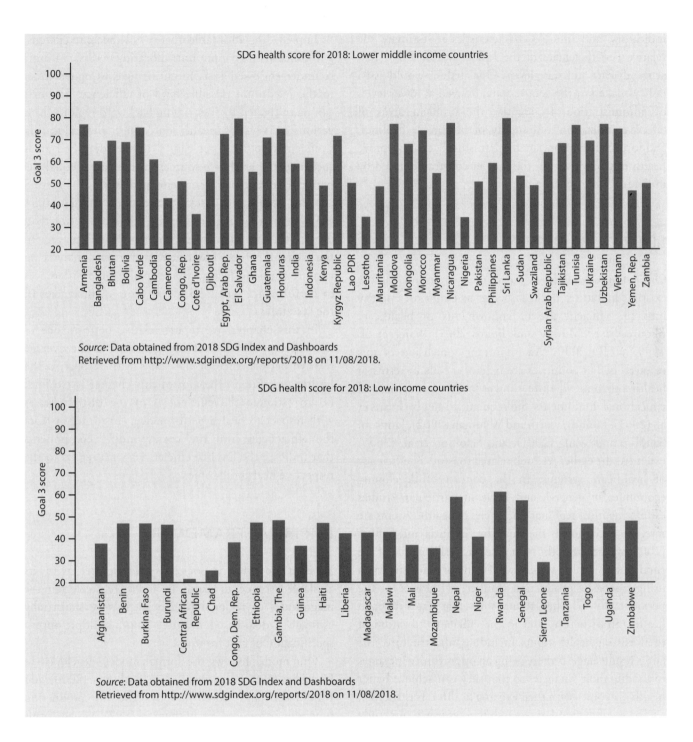

SDG health score for 2018: Lower middle income countries

Source: Data obtained from 2018 SDG Index and Dashboards
Retrieved from http://www.sdgindex.org/reports/2018 on 11/08/2018.

SDG health score for 2018: Low income countries

Source: Data obtained from 2018 SDG Index and Dashboards
Retrieved from http://www.sdgindex.org/reports/2018 on 11/08/2018.

infrastructure, personnel, and consumables (such as pharmaceutical drugs and assists), as well as from the relative (in)efficiency in utilization of inputs.

For many countries, information on health inputs and outcomes is available at the national and sub-national levels from different health surveys. But estimating the extent of (in)efficiency in utilization of available resources requires developing a model that relates health inputs with associated health outcomes. As India seeks to achieve UHC, studies such as the current one would be increasingly relevant (Lahariya 2018).

In this chapter, we develop an empirical model for multidimensional health outcomes that uses various inputs like access to health personnel and facilities, household indicators, and lifestyle characteristics to estimate the relative (in)efficiencies of the Indian healthcare system at the district and state levels. Our analysis would assist policy-makers at the centre, state, or even at lower levels of administration, to identify the problem areas of effective utilization and supply of healthcare facilities, and formulate appropriate mechanisms that can improve health outcomes within the budget constraints faced by individual state governments.

LITERATURE SURVEY

Our empirical model is based on two strands of the existing literature; the first being an empirical enquiry into the efficient use of endowments of healthcare resources (see Murray and Frenk 2001; Wang et al. 1999, WHO 2000). An important conclusion of this research is that countries are heterogeneous in terms of health outcomes despite similar levels of income and educational attainments. Subsequent studies by Evans et al. (2001), Hollingsworth and Wildman (2002), Jamison, Sandbu, and Wang (2001), and Salomon et al. (2001) extended the earlier research related to issues of efficiency of healthcare systems. In the context of developing economies in general, and India in particular, studies estimating intra-regional efficiencies of health systems are rare. An exception is the study by Kathuria and Sankar (2005) where the authors analyse the performance of the rural public health systems of 16 major states in India using stochastic production frontier techniques for the period 1986–97. Their results show that states differ in health infrastructure, and in the efficient utilization of their existing health inputs, including infrastructure. The latter result suggests there being an opportunity for states to modify their strategies so that they can achieve better health outcomes with their existing health infrastructure.

The second strand of research that we use in our study are those that develop methodologies to estimate multi-input, multi-output 'production' technologies. In this literature, single output stochastic frontier production models (Aigner, Lovell, and Schmidt 1977; Meeusen and van den Broeck 1977) are extended to incorporate multiple output models (Henningsen, Henningsen, and Jensen 2015; Kumbhakar and Lovell 2003; Löthgren 1997; Zhang and Garvey 2008), among others.

In providing affordable quality healthcare to citizens, two concerns are paramount: allocating necessary inputs to under-endowed areas and utilizing existing resources to the maximum possible level of efficiency. The first can be mitigated by identifying backward regions from various surveys of health outcomes, and allocating sufficient resources 'per capita' in the identified areas such that the level of resources in these areas equal the national average or some predefined levels. The second concern necessitates a statistical enquiry that identifies the systems that are performing relatively better than others, that is, identify the more efficient players in the system. Once identified, a further analysis to enquire into the factors that explain these differences in performance will help identify the inefficiencies in the system.

In this chapter, we report relative performance of the different districts of India as well as the average relative performance of the states with respect to the healthcare system. The aim of this chapter is twofold: (a) to estimate the efficiencies of the districts/states with respect to health performance; (b) to deconstruct the efficiencies into the corresponding components that indicate the level of efficiencies with regard to the respective health outcomes.

EMPIRICAL FRAMEWORK

To measure what a society could achieve with its available resources in healthcare and thereby ascertain the magnitudes of regional (in)efficiencies, we statistically estimate a dual-based multiple-input, multiple-output specification of cost frontiers.

Our model follows the formal models developed in Löthgren (1997) and detailed in Löthgren (2000) and Kumbhakar and Lovell (2003). The ray production function introduced in Löthgren (1997), which forms the basis of our stochastic frontier model, formulates the Euclidean norm of the frontier output vector as a function of the inputs and the output polar-coordinate angles. In the present exercise, we apply the inverse of this procedure and deconstruct the estimate of inefficiencies into the components corresponding to the inefficiencies associated with the outcome. Box 3.2 gives the underlying technical details of the model.

> **BOX 3.2** The Formal Stochastic Model
>
> The primal version of our model is founded on the ray production function. The ray production function is a scalar-valued representation of a multiple input, multiple output technology that formulates the Euclidean norm of the frontier output vector as a function of the inputs and the output mix, represented by the output polar coordinate angles. The same can be represented by: $\|y\| = F(x, \theta)$ where $\|\ \|$ denotes the Euclidean norm of the output vector y, x represents the vector of inputs while θ represents the vector of output polar coordinate angles. Formally:
>
> $\|y\| \equiv \sqrt[n]{\sum_{i=1}^{n} y_i^2}$ where $y_i \forall i = 1.. n$ denotes the individual components of the output vector y, and the vector of polar coordinate angles (in radians) is related to the output vector following the expression: $\theta \equiv \left\{ \theta_j \forall j = 1..(n-1) / \left(\sqrt[n]{\sum_{i=j}^{n} y_i^2} \right) \cos \theta_j y_j \right\}$ from which it is recursively generated. Note that in our formulation, the functional form of $F(\cdot, \cdot)$ interacts with the vector of output polar coordinate angles θ up to a quadratic term. In addition to the ray production function, the statistical model used in this analysis allows for a non-negative technical inefficiency component 'v' and an idiosyncratic random shock component 'u' to affect the output. This model coined as the stochastic ray frontier model, is obtained by introducing a composite error term '$\varepsilon \equiv u - v$' in the original ray frontier model which can now be represented by: $\|y\| = F(x, \theta)e^\varepsilon$. Taking the natural log of both sides and assuming a log-linear functional form of $F(x, \theta)$ yields: $\ln\|y\| = \ln x + \log\theta + u - v$. Kumbhakar and Lovell (2003) show that performing an analogous derivation in the dual cost function problem allows us to reformulate the problem as: $\ln\|c\| = \ln x + \ln \theta + u + v$, where c denotes the associated cost instead of output (the output variable now constitutes a part of the input vector x). Our model specification assumes u to follow a normal distribution with zero mean and some arbitrary variance, and the inefficiency term v to follow a truncated–normal distribution. In our model, technical inefficiency is defined as the estimated value of: $F(x, \theta)E(e^v) - F(x, \theta)$ (conditional on the data) where $E(\ )$ denotes the expected value of the term in the parentheses. To deconstruct the estimate of inefficiencies 'TI' into the components corresponding to the inefficiencies associated with the outcomes, we follow the inverse of the procedure used to obtain the polar coordinate angles corresponding to the output vector. Formally: $TI_i = RI_i \cos\theta_i \forall i = 1.. n - 1$, $TI_n = RI_n$ where $RI_1 = TE$ and $RI_{i+1} = RI_i \sin\theta_i \forall i = 1.. n - 1$.

DATA DESCRIPTION

We use data from 451 districts of India. The information is collated from various rounds of Annual Health Surveys (AHS), District Level Household Surveys (DLHS), National Family Health Surveys (NFHS), and National Sample Surveys (NSS). We compile a host of input and outcome variables.

We consider three health outcomes—child mortality ratio, rate of adult chronic illness, and rate of adult acute illness. The control variables used in our analysis include several aggregates of individual and household-level characteristics as well as observations on various measures of physical infrastructure and human resources of sub-regional public health facilities.

RESULTS AND DISCUSSION

Table 3.1 lists the dependent variables along with the sources of data. Table 3.2 reports summary statistics of the health outcomes as well as some input variables used

in our analysis. The estimates of the stochastic frontier model are reported in Table 3.3. The estimates of technical inefficiencies over the districts are summarized in Table A1 of the statistical appendix. State-level aggregates of the technical inefficiencies can be obtained from Table A2 of the statistical appendix. In Tables A1 and A2, we also report the magnitudes of technical inefficiencies across the individual outcomes. From these two tables, the relative rankings of the states and/or districts in terms of overall inefficiency and technical inefficiencies with respect to individual inefficiencies can be easily computed. Moreover, the reported estimated figures can also be used to compute the degree of inequality in technical inefficiency both within and across the states. This may also suggest the extent of failure of spatial transmission of healthcare reforms aimed at improving efficiency in the provision of healthcare within and across states, respectively. This last result is apparent especially from Figure 3.1 that presents the results reported in Table A2 pictorially. Another interesting observation from the figures is that the extent of technical inefficiency across the districts and states shows an inherent tendency of

TABLE 3.1 List of Dependent and Independent Variables and Their Sources

Variable groups	Type	Sources	Comments
Mortality rates of children.	Dependent outcome variable	NFHS-4 (2014–15)	Constructed from child mortality rates (CMR), infant mortality rates (IMR), and neonatal mortality rates (NMR) following the formula: [CMR (1-IMR) (1-NMR) + IMR (1-NMR) + NMR)]. Variables considered as a fraction.
Rate of adult chronic illness and rate of adult acute illness.	Dependent outcome variables	DLHS-4 (2012–13), AHS (2012–13)	Variables considered as a fraction.
Total population in the district.	Independent control variable	DLHS-4, AHS (2012–13)	Variable considered in logarithms.
Total number of medical specialists, obstetricians/gynaecologists, paediatricians, surgery specialists, and general duty doctors per bed in district hospital/s.	Independent control variables	DLHS-3 (2007–8)	Termed as index of clinical medical personnel.
Total number of anaesthetists, pathologists/microbiologists, radiologists, dermatologists, ophthalmologists, nurses, compounders, technicians, radiographers, pharmacists, and physiotherapists per bed in district hospital/s.	Independent control variables	DLHS-3 (2007–8)	Termed as index of supporting clinical medical personnel.
Percentage of population who chew tobacco; percentage of population who smoke; percentage of population who consume alcohol; percentage of adult literates; percentage of households with medical insurance of some type; percentage of households with improved drinking water facilities; percentage of households with improved sanitation facilities.	Independent control variables	NFHS-4 (2014–15)	Variables considered as a fraction.
Availability of facilities of haematology, urine analysis, stool analysis, pap smear, sputum, histopathology, microbiology, blood sugar, blood urea, blood creatinine, Widal test, Elisa test for HIV, R A factor test, venereal disease research laboratory (VDRL) test, electrocardiogram (ECG), stress test (treadmill test (TMT)), 2d-echo, X-ray, ultrasound, fully operational blood bank, fully functional physiotherapy unit, and pharmacy.	Independent control variable	DLHS-3 (2007–8)	These variables are considered as an index. The construction of the index follows Filmer and Pritchett (1998, 1999). Termed as index of diagnostics.
Availability of facilities of pregnancy test, Coomb's test.	Independent control variable	DLHS-3 (2007–8)	These variables are considered as an index. The construction of the index follows Filmer and Pritchett (1998, 1999). Termed as index of diagnostics (child).
Availability of facilities of water supply for 24 hours; three-phase electricity connection; standby facility of generator/inverter available in working condition; telephone facility available in all the sections of the hospital; personal computer; central sterile and supply department; biomedical waste disposal facility; ambulance; elective, emergency, and ophthalmology operation theatre; total beds; general medicine; surgery; intensive care unit (ICU), post-operation wards; number of beds in post-partum and burn wards.	Independent control variable	DLHS-3 (2007–8)	These variables are considered as an index. The construction of the index follows Filmer and Pritchett (1998, 1999). Termed as index of physical infrastructure.

Availability of paediatric ward, labour room, delivery room, and neonatal room; number of beds in post-, ante-natal care units	Independent control variable	DLHS-3 (2007–8)	These variables are considered as an index. The construction of the index follows Filmer and Pritchett (1998, 1999). Termed as index of physical infrastructure (child).
Availability of anaesthetist and surgery for 24 hours; availability and cleanliness of outpatient department (OPD), rooms, wards, and premises; score indexed from 1 to 3	Independent control variable	DLHS-3 (2007–8)	These variables are considered as an index. The construction of the index follows Filmer and Pritchett (1998, 1999). Termed as index of efficiency.
Availability of obstetrician/gynaecologist and nurse for 24 hours	Independent control variable	DLHS-3 (2007–8)	These variables are considered as an index. The construction of the index follows Filmer and Pritchett (1998, 1999). Termed as index of efficiency (child).
Public to private hospitals attendance ratio; public to private hospitals attendance ratio for child	Independent control variables	NFHS-4 (2014–15)	Ratio of number of cases at the state level.

TABLE 3.2 Statistics of the Outcome Variables and Some Input Variables

State	Average percentage of child mortality	Average percentage of adults with chronic illness	Average percentage of adults with acute illness	Average percentage of people chewing tobacco	Average percentage of smokers	Average percentage of people drinking alcohol	Average percentage of adult literates	Total population (in million)
Andhra Pradesh	1.2840	11.9757	9.7357	4.0713	2.6237	2.7816	71.1417	49.3868
Assam	15.8037	18.0488	10.9255	70.8208	1.1669	8.0919	76.4862	27.6877
Bihar	14.2842	13.4370	14.9549	2.4599	1.0468	0.5831	64.1246	103.3986
Chhattisgarh	13.1693	4.1932	10.7210	21.5898	0.3935	6.9504	75.9396	25.1501
Haryana	2.3092	16.2306	13.3792	0.4813	0.7310	0.4642	83.3994	24.3088
Himachal Pradesh	0.6732	2.7747	2.1901	0.8270	1.0440	0.9020	92.2508	6.8646
Jharkhand	10.5295	8.4481	6.8195	6.6018	0.4892	5.5259	69.4921	28.3242
Karnataka	1.7434	6.0786	5.3476	18.8133	0.7767	0.9339	78.9135	57.5833
Kerala	0.5400	6.9084	8.1834	0.9253	0.5700	0.6775	98.2812	33.4061
Madhya Pradesh	17.3111	6.9476	8.9816	6.2421	0.4938	1.0627	71.3601	68.3674
Maharashtra	1.1269	8.1650	8.6486	5.3593	0.7235	0.7951	85.5496	99.9320
Odisha	16.0067	10.5585	10.2158	21.0632	0.5930	4.6859	75.8444	41.9742
Punjab	1.0640	10.0289	3.9701	0.7165	0.2624	0.8144	84.5875	27.7433
Rajasthan	15.8243	4.6289	5.4795	3.9357	0.7988	0.4110	71.5323	67.6806
Tamil Nadu	0.6024	3.6642	3.4866	4.7105	0.4451	0.5505	83.7150	63.1414
Uttar Pradesh	19.2496	12.3877	12.0827	6.0555	1.1191	0.5296	71.9887	198.3756
Uttarakhand	11.3702	10.4581	8.7292	1.4016	0.9319	0.4425	83.9201	10.0863
West Bengal	1.4986	14.0676	16.5171	15.7313	1.9998	1.7586	75.6699	86.7794
All India	**12.3439**	**9.9593**	**10.0379**	**9.1047**	**0.9880**	**1.5125**	**75.8684**	**1,020.1904**

Source: Data compiled from DLHS-3 (2007–8), AHS (2012–13), DLHS-4 (2012–13) and NFHS-4 (2014–15).

TABLE 3.3 Estimation Results

Model Coefficients	Estimates	Model Coefficients	Estimates
θ_1	0.9445**	Proportion of households with sanitation facilities	−0.0012
	(0.4045)		(0.0016)
θ_2	−0.9009	Index of clinical medical personnel	0.2572
	(0.5497)		(0.2245)
$\theta_1 \times \theta_1$	−0.5440***	Index of supporting clinical medical personnel	−2.3702
	(0.1911)		(2.0268)
$\theta_1 \times \theta_2$	−0.1512	Index of diagnostics	−0.0443
	(0.2334)		(0.0372)
$\theta_2 \times \theta_2$	0.7493**	Index of diagnostics (child)	0.0614**
	(0.2919)		(0.0260)
ln(total population)	0.1953***	Index of physical infrastructure	−0.0801***
	(0.0352)		(0.0310)
Proportion chewing tobacco	0.0050***	Index of physical infrastructure (child)	0.0028
	(0.0018)		(0.0249)
Proportion smoking	0.0646***	Index of efficiency	0.0049
	(0.0245)		(0.0230)
Proportion drinking alcohol	0.0003	Index of efficiency (child)	−0.0776***
	(0.0061)		(0.0287)
Proportion of adult literates	−0.0072**	Public to private hospitals attendance ratio	0.6423**
	(0.0032)		(0.3044)
Proportion of households with insurance	−0.0079***	Public to private hospitals attendance ratio for child	−0.5134
	(0.0011)		(0.4265)
Proportion of households with drinking water facilities	−0.0014	Constant	−3.7567***
	(0.0021)		(0.7159)

Note: ** and *** indicate significance at 5 per cent and 1 per cent, respectively.

Source: Authors' calculations based on data from DLHS-3 (2007–8), AHS (2012–13), DLHS-4 (2012–13) and NFHS-4 (2014–15).

being spatially correlated both in terms of the overall magnitude and also across the individual dimensions: possibly indicating the influence of other socio-economic factors that play a deterministic role in dictating the extent of inefficiency of the healthcare system. Both these observations warrant future investigations to ascertain the causes of these phenomena.

* * *

The Government of India in 2017 set a target of raising annual health spending to 2.5 per cent of India's gross domestic product (GDP) by 2025, from the 2018 value of 1.15 per cent—one of the lowest proportions in the world (Thomson Reuters 2018). Since resources

are limited, it is important that they be used efficiently. Decreasing inefficiencies and providing more health infrastructure are two ways of achieving an increase in health outcomes. Using data from national sources, the current study estimates the relative inefficiencies in the performance of healthcare systems across the districts of India in terms of the outcomes of child mortality rates, and adult morbidity rates of acute and chronic illnesses. An important observation of the present study is that the estimates of overall and component-wise inefficiencies exhibit significant intra- and inter-state regional disparities as well as a substantial spatial dependence.

A significant shortcoming of the present analysis is that, because of non-availability of data on private-sector healthcare facilities, our estimates of technical

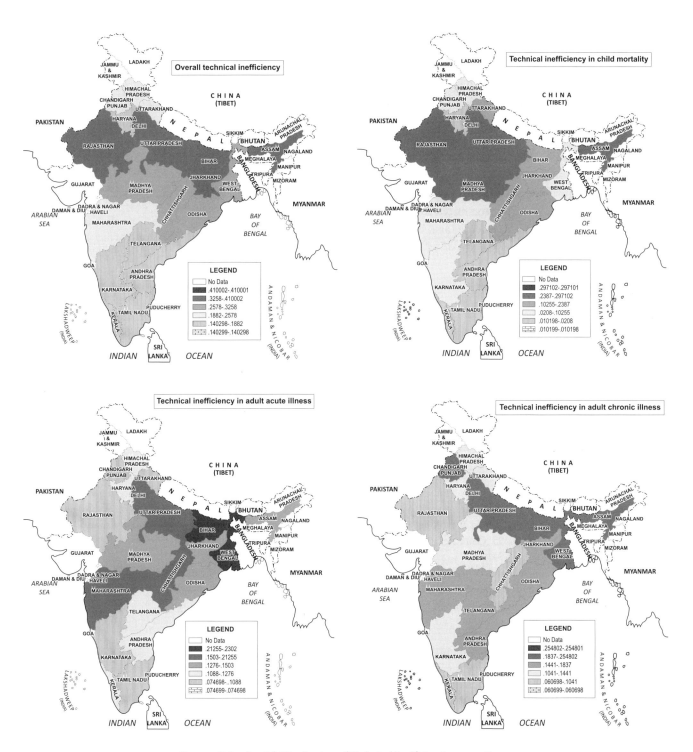

FIGURE 3.1 Spatial Distribution of Technical Inefficiencies across States

Note: These maps are not to scale and do not represent authentic international boundaries.
Source: Based on author's calculations from NFHS-4, DLHS-4, DLHS-3 and AHS (2012–13) data.

efficiencies might exhibit some aberrations. The exclusion of this complementary sector from our analysis would result in a negative bias in the estimated inefficiencies, particularly for those states that have a large private sector. Thus this research also highlights the necessity of collecting and disbursing information on the qualitative and quantitative aspects of private healthcare facilities and service providers. Contingent on the availability of data, a further improvement can be incorporated in our model by controlling for interregional migration of patients. Intuitively, accounting for interregional patient mobility would lead to a rise in interregional inequality in technical inefficiencies, the magnitude of which needs to be ascertained empirically.

REFERENCES

Aigner, D.J., C.A. Lovell, and P. Schmidt. 1977. 'Formulation and Estimation of Stochastic Frontier Production Function Models', *Journal of Econometrics*, 6(1): 21–37.

Evans, D.B., A. Tandon, C.J. Murray, and J.A. Lauer. 2001. *The Comparative Efficiency of National Health Systems in Producing Health: An Analysis of 191 Countries*. Geneva: GPE Discussion Paper Series No. 29, WHO, EIP/GPE/EQC.

Filmer, D. and L. Pritchett. 1998. 'Estimating Wealth Effects without Expenditure Data—Or Tears: With an Application to Educational Enrolments in States of India'. World Bank Policy Research Working Paper 1994.

———. 1999. 'The Effect of Household Wealth on Educational Attainment: Evidence from 35 Countries', *Population and Development Review*, 25(1): 85–120.

Henningsen, G., A. Henningsen, and U. Jensen. 2015. 'A Monte Carlo Study on Multiple Output Stochastic Frontiers: A Comparison of Two Approaches', *Journal of Productivity Analysis*, 44(3): 309–20.

Hollingsworth, B. and J. Wildman. 2002. 'The Efficiency of Health Production: Reestimating the WHO Panel Data Using Parametric and Nonparametric Approaches to Provide Additional Information'. Centre for Health Program Evaluation Working Paper No. 131. Melbourne: Monash University.

Jamison, D.T., M. Sandbu, and J. Wang. 2001. 'Cross Country Variation in Mortality Decline, 1962–87: The Role of Country Specific Technical Progress'. Commission on Macroeconomics and Health Working Paper No. WGI: 4. Geneva: WHO.

Kathuria, V. and D. Sankar. 2005. 'Inter-state Disparities in Health Outcomes in Rural India: An Analysis Using a Stochastic Production Frontier Approach', *Development Policy Review*, 23(2): 145–63.

Kumbhakar, S.C. and C.K. Lovell. 2003. *Stochastic Frontier Analysis*. Cambridge, New York: Cambridge University Press.

Lahariya, C. 2018. 'Taking the Road Less Traveled: Economic Analyses for Advancing Universal Health Coverage', *Journal of Postgraduate Medicine*, 64(3): 134–5.

Löthgren, M. 1997. 'Generalized Stochastic Frontier Production Models', *Economics Letters*, 57(3): 255–9.

———. 2000. 'Specification and Estimation of Stochastic Multiple-output Production and Technical Inefficiency', *Applied Economics*, 32(12): 1533–40, doi:10.1080/000368400418943.

Meeusen, W. and J. van den Broeck. 1977. 'Efficiency Estimation from Cobb Douglas Production Functions with Composed Error', *International Economic Review*, 18(2): 435–44.

Murray, C.J. and J. Frenk. 2001. 'World Health Report 2000: A Step towards Evidence-Based Health Policy', *The Lancet*, 357(9269): 1698–1700.

Planning Commission, Government of India. 2002. *National Human Development Report 2001*.

Salomon, J.A., C.D. Mathers, C.J. Murray, and B. Ferguson. 2001. 'Method for Life Expectancy and Healthy Life Expectancy Uncertainty Analysis'. Global Programme on Evidence for Health Policy Working Paper No. 10. Geneva: WHO.

Thomson Reuters. 2018. 'India Plans to Raise Health Spending by 11 Percent in Budget; Less than Requested', 18 January, https://www.reuters.com/article/us-india-budget-health-exclusive/india-plans-to-raise-health-spending-by-11-percent-in-budget-less-than-requested-idUSKBN1F711N; 18 January 2019.

Wang, J., D.T. Jamison, E. Bos, A. Preker, and J. Peaboy. 1999. *Measuring Country Performance on Health: Selected Indicators for 115 Countries*. Washington, DC: Human Development Network, Health, Nutrition and Population Studies, World Bank.

World Health Organisation (WHO). 1946. *The Constitution of the World Health Organization*, opened for signature July 22, 1946, 62 Stat. 2679, 14 U.N.T.S. 186.

———. 2000. *World Health Report: Health Systems: Improving Performance*. Geneva: WHO.

Zhang, T. and E. Garvey. 2008. 'A Comparative Analysis of Multi-output Frontier Models', *Journal of Zhejiang University-SCIENCE A*, 9(10): 1426–36.

Statistical Appendix
A Compendium of Health-Related Statistics

TABLE A1   District-Wise Estimates of Inefficiencies (statistical estimates obtained from the statistical model described in Box 3.2)

State	District	Overall technical inefficiency	Technical inefficiency in child mortality	Technical inefficiency in adult chronic illness	Technical inefficiency in adult acute illness
Andhra Pradesh	Anantapur	0.2076	0.0169	0.1869	0.0889
	Chittoor	0.2039	0.0212	0.1551	0.1307
	East Godavari	0.2334	0.0165	0.1764	0.1519
	Guntur	0.2198	0.0184	0.1635	0.1458
	Krishna	0.1217	0.0000	0.0849	0.0871
	Kurnool	0.2325	0.0293	0.1756	0.1496
	Prakasam	0.1573	0.0030	0.1072	0.1151
	Sri Potti Sriramulu Nellore	0.1765	0.0063	0.1296	0.1197
	Srikakulam	0.2131	0.0209	0.1955	0.0822
	Vishakapatnam	0.2399	0.0360	0.1835	0.1504
	Vizianagaram	0.1784	0.0230	0.1420	0.1056
	West Godavari	0.1897	0.0157	0.1492	0.1162
Assam	Barpeta	0.4587	0.3311	0.2990	0.1064
	Darrang	0.4437	0.3842	0.2109	0.0696
	Dhemaji	0.4250	0.3115	0.2287	0.1770
	Dhubri	0.5397	0.4406	0.2887	0.1175
	Dibrugarh	0.4108	0.1738	0.3155	0.1975
	Goalpara	0.4912	0.3672	0.3014	0.1250
	Golaghat	0.4454	0.1912	0.3504	0.1976

(Cont'd)

TABLE A1 (*Cont'd*)

State	District	Overall technical inefficiency	Technical inefficiency in child mortality	Technical inefficiency in adult chronic illness	Technical inefficiency in adult acute illness
	Hailakandi	0.4788	0.2181	0.3458	0.2491
	Jorhat	0.3750	0.1269	0.3183	0.1523
	Kamrup	0.2474	0.1697	0.1654	0.0713
	Karbi Anglong	0.4767	0.2635	0.3076	0.2514
	Karimganj	0.4317	0.2105	0.2996	0.2286
	Kokrajhar	0.4097	0.3781	0.1302	0.0886
	Lakhimpur	0.4116	0.2972	0.2668	0.0997
	Marigaon	0.4456	0.3502	0.2575	0.0980
	Nagaon	0.5058	0.2269	0.3447	0.2925
	Nalbari	0.3996	0.3127	0.2327	0.0876
	North Cachar Hills	0.3836	0.2422	0.2472	0.1654
	Sibsagar	0.3734	0.1843	0.2909	0.1444
	Sonitpur	0.4779	0.4198	0.2171	0.0706
	Tinsukia	0.4457	0.1999	0.3375	0.2118
Bihar	Araria	0.6675	0.3472	0.3269	0.4670
	Aurangabad	0.3255	0.1755	0.2247	0.1571
	Banka	0.4083	0.2314	0.2560	0.2183
	Begusarai	0.3731	0.1379	0.2864	0.1954
	Bhagalpur	0.3489	0.2038	0.1979	0.2026
	Bhojpur	0.3100	0.2251	0.1841	0.1073
	Buxar	0.3523	0.2143	0.2469	0.1311
	Darbhanga	0.3505	0.1788	0.1341	0.2701
	Gaya	0.5794	0.3243	0.3839	0.2883
	Gopalganj	0.3555	0.2241	0.1910	0.1991
	Jehanabad	0.3250	0.2363	0.1612	0.1542
	Kaimur (Bhabua)	0.2838	0.1890	0.1503	0.1490
	Katihar	0.4195	0.2312	0.2309	0.2632
	Khagaria	0.4276	0.3258	0.2277	0.1576
	Kishanganj	0.5209	0.2693	0.1901	0.4033
	Lakhisarai	0.3531	0.1562	0.2660	0.1720
	Madhepura	0.4720	0.3487	0.2196	0.2301
	Madhubani	0.4043	0.2252	0.2079	0.2637
	Munger	0.3380	0.2133	0.2095	0.1578
	Muzaffarpur	0.4689	0.2912	0.2505	0.2690
	Nalanda	0.3628	0.2009	0.2063	0.2206
	Nawada	0.3283	0.1721	0.2273	0.1628
	Pashchim Champaran	0.4351	0.1943	0.2295	0.3144
	Purba Champaran	0.4830	0.2209	0.2021	0.3791
	Purnia	0.5208	0.2713	0.1907	0.4016
	Rohtas	0.4218	0.1921	0.3167	0.2018

	Saharsa	0.4288	0.2740	0.1968	0.2646
	Samastipur	0.4998	0.2776	0.3377	0.2423
	Saran	0.4167	0.2792	0.2470	0.1863
	Sheikhpura	0.2696	0.1453	0.1791	0.1396
	Sheohar	0.4763	0.1930	0.1530	0.4076
	Sitamarhi	0.5812	0.3099	0.2243	0.4375
	Siwan	0.3490	0.2983	0.1163	0.1391
	Vaishali	0.4101	0.2092	0.2295	0.2678
Chhattisgarh	Bastar	0.3033	0.2766	0.0489	0.1142
	Bilaspur	0.2713	0.1950	0.0760	0.1726
	Dantewada	0.3637	0.3037	0.0459	0.1948
	Dhamtari	0.1857	0.0974	0.0725	0.1405
	Durg	0.2215	0.1762	0.0674	0.1160
	Janjgir–Champa	0.2261	0.1441	0.0581	0.1643
	Jashpur	0.2525	0.1683	0.0745	0.1729
	Kanker	0.1869	0.1629	0.0420	0.0815
	Kawardha	0.3265	0.2322	0.0646	0.2203
	Korba	0.2545	0.1929	0.0583	0.1554
	Koriya	0.2399	0.2074	0.0571	0.1062
	Mahasamund	0.2665	0.1569	0.0458	0.2105
	Raigarh	0.2699	0.1708	0.0721	0.1962
	Raipur	0.3206	0.2881	0.0610	0.1268
	Rajnandgaon	0.2149	0.1253	0.0483	0.1677
	Surguja	0.3092	0.2644	0.0506	0.1522
Haryana	Faridabad	0.1976	0.0270	0.1537	0.1211
	Fatehabad	0.2082	0.0258	0.1291	0.1614
	Gurgaon	0.1898	0.0166	0.1246	0.1422
	Hisar	0.2267	0.0320	0.1909	0.1180
	Jhajjar	0.2007	0.0106	0.1658	0.1126
	Jind	0.2030	0.0119	0.1513	0.1348
	Kaithal	0.1821	0.0148	0.1436	0.1110
	Karnal	0.2017	0.0217	0.1414	0.1421
	Kurukshetra	0.1755	0.0051	0.1356	0.1113
	Mahendragarh	0.1798	0.0238	0.1516	0.0937
	Mewat	0.3001	0.0454	0.1676	0.2447
	Panchkula	0.1708	0.0142	0.1569	0.0659
	Panipat	0.2268	0.0276	0.1657	0.1525
	Rewari	0.1807	0.0119	0.1270	0.1280
	Rohtak	0.1836	0.0150	0.1337	0.1249
	Sirsa	0.2226	0.0259	0.1816	0.1260
	Sonipat	0.2107	0.0285	0.1511	0.1440
	Yamunanagar	0.1862	0.0264	0.1477	0.1103
Himachal Pradesh	Bilaspur	0.2130	0.0947	0.1411	0.1283
	Chamba	0.1650	0.0000	0.1577	0.0485

(Cont'd)

TABLE A1 (*Cont'd*)

State	District	Overall technical inefficiency	Technical inefficiency in child mortality	Technical inefficiency in adult chronic illness	Technical inefficiency in adult acute illness
	Hamirpur	0.1435	0.0117	0.1117	0.0894
	Kangra	0.1987	0.0377	0.1446	0.1309
	Kinnaur	0.1970	0.1389	0.1124	0.0828
	Kullu	0.2304	0.0738	0.1444	0.1636
	Lahul & Spiti	0.1156	0.0000	0.0945	0.0667
	Mandi	0.1815	0.0000	0.1007	0.1510
	Shimla	0.2193	0.0958	0.1729	0.0951
	Sirmaur	0.2012	0.0524	0.1310	0.1435
	Solan	0.1609	0.0000	0.1395	0.0802
	Una	0.2171	0.0353	0.2069	0.0554
Jharkhand	Bokaro	0.3325	0.2068	0.2401	0.1006
	Chatra	0.4965	0.3664	0.2308	0.2430
	Deoghar	0.2843	0.2147	0.1473	0.1142
	Dhanbad	0.2653	0.1137	0.2164	0.1029
	Dumka	0.3969	0.2544	0.2849	0.1079
	Garhwa	0.3184	0.2464	0.1442	0.1408
	Giridih	0.3343	0.2369	0.1768	0.1561
	Godda	0.4708	0.4051	0.2019	0.1295
	Gumla	0.3219	0.2302	0.1493	0.1685
	Hazaribagh	0.2805	0.1673	0.1198	0.1906
	Kodarma	0.3010	0.2206	0.1514	0.1379
	Lohardaga	0.2631	0.1875	0.1400	0.1202
	Pakaur	0.3557	0.3073	0.1047	0.1455
	Palamu	0.2894	0.2276	0.1315	0.1212
	Pashchimi Singhbhum	0.4583	0.3203	0.2351	0.2284
	Purbi Singhbhum	0.2384	0.1288	0.1167	0.1631
	Ranchi	0.3495	0.2259	0.2134	0.1599
	Sahibganj	0.3570	0.3127	0.1213	0.1225
Karnataka	Bagalkot	0.2527	0.2107	0.0946	0.1025
	Belgaum	0.2819	0.0931	0.1436	0.2240
	Bellary	0.3060	0.1244	0.2236	0.1677
	Bidar	0.2172	0.0448	0.1841	0.1062
	Chamarajanagar	0.2108	0.0647	0.1562	0.1259
	Chikmagalur	0.1741	0.0000	0.1407	0.1025
	Chitradurga	0.2083	0.1348	0.1400	0.0750
	Dakshina Kannada	0.1739	0.0038	0.1547	0.0792
	Davanagere	0.2107	0.0237	0.1359	0.1593
	Dharwad	0.2091	0.0539	0.1220	0.1610
	Gadag	0.2663	0.0864	0.0941	0.2336
	Gulbarga	0.2725	0.1547	0.1561	0.1611

	Hassan	0.1785	0.0129	0.1155	0.1354
	Haveri	0.2354	0.0796	0.1334	0.1768
	Kodagu	0.1243	0.0000	0.0783	0.0965
	Kolar	0.2029	0.0503	0.1436	0.1343
	Koppal	0.2575	0.1631	0.1262	0.1543
	Mandya	0.1617	0.0182	0.1214	0.1054
	Mysore	0.1738	0.0030	0.1487	0.0900
	Raichur	0.2692	0.0849	0.1806	0.1806
	Shimoga	0.1779	0.0120	0.1676	0.0586
	Tumkur	0.2419	0.0709	0.1746	0.1516
	Udupi	0.1472	0.0068	0.1272	0.0737
	Uttara Kannada	0.2117	0.0094	0.2059	0.0484
Kerala	Alappuzha	0.1711	0.0060	0.1230	0.1187
	Ernakulam	0.1686	0.0045	0.1255	0.1126
	Kannur	0.1375	0.0000	0.1025	0.0917
	Kollam	0.1592	0.0027	0.0892	0.1319
	Kottayam	0.1306	0.0000	0.1102	0.0701
	Kozhikode	0.1420	0.0043	0.0747	0.1207
	Mallappuram	0.1940	0.0101	0.0755	0.1784
	Palakkad	0.2953	0.0820	0.0383	0.2811
	Pathanamthitta	0.1647	0.0000	0.0663	0.1508
	Thiruvananthapuram	0.1553	0.0060	0.1178	0.1010
	Thrissur	0.1887	0.0000	0.1717	0.0783
	Wayanand	0.1151	0.0000	0.0778	0.0849
Madhya Pradesh	Balaghat	0.3752	0.2394	0.1166	0.2644
	Barwani	0.3918	0.3492	0.0714	0.1627
	Betul	0.3496	0.2395	0.0778	0.2425
	Bhind	0.3042	0.2760	0.0980	0.0821
	Bhopal	0.2441	0.1818	0.1343	0.0923
	Chhatarpur	0.3723	0.3073	0.1186	0.1735
	Chhindwara	0.3963	0.3206	0.0862	0.2164
	Damoh	0.4027	0.3161	0.1322	0.2116
	Datai	0.2407	0.2295	0.0535	0.0489
	Dewas	0.2517	0.2300	0.0912	0.0457
	Dindori	0.3203	0.1976	0.2056	0.1458
	East Nimar	0.3566	0.3127	0.0641	0.1589
	Guna	0.3489	0.3196	0.0730	0.1195
	Gwalior	0.2825	0.2558	0.0925	0.0762
	Harda	0.2769	0.2510	0.0668	0.0960
	Hoshangabad	0.3056	0.2220	0.0811	0.1937
	Indore	0.3209	0.2409	0.1878	0.0985
	Jabalpur	0.2942	0.2193	0.1396	0.1378
	Jhabua	0.4421	0.4226	0.0671	0.1112

(Cont'd)

TABLE A1 (*Cont'd*)

State	District	Overall technical inefficiency	Technical inefficiency in child mortality	Technical inefficiency in adult chronic illness	Technical inefficiency in adult acute illness
	Katni	0.3167	0.2471	0.0900	0.1765
	Mandla	0.3019	0.1955	0.1339	0.1871
	Mandsaur	0.2970	0.2414	0.1306	0.1134
	Morena	0.2711	0.2432	0.0847	0.0849
	Narsimhapur	0.3279	0.2604	0.1074	0.1680
	Neemuch	0.2971	0.2368	0.1221	0.1316
	Panna	0.3414	0.3019	0.1228	0.1016
	Raisen	0.3007	0.2676	0.0664	0.1200
	Rajgarh	0.3138	0.2681	0.0954	0.1324
	Ratlam	0.2795	0.2547	0.0859	0.0767
	Rewa	0.3930	0.2800	0.1775	0.2110
	Sagar	0.3437	0.2881	0.1300	0.1351
	Satna	0.2727	0.2441	0.0867	0.0851
	Sehore	0.2899	0.2691	0.0579	0.0910
	Seoni	0.3234	0.2053	0.1297	0.2135
	Shahdol	0.3803	0.2965	0.0889	0.2210
	Shajapur	0.3075	0.2664	0.1224	0.0929
	Sheopur	0.2731	0.2603	0.0639	0.0526
	Shivpuri	0.3552	0.3433	0.0542	0.0734
	Sidhi	0.3731	0.3128	0.0709	0.1905
	Tikamgarh	0.3551	0.3155	0.0834	0.1400
	Ujjain	0.3233	0.2570	0.1551	0.1200
	Umaria	0.2861	0.2169	0.0938	0.1612
	Vidisha	0.4010	0.3054	0.1086	0.2361
	West Nimar	0.3185	0.2830	0.0919	0.1135
Maharashtra	Ahmadnagar	0.2175	0.0150	0.1779	0.1241
	Akola	0.1773	0.0059	0.1510	0.0927
	Amravati	0.2031	0.0404	0.1585	0.1205
	Aurangabad	0.3040	0.0129	0.1599	0.2582
	Bhandara	0.1860	0.0203	0.1386	0.1223
	Bid	0.2414	0.0102	0.1096	0.2149
	Buldana	0.2535	0.0210	0.1196	0.2225
	Chandrapur	0.2728	0.0925	0.2346	0.1042
	Dhule	0.2193	0.0252	0.1290	0.1755
	Gadchiroli	0.2312	0.0403	0.2113	0.0849
	Gondiya	0.3213	0.1558	0.1633	0.2286
	Hingoli	0.2316	0.0099	0.1272	0.1933
	Jalgaon	0.2352	0.0197	0.1486	0.1812
	Jalna	0.2387	0.0410	0.1222	0.2010
	Kolhapur	0.2092	0.0031	0.1003	0.1835

	Latur	0.1988	0.0102	0.1497	0.1304
	Nagpur	0.2510	0.0385	0.0937	0.2296
	Nandurbar	0.3348	0.1107	0.1984	0.2460
	Nashik	0.2215	0.0191	0.1745	0.1350
	Osmanabad	0.2569	0.0397	0.1083	0.2296
	Parbhani	0.2811	0.0524	0.0798	0.2644
	Pune	0.1936	0.0081	0.1767	0.0787
	Raigarh	0.2018	0.0135	0.1823	0.0854
	Ratnagiri	0.2210	0.0032	0.1031	0.1955
	Sangli	0.1768	0.0061	0.1190	0.1307
	Satara	0.2147	0.0085	0.1137	0.1819
	Sindhudurg	0.1852	0.0329	0.1575	0.0917
	Solapur	0.2105	0.0115	0.1233	0.1702
	Thane	0.2879	0.0368	0.2294	0.1701
	Wardha	0.1906	0.0189	0.1250	0.1426
	Washim	0.2071	0.0038	0.1900	0.0821
	Yavatmal	0.2115	0.0289	0.1701	0.1223
Odisha	Anugul	0.2277	0.1639	0.0634	0.1448
	Balangir	0.4645	0.4094	0.1355	0.1726
	Baleshwar	0.3274	0.1942	0.0750	0.2527
	Bargarh	0.2621	0.1937	0.1262	0.1236
	Baudh	0.3245	0.2423	0.1510	0.1542
	Bhadrak	0.2679	0.1279	0.1566	0.1757
	Cuttack	0.3620	0.2697	0.2020	0.1323
	Debagarh	0.3245	0.2082	0.1712	0.1808
	Dhenkanal	0.2458	0.1631	0.1211	0.1384
	Gajapati	0.2541	0.1978	0.1297	0.0929
	Ganjam	0.3393	0.2566	0.1869	0.1199
	Jagatsinghapur	0.2091	0.1284	0.1427	0.0828
	Jajapur	0.2518	0.1382	0.1523	0.1453
	Jharsuguda	0.3492	0.1921	0.2248	0.1858
	Kalahandi	0.2891	0.2173	0.1600	0.1037
	Kandhamal	0.3890	0.3303	0.1586	0.1305
	Kendrapara	0.2060	0.1418	0.1147	0.0959
	Kendujhar	0.3391	0.2720	0.0575	0.1942
	Khordha	0.3045	0.2240	0.1774	0.1053
	Koraput	0.3596	0.3109	0.1482	0.1032
	Malkangiri	0.6019	0.4115	0.1910	0.3955
	Mayurbhanj	0.3922	0.2745	0.1375	0.2441
	Nabarangapur	0.3670	0.3217	0.1463	0.0991
	Nayagarh	0.3260	0.1536	0.2404	0.1579
	Nuapada	0.3841	0.3524	0.0812	0.1294
	Puri	0.2176	0.1538	0.1390	0.0660

(Cont'd)

TABLE A1   (*Cont'd*)

State	District	Overall technical inefficiency	Technical inefficiency in child mortality	Technical inefficiency in adult chronic illness	Technical inefficiency in adult acute illness
	Rayagada	0.4339	0.4078	0.0879	0.1195
	Sambalpur	0.3016	0.2049	0.1331	0.1768
	Sonapur	0.1814	0.1366	0.1068	0.0534
	Sundargarh	0.4376	0.3524	0.1846	0.1823
Punjab	Amritsar	0.2422	0.0262	0.2340	0.0567
	Barnala	0.1997	0.0174	0.1740	0.0964
	Bhathinda	0.1885	0.0162	0.1548	0.1063
	Faridkot	0.1709	0.0256	0.1552	0.0669
	Fatehgarh Sahib	0.1693	0.0242	0.1613	0.0454
	Firozpur	0.2449	0.0615	0.2138	0.1025
	Gurdaspur	0.1861	0.0076	0.1604	0.0942
	Hoshiarpur	0.2054	0.0152	0.1966	0.0574
	Jalandhar	0.2327	0.0206	0.2266	0.0487
	Kapurthala	0.1681	0.0098	0.1452	0.0841
	Ludhiana	0.2431	0.0248	0.2311	0.0710
	Mansa	0.1668	0.0220	0.1367	0.0930
	Moga	0.2001	0.0270	0.1903	0.0557
	Muktsar	0.1941	0.0259	0.1753	0.0793
	Patiala	0.1847	0.0063	0.1614	0.0896
	Rupnagar	0.1507	0.0138	0.1424	0.0475
	SAS Nagar	0.2087	0.0283	0.1999	0.0530
	Sangrur	0.2326	0.0289	0.2083	0.0994
	Shahid Bhagat Singh Nagar	0.1660	0.0076	0.1579	0.0506
	Taran Taran	0.1764	0.0043	0.1716	0.0406
Rajasthan	Ajmer	0.3019	0.2729	0.0946	0.0877
	Alwar	0.3328	0.3137	0.0577	0.0950
	Banswara	0.3004	0.2960	0.0325	0.0400
	Baran	0.3056	0.2449	0.0887	0.1599
	Barmer	0.4301	0.4011	0.0874	0.1286
	Bharatpur	0.3905	0.3500	0.0764	0.1552
	Bhilwara	0.2992	0.2749	0.0852	0.0818
	Bikaner	0.3216	0.2975	0.0942	0.0776
	Bundi	0.2948	0.2667	0.0931	0.0843
	Chittaurgarh	0.4461	0.3737	0.1067	0.2190
	Churu	0.2860	0.2672	0.0619	0.0810
	Dausa	0.4053	0.3316	0.1332	0.1913
	Dhaulpur	0.2498	0.2335	0.0558	0.0687
	Dungarpur	0.3190	0.3073	0.0619	0.0590
	Ganganagar	0.3165	0.2885	0.0602	0.1155
	Hanumangarh	0.3147	0.2845	0.0692	0.1154

	Jaipur	0.3460	0.2902	0.1452	0.1202
	Jaisalmer	0.3320	0.2901	0.0669	0.1470
	Jalore	0.3643	0.3443	0.0804	0.0877
	Jhalawar	0.2662	0.2199	0.0726	0.1312
	Jhunjhunu	0.2715	0.2544	0.0855	0.0413
	Jodhpur	0.3154	0.2983	0.0706	0.0743
	Karauli	0.3055	0.2867	0.0685	0.0804
	Kota	0.3284	0.2323	0.1549	0.1728
	Nagaur	0.3046	0.3010	0.0439	0.0168
	Pali	0.2835	0.2396	0.1286	0.0802
	Rajsamand	0.3926	0.3337	0.0856	0.1883
	Sawai Madhopur	0.2652	0.2502	0.0664	0.0579
	Sikar	0.3272	0.2888	0.0980	0.1185
	Sirohi	0.2729	0.2548	0.0665	0.0715
	Tonk	0.3234	0.2768	0.0793	0.1473
	Udaipur	0.3091	0.2792	0.0743	0.1100
Tamil Nadu	Ariyalur	0.1095	0.0034	0.0691	0.0849
	Coimbatore	0.1208	0.0000	0.0777	0.0924
	Cuddalore	0.1441	0.0282	0.1176	0.0784
	Dharmapuri	0.1235	0.0166	0.0726	0.0986
	Dindigul	0.1336	0.0050	0.0969	0.0919
	Erode	0.1338	0.0073	0.0821	0.1053
	Kancheepuram	0.1722	0.0621	0.1116	0.1154
	Kanniyakumari	0.1018	0.0000	0.0686	0.0753
	Karur	0.1022	0.0065	0.0866	0.0538
	Madurai	0.1799	0.0448	0.1400	0.1036
	Nagapattinam	0.1647	0.0343	0.1366	0.0854
	Namakkal	0.1344	0.0000	0.0950	0.0950
	Nilgiris	0.1098	0.0191	0.0900	0.0600
	Perambalur	0.1200	0.0400	0.0908	0.0675
	Pudukkottai	0.1123	0.0077	0.0764	0.0820
	Ramanathapuram	0.1326	0.0173	0.0890	0.0968
	Salem	0.1263	0.0086	0.0934	0.0846
	Sivaganga	0.1208	0.0123	0.0671	0.0996
	Thanjavur	0.1508	0.0295	0.1117	0.0969
	Theni	0.1051	0.0197	0.0876	0.0546
	Thiruvallur	0.1614	0.0310	0.1174	0.1063
	Thiruvarur	0.1022	0.0043	0.0755	0.0688
	Thoothukkudi	0.1930	0.0758	0.1347	0.1155
	Tiruchirappalli	0.1422	0.0000	0.1024	0.0986
	Tirunelveli	0.1259	0.0171	0.1033	0.0700
	Tiruvannamalai	0.1514	0.0000	0.1056	0.1085

(Cont'd)

TABLE A1 (*Cont'd*)

State	District	Overall technical inefficiency	Technical inefficiency in child mortality	Technical inefficiency in adult chronic illness	Technical inefficiency in adult acute illness
	Vellore	0.1427	0.0188	0.1074	0.0921
	Viluppuram	0.1536	0.0229	0.0830	0.1272
	Virudhunagar	0.1324	0.0059	0.0804	0.1051
Uttar Pradesh	Agra	0.5594	0.3047	0.2454	0.3998
	Aligarh	0.5347	0.3948	0.2309	0.2770
	Allahabad	0.4120	0.3112	0.2518	0.0976
	Ambedkar Nagar	0.3958	0.2283	0.2514	0.2034
	Auraiya	0.3149	0.2761	0.1263	0.0836
	Azamgarh	0.4029	0.2442	0.2203	0.2326
	Bahraich	0.5368	0.5006	0.1660	0.1003
	Ballia	0.3721	0.2502	0.2554	0.1031
	Balrampur	0.5167	0.3901	0.3084	0.1401
	Banda	0.3392	0.2952	0.1484	0.0767
	Bara Banki	0.4027	0.3426	0.1534	0.1457
	Bareilly	0.5332	0.3766	0.1916	0.3251
	Basti	0.3445	0.2668	0.1976	0.0918
	Bijnor	0.6129	0.4213	0.2265	0.3831
	Budaun	0.6268	0.3918	0.1712	0.4583
	Chandauli	0.3923	0.2615	0.1846	0.2269
	Chitrakoot	0.3878	0.3528	0.1511	0.0553
	Deoria	0.3531	0.2379	0.2401	0.1023
	Etah	0.3939	0.2158	0.1025	0.3132
	Etawah	0.2587	0.2398	0.0819	0.0519
	Faizabad	0.3512	0.2791	0.1865	0.1035
	Farrukhabad	0.2824	0.2623	0.0789	0.0686
	Fatehpur	0.3888	0.3290	0.1621	0.1290
	Firozabad	0.4579	0.3445	0.1563	0.2581
	Gautam Buddha Nagar	0.3337	0.1969	0.1114	0.2453
	Ghaziabad	0.4392	0.2428	0.1615	0.3284
	Ghazipur	0.3481	0.2255	0.1813	0.1937
	Gonda	0.3692	0.3447	0.0999	0.0865
	Gorakhpur	0.3465	0.2157	0.2591	0.0804
	Hamirpur	0.2830	0.2523	0.1147	0.0571
	Hardoi	0.4966	0.4511	0.1672	0.1229
	Hathras	0.3353	0.2150	0.1437	0.2135
	Jalaun	0.3326	0.3126	0.1094	0.0306
	Jaunpur	0.3782	0.2770	0.2360	0.1031
	Jhansi	0.2997	0.2711	0.1074	0.0693
	Kannauj	0.4423	0.2813	0.2039	0.2738
	Kanpur Dehat	0.3039	0.2703	0.1072	0.0881

	Kanpur Nagar	0.2892	0.1767	0.1838	0.1365
	Kheri	0.5595	0.5039	0.1698	0.1743
	Kushinagar	0.3711	0.2646	0.2352	0.1113
	Lalitpur	0.2940	0.2811	0.0487	0.0712
	Lucknow	0.2976	0.2339	0.1404	0.1189
	Mahoba	0.3206	0.2935	0.1227	0.0398
	Mahrajganj	0.6217	0.4354	0.4142	0.1594
	Mainpuri	0.4398	0.2877	0.1746	0.2832
	Mathura	0.4551	0.2166	0.1883	0.3532
	Mau	0.3555	0.2094	0.1980	0.2081
	Meerut	0.4091	0.2313	0.1962	0.2745
	Mirzapur	0.3476	0.2629	0.2050	0.0982
	Moradabad	0.5284	0.4173	0.1657	0.2787
	Muzaffarnagar	0.5578	0.3081	0.1754	0.4306
	Pilibhit	0.5543	0.3413	0.2262	0.3737
	Pratapgarh	0.3936	0.2804	0.2395	0.1375
	Rae Bareli	0.3438	0.3007	0.1272	0.1076
	Rampur	0.5539	0.2410	0.1508	0.4754
	Saharanpur	0.5618	0.4401	0.1921	0.2915
	Sant Kabir Nagar	0.4206	0.3003	0.2735	0.1096
	Sant Ravidas Nagar (Bhadohi)	0.4006	0.3395	0.1976	0.0785
	Shahjahanpur	0.4320	0.3093	0.1534	0.2596
	Shrawasti	0.5974	0.4484	0.3255	0.2235
	Siddharthnagar	0.4185	0.3225	0.2367	0.1227
	Sitapur	0.5069	0.4363	0.2060	0.1554
	Sonbhadra	0.4182	0.2562	0.2298	0.2377
	Sultanpur	0.3904	0.3052	0.1813	0.1626
	Unnao	0.3988	0.3424	0.1861	0.0850
	Varanasi	0.3476	0.2387	0.1955	0.1601
Uttarakhand	Almora	0.2315	0.1390	0.1777	0.0519
	Bageshwar	0.1761	0.0980	0.1361	0.0537
	Chamoli	0.2269	0.1310	0.1651	0.0841
	Champawat	0.2270	0.1211	0.1830	0.0583
	Dehradun	0.2033	0.1180	0.1512	0.0673
	Garhwal	0.2195	0.1339	0.1674	0.0469
	Hardwar	0.3786	0.1935	0.1345	0.2964
	Nainital	0.1964	0.1333	0.1187	0.0820
	Pithoragarh	0.1957	0.0768	0.1734	0.0485
	Rudraprayag	0.1568	0.0688	0.1188	0.0759
	Tehri Garhwal	0.2126	0.1515	0.1276	0.0772
	Udham Singh Nagar	0.2658	0.2220	0.1320	0.0624
	Uttarkashi	0.1878	0.1209	0.1212	0.0772

(Cont'd)

TABLE A1 (*Cont'd*)

State	District	Overall technical inefficiency	Technical inefficiency in child mortality	Technical inefficiency in adult chronic illness	Technical inefficiency in adult acute illness
West Bengal	Bankura	0.2342	0.0135	0.1759	0.1541
	Burdwan	0.4214	0.0391	0.2397	0.3444
	Birbhum	0.3645	0.0175	0.2039	0.3016
	Dakshin Dinajpur	0.2380	0.0209	0.1649	0.1704
	Darjeeling	0.2661	0.0179	0.1707	0.2034
	Howrah	0.2275	0.0025	0.1817	0.1368
	Hooghly	0.2297	0.0209	0.1557	0.1676
	Jalpaiguri	0.3769	0.0300	0.2170	0.3066
	Cooch Behar	0.2783	0.0063	0.1419	0.2394
	Maldah	0.2966	0.0104	0.2076	0.2116
	Murshidabad	0.2448	0.0350	0.1466	0.1929
	Nadia	0.2913	0.0200	0.2082	0.2027
	North 24 Parganas	0.3407	0.0368	0.2294	0.2492
	Paschim Medinipur	0.2445	0.0000	0.1506	0.1926
	Purba Medinipur	0.2670	0.0084	0.1807	0.1964
	Purulia	0.3485	0.0039	0.1762	0.3006
	South 24 Parganas	0.3231	0.0152	0.2207	0.2355
	Uttar Dinajpur	0.3738	0.0415	0.2560	0.2692

TABLE A2 State-Wise Estimates of Inefficiencies (statistical estimates obtained from the statistical model described in Box 3.2)

State	Overall technical inefficiency	Technical inefficiency in child mortality	Technical inefficiency in adult chronic illness	Technical inefficiency in adult acute illness
Andhra Pradesh	0.1882	0.0163	0.1458	0.1159
Assam	0.4014	0.2544	0.2548	0.1424
Bihar	0.3876	0.2182	0.2090	0.2302
Chhattisgarh	0.2676	0.2069	0.0607	0.1503
Haryana	0.1813	0.0197	0.1349	0.1172
Himachal Pradesh	0.1932	0.0388	0.1428	0.1126
Jharkhand	0.3326	0.2292	0.1789	0.1460
Karnataka	0.1745	0.0530	0.1159	0.1065
Kerala	0.1617	0.0102	0.0928	0.1216
Madhya Pradesh	0.3155	0.2586	0.1041	0.1336
Maharashtra	0.2250	0.0246	0.1511	0.1541
Odisha	0.3253	0.2387	0.1448	0.1488
Punjab	0.2086	0.0219	0.1914	0.0747
Rajasthan	0.3258	0.2925	0.0864	0.1030
Tamil Nadu	0.1403	0.0200	0.0991	0.0945
Uttar Pradesh	0.4100	0.2971	0.1837	0.1848
Uttarakhand	0.2480	0.1521	0.1434	0.1088
West Bengal	0.3031	0.0208	0.1949	0.2292

TABLE B1 Out-of-Pocket Expenses as a Percentage of Monthly Consumption Expenditure (MCE) across Religion, Social Group, and Quintiles of Usual MCE for NSS 60th (2004) and 71st (2014) Rounds

	NSS 60th Round						NSS 71st Round					
	Inpatients		Outpatients		All		Inpatients		Outpatients		All	
	Insured	Uninsured	Insured	Uninsured	Insured	Uninsured	Insured	Uninsured	Insured	Uninsured	Insured	Uninsured
Religion												
Hinduism	15.24	24.38	12.28	30.07	15.35	31.92	14.85	20.04	20.69	34.97	20.16	32.18
Islam	55.33	31.24	14.40	32.93	31.19	36.88	12.92	15.89	31.29	37.25	27.66	32.24
Others	63.07	63.34	16.17	31.95	47.65	50.36	13.01	22.26	15.65	54.68	15.53	47.27
Social Group												
Scheduled tribe	6.24	39.28	8.98	26.09	12.11	32.88	16.69	12.22	42.44	104.79	30.68	69.00
Scheduled caste	19.96	20.79	14.20	28.95	19.30	29.77	14.58	16.28	17.86	32.90	18.73	28.75
Other backward classes	39.64	28.84	8.81	33.02	25.50	35.85	14.61	19.84	21.36	31.13	20.90	29.33
Others	18.05	27.76	15.96	28.02	18.30	31.98	13.92	22.31	19.23	31.68	18.39	32.23
Quartiles of MCE												
1st	10.43	42.53	2.35	49.14	10.67	51.06	20.42	26.16	45.41	63.76	39.96	55.01
2nd	2.98	28.96	12.46	31.33	8.81	34.37	20.65	19.34	19.20	29.53	21.77	28.26
3rd	69.72	27.29	13.05	30.31	32.16	33.47	14.88	15.97	15.30	23.39	17.26	22.55
4th	20.52	21.26	12.92	22.44	19.39	25.58	10.88	17.81	12.26	23.20	12.90	24.38
Total	**23.36**	**27.61**	**12.90**	**30.47**	**20.48**	**33.54**	**14.90**	**19.66**	**21.23**	**36.34**	**20.39**	**32.90**

TABLE B2a Out-of-Pocket Expenses as a Percentage of Monthly Consumption Expenditure across States and Sectors for NSS 60th Round (2004)

State	Inpatients						Outpatients						All					
	Insured households			Uninsured households			Insured households			Uninsured households			Insured households			Uninsured households		
	Rural	Urban	Total	Rural	Urban	Total	Rural	Urban	Total	Rural	Urban	Total	Rural	Urban	Total	Rural	Urban	Total
Jammu & Kashmir				11.39	16.71	11.73				15.24	25.27	15.69				14.45	24.58	14.92
Himachal Pradesh	15.00		15.00	27.48	20.03	26.68				32.46	6.74	29.37	15.00		15.00	33.70	12.83	31.21
Punjab	7.82		7.82	30.88	55.04	39.29				20.21	10.33	15.74	7.82		7.82	25.19	20.80	23.31
Uttarakhand				51.00	4.85	16.08					0.00	0.00				51.00	4.85	16.08
Haryana		45.85	45.85	42.31	30.02	37.65		52.78	52.78	20.98	20.14	20.56		73.79	73.79	38.42	26.87	32.97
Rajasthan	4.59	4.86	4.71	29.94	21.40	27.32	15.52	27.14	19.45	48.61	26.74	41.95	13.30	22.45	16.45	47.80	28.73	42.09
Uttar Pradesh	71.28	1.67	38.54	41.29	21.57	30.45				26.35	0.00	25.00	71.28	1.67	38.54	28.60	16.44	26.79
Bihar		0.89	0.89	19.02	8.83	17.19				72.75	27.39	69.44		0.89	0.89	60.55	19.45	56.29
Sikkim				8.95	5.38	8.56				9.13		9.13				9.90	5.38	9.44
Arunachal Pradesh	0.57		0.57	18.17	4001.72	3448.38					2.35	2.35	0.57		0.57	18.17	2161.74	1990.00
Nagaland		28.21	28.21	3.14	3.51	3.38	10.72		10.72		7.64	7.64		28.21	28.21	3.14	5.80	5.29
Manipur				7.48	5.34	6.65				8.18	12.22	10.07				8.60	10.78	9.56
Mizoram				1.00	4.08	3.38										1.00	4.08	3.38
Tripura				16.48		16.48				14.98		14.98				17.59		17.59
Meghalaya				8.28	28.73	23.05					62.19	62.19				8.28	38.49	31.29
Assam	4.65		4.65	22.50	2.58	13.53				30.98	2.89	28.19	10.22		10.22	29.18	2.69	23.40
West Bengal	93.48	15.58	24.00	18.14	23.17	19.93	11.88	1.58	8.56	25.31	19.47	24.03	23.71	12.18	16.64	25.45	24.59	25.25
Jharkhand	0.21		0.21	58.23	6.61	34.52				33.47	2.89	22.53	0.21		0.21	38.70	4.22	26.06
Odisha		6.81	6.81	33.03	31.03	32.51				39.94	10.22	38.16		6.81	6.81	39.60	26.34	37.83
Chhattisgarh				106.92	25.18	63.88				40.33	56.49	46.17				58.61	48.37	54.51
Madhya Pradesh		47.26	47.26	20.93	15.05	19.23		2.69	2.69	31.78	20.63	28.62		13.70	13.70	30.97	21.63	28.39
Gujarat	0.35	2.56	2.36	8.39	12.05	9.63	0.00	3.33	1.09	13.98	10.96	11.96	0.35	2.63	2.43	13.67	11.78	12.56
Maharashtra	16.63	13.03	13.34	34.89	26.12	31.00	10.00	15.84	14.88	38.97	26.46	31.83	12.97	15.17	14.90	41.23	30.11	35.44
Andhra Pradesh	2.92	10.31	10.19	30.07	13.82	22.66		7.68	7.68	31.23	18.22	24.65	2.92	9.67	9.60	36.21	19.04	27.57
Karnataka	11.34	9.38	9.98	23.70	13.95	20.83	17.22	32.04	27.83	35.28	18.87	30.53	18.44	20.19	19.71	35.40	19.81	30.92
Goa					37.94	37.94					13.92	13.92					26.04	26.04
Kerala	1.28	64.17	35.40	30.30	37.46	32.39	10.43	10.64	10.49	24.43	26.25	25.00	5.66	62.43	28.34	33.99	39.08	35.53
Tamil Nadu	26.47	88.11	78.89	25.35	30.37	26.82	0.77	13.47	7.99	27.43	22.47	25.65	8.80	77.76	56.00	30.75	28.74	30.07
All India	**15.61**	**25.12**	**23.36**	**27.93**	**26.95**	**27.61**	**10.86**	**14.11**	**12.90**	**34.75**	**22.62**	**30.47**	**13.36**	**23.23**	**20.48**	**36.68**	**27.54**	**33.54**

TABLE B2b Out-of-Pocket Expenses as a Percentage of Monthly Consumption Expenditure across States and Sectors for NSS 71st Round (2014)

State	Inpatients						Outpatients						All					
	Insured Households			Uninsured Households			Insured Households			Uninsured Households			Insured Households			Uninsured Households		
	Rural	Urban	Total	Rural	Urban	Total	Rural	Urban	Total	Rural	Urban	Total	Rural	Urban	Total	Rural	Urban	Total
Jammu & Kashmir	7.12	8.43	7.57	8.92	12.34	9.58	35.91	65.12	37.05	48.07	44.89	47.74	20.00	10.22	16.60	35.09	26.41	33.70
Himachal Pradesh	6.91	13.33	7.30	21.58	24.93	21.76	47.20	14.42	46.68	14.26	18.69	14.64	13.97	13.38	13.94	18.79	22.86	19.07
Punjab	8.27	16.31	12.77	43.30	23.11	35.41	7.58	82.29	25.16	32.65	25.51	30.80	8.40	30.68	18.22	40.03	26.93	36.06
Uttarakhand		2.54	2.54	19.55	22.54	19.95		2.11	2.11	30.58	28.80	30.24		2.73	2.73	31.51	29.10	31.06
Haryana	7.15	12.44	12.39	13.84	22.06	18.04		20.21	20.21	4.71	34.30	29.01	7.15	15.43	15.36	9.79	34.17	27.51
Rajasthan	9.04	4.21	7.35	13.14	16.23	13.84	33.31	13.13	29.31	25.53	11.24	20.68	21.21	6.89	16.73	20.65	15.63	19.30
Uttar Pradesh	21.53	9.97	14.92	17.82	22.84	18.56	31.73	10.34	15.55	26.12	19.00	24.89	29.87	11.69	17.48	25.25	23.27	24.93
Bihar	22.55	16.27	21.95	14.02	27.67	15.10	45.38	13.01	43.04	39.91	32.61	39.62	39.40	15.09	37.25	30.03	32.24	30.15
Sikkim	19.61	14.49	15.37	13.57	15.99	14.07	82.96	22.16	24.23	9.76	14.16	11.28	45.78	21.15	22.95	12.86	16.51	13.88
Arunachal Pradesh	0.21	4.66	2.96	14.72	4.90	13.27		24.59	24.59	50.04	35.30	49.28	0.21	6.27	4.05	37.87	15.54	35.82
Nagaland	4.94	2.75	4.13	6.46	6.02	6.34	28.24	2.94	7.02	19.81	8.59	18.59	10.64	2.94	5.81	15.67	7.16	14.24
Manipur	23.23	14.47	19.44	14.71	13.52	14.47				95.22	37.31	76.12	23.23	14.47	19.44	21.32	17.03	20.39
Mizoram	6.17	2.43	4.28	6.19	9.14	7.67	8.86	2.77	5.41	31.19	25.68	30.34	6.98	2.61	4.72	22.82	14.70	20.22
Tripura	4.72	3.24	4.48	4.22	7.16	5.13	50.14	29.00	49.80	31.86	28.71	31.55	18.66	4.17	16.84	19.94	12.83	18.51
Meghalaya	4.50	15.37	7.12	2.58	8.69	3.08	7.89		7.89	10.43	22.00	14.17	6.11	15.37	7.66	4.66	17.46	6.72
Assam	9.52	10.41	9.93	11.39	24.60	13.86	0.80	10.20	5.71	18.68	91.41	37.91	4.29	10.73	7.43	16.16	69.70	28.49
West Bengal	14.40	10.61	12.90	17.81	23.96	19.16	23.09	11.38	20.27	50.84	23.76	44.83	24.08	12.71	20.76	46.02	27.72	42.02
Jharkhand	9.02	5.64	7.02	11.09	12.34	11.31		3.71	3.71	17.90	56.80	37.85	9.02	4.21	4.62	14.83	50.11	27.22
Odisha	16.12	11.87	15.68	18.91	22.23	19.31	61.39	12.63	58.33	65.42	31.62	59.86	39.06	13.32	37.04	56.11	32.29	52.41
Chhattisgarh	11.65	5.49	9.53	16.56	20.87	17.46	10.25	10.35	10.25	1177.77	61.78	792.04	11.30	5.60	10.04	604.43	51.81	454.56
Madhya Pradesh	11.99	6.58	7.66	11.82	23.10	15.29		46.91	46.91	27.01	64.13	45.43	11.99	34.01	32.21	18.34	48.55	29.98
Gujarat	4.34	4.90	4.80	9.03	12.99	10.60	6.95	3.09	4.49	17.78	3.86	9.43	5.93	4.70	4.92	14.02	7.74	13.84
Maharashtra	36.11	10.47	15.37	28.59	19.11	26.14	12.12	12.22	12.21	27.46	20.76	25.50	37.88	11.65	15.84	32.94	22.61	30.01
Andhra Pradesh	17.59	18.91	18.05	23.81	20.50	22.16	20.83	13.53	18.13	19.24	24.60	22.38	22.38	17.52	20.64	24.04	25.69	24.98
Karnataka	39.79	11.13	21.27	19.16	20.32	19.53	18.72	13.78	14.97	39.56	16.84	30.26	36.56	14.03	21.32	33.53	20.96	23.88
Goa	38.75	32.86	36.57	29.69	11.99	16.61	4.39	5.73	5.01	27.94	17.43	20.82	18.81	14.02	16.67	30.79	18.18	22.17
Kerala	9.38	9.57	9.50	17.39	22.96	19.37	14.41	14.27	14.32	11.93	11.48	11.69	14.19	12.93	13.39	17.10	15.96	16.54
Tamil Nadu	35.80	18.17	21.39	24.85	50.55	38.10	5.63	24.09	20.02	15.29	18.49	17.43	19.89	22.79	22.23	21.96	30.68	27.37
All India	**17.14**	**11.87**	**14.53**	**18.36**	**22.73**	**19.36**	**25.98**	**14.36**	**21.23**	**40.11**	**26.76**	**36.35**	**25.15**	**14.57**	**20.39**	**34.50**	**28.35**	**32.90**

TABLE B3a Average Days of Hospitalization across Perception of Absolute State of Health over Sectors and Quintiles of Usual Monthly Consumption Expenditure

	NSS 60th Round											
	Uninsured				Insured				All			
	1	2	3	Total	1	2	3	Total	1	2	3	Total
Sector												
Rural	7.41	10.10	12.92	11.30		8.26	7.76	8.01	7.41	10.10	12.91	11.29
Urban	9.91	8.88	13.59	10.78	8.58	8.86	12.08	9.99	9.88	8.88	13.53	10.74
Quartiles of MCE												
1st	8.40	9.91	11.98	10.81		15.00	18.00	17.41	8.40	9.92	12.01	10.83
2nd	8.48	8.17	11.57	9.65		10.00	12.00	11.78	8.48	8.18	11.57	9.65
3rd	9.21	9.11	12.34	10.53		22.31	24.00	22.54	9.21	9.25	12.36	10.61
4th	8.67	10.37	14.66	12.04	8.58	6.76	10.49	8.17	8.67	10.23	14.52	11.90
Total	**8.76**	**9.69**	**13.13**	**11.13**	**8.58**	**8.80**	**11.43**	**9.77**	**8.76**	**9.67**	**13.10**	**11.10**
	NSS 71st Round											
	Uninsured				Insured				All			
	1	2	3	Total	1	2	3	Total	1	2	3	Total
Sector												
Rural	6.10	7.70	10.63	8.95	6.35	8.64	12.83	10.49	6.13	7.89	11.09	9.26
Urban	7.60	7.03	10.27	8.37	5.87	8.26	10.73	9.17	7.15	7.36	10.39	8.58
Quartiles of MCE												
1st	4.49	7.06	9.65	8.11	3.12	6.27	12.71	9.03	4.40	6.88	10.28	8.31
2nd	10.87	7.56	9.24	8.37	8.70	7.61	14.20	10.19	10.49	7.57	10.03	8.69
3rd	5.92	7.71	10.13	8.70	8.95	10.49	10.88	10.61	7.13	8.37	10.30	9.14
4th	6.89	7.43	11.62	9.19	4.41	8.64	11.61	9.87	6.46	7.73	11.62	9.36
Total	**6.56**	**7.44**	**10.51**	**8.74**	**6.08**	**8.46**	**11.97**	**9.90**	**6.48**	**7.68**	**10.84**	**9.00**

Note: Code: 1: excellent/very good; 2: good/fair; 3: poor.

TABLE B3b Number of Persons (aged 60 and above) across Perception of Absolute State of Health over Sectors and Quintiles of Usual Monthly Consumption Expenditure

NSS 60th Round

	Uninsured				Insured				All			
	1	2	3	Total	1	2	3	Total	1	2	3	Total
Sector												
Rural	31,271	1,471,362	1,151,653	2,654,286	0	4,092	4,088	8,180	31,271	1,475,455	1,155,741	2,662,466
Urban	36,615	743,963	516,187	1,296,765	780	41,082	22,722	64,583	37,394	785,045	538,909	1,361,348
Quartiles of MCE												
1st	5,875	386,739	312,059	704,674	0	384	1,561	1,945	5,875	387,123	313,620	706,618
2nd	2,876	293,971	226,811	523,658		96	785	880	2,876	294,067	227,596	524,539
3rd	15,203	538,198	435,575	988,975	0	5,706	909	6,615	15,203	543,904	436,484	995,590
4th	43,931	996,417	693,396	1,733,743	780	38,988	23,555	63,323	44,710	1,035,405	716,950	1,797,066
Total	**67,885**	**2,215,325**	**1,667,841**	**3,951,050**	**780**	**45,174**	**26,809**	**72,763**	**68,665**	**2,260,499**	**1,694,650**	**4,023,813**

NSS 71st Round

	Uninsured				Insured				All			
	1	2	3	Total	1	2	3	Total	1	2	3	Total
Sector												
Rural	106,011	1,804,690	1,520,700	3,431,402	13,220	479,849	401,772	894,841	119,231	2,284,539	1,922,473	4,326,242
Urban	46,572	1,110,936	799,667	1,957,175	16,617	416,875	275,846	709,339	63,189	1,527,811	1,075,514	2,666,514
Quartiles of MCE												
1st	53,034	541,143	496,519	1,090,696	3,618	164,971	129,377	297,966	56,652	706,114	625,896	1,388,662
2nd	21,965	494,798	396,591	913,354	4,590	115,302	75,677	195,568	26,555	610,100	472,268	1,108,923
3rd	11,613	609,890	441,646	1,063,149	7,694	190,226	127,214	325,135	19,307	800,116	568,860	1,388,284
4th	65,971	1,269,795	985,612	2,321,378	13,935	426,225	345,209	785,368	79,906	1,696,020	1,330,820	3,106,746
Total	**152,583**	**2,915,626**	**2,320,368**	**5,388,577**	**29,837**	**896,724**	**677,477**	**1,604,037**	**182,420**	**3,812,350**	**2,997,844**	**6,992,615**

Note: Code: 1: excellent/very good; 2: good/fair; 3: poor.

TABLE B4a   Total Per Day Loss of Income Due to Ailment across Usual Monthly Consumption Expenditure Quintiles for NSS 60th Round (2004) (in INR at 2004 prices)

Quartiles of MCE	Uninsured	Insured	Total
1st	40.96	77.39	41.00
2nd	41.15	8.59	40.75
3rd	51.64	11.00	51.25
4th	34.79	45.73	35.57
Total	**42.07**	**39.06**	**41.98**

TABLE B4b   Total Per Day Loss of Income Due to Ailment across Usual Monthly Consumption Expenditure Quintiles for NSS 71st Round (2014) (in INR at 2004 prices)

Quartiles of MCE	Uninsured	Insured	Total
1st	36.43	22.82	33.74
2nd	42.54	26.83	38.98
3rd	44.02	25.47	38.70
4th	24.21	45.96	29.69
Total	**36.20**	**31.64**	**35.09**

TABLE B5a   Total Loss of Per Day Income Due to Ailment across Sectors and States for NSS 60th Round (2004) (in INR at 2004 prices)

State	Uninsured			Insured			All		
	Rural	Urban	Total	Rural	Urban	Total	Rural	Urban	Total
Jammu & Kashmir	49.75	112.46	62.13				49.75	112.46	62.13
Himachal Pradesh	45.98	12.09	44.55	0.00		0.00	45.94	12.09	44.51
Punjab	28.07	55.53	36.45	0.00	0.00	0.00	28.01	55.40	36.37
Uttarakhand	17.59	49.79	23.25				17.59	49.79	23.25
Haryana	56.30	76.20	61.29		199.78	199.78	56.30	77.24	61.59
Rajasthan	22.73	9.91	19.60	0.03	1.32	0.76	22.58	9.69	19.38
Uttar Pradesh	75.94	55.77	71.19	126.79	6.54	121.60	77.36	55.57	72.32
Bihar	65.49	53.89	63.55				65.49	53.89	63.55
Sikkim	15.62	33.02	15.76				15.62	33.02	15.76
Arunachal Pradesh	147.19	796.24	184.76				147.19	796.24	184.76
Nagaland	125.54	147.73	129.90	2,714.93	89.43	2,403.95	382.14	144.41	337.08
Manipur	110.94	18.81	90.92				110.94	18.81	90.92
Mizoram	0.00	59.66	48.54				0.00	59.66	48.54
Tripura	80.03	197.42	89.57				80.03	197.42	89.57
Meghalaya	81.90	149.17	91.47		0.00	0.00	81.90	138.49	90.47
Assam	93.69	143.62	101.37	268.73		268.73	98.70	143.62	105.44
West Bengal	45.51	36.69	43.23	10.64	18.93	14.71	44.68	35.58	42.26
Jharkhand	56.01	97.77	67.73				56.01	97.77	67.73
Odisha	60.73	117.26	64.68				60.73	117.26	64.68
Chhattisgarh	63.72	28.94	59.67				63.72	28.94	59.67

Madhya Pradesh	39.63	57.05	43.58		101.88	101.88	39.63	58.84	44.13
Gujarat	26.92	29.37	27.81	0.00	71.19	68.28	26.74	38.73	31.80
Maharashtra	40.56	17.67	30.00	0.00	13.81	13.26	40.33	17.15	28.83
Andhra Pradesh	42.59	31.48	39.25	0.00	0.06	0.06	42.58	28.26	37.94
Karnataka	31.63	33.70	32.20	0.00	0.00	0.00	31.43	32.49	31.73
Goa	161.80	75.84	111.42				161.80	75.84	111.42
Kerala	37.82	27.64	35.53	14.12	300.50	108.28	37.47	34.36	36.77
Tamil Nadu	23.60	29.34	25.40	5.54	3.33	4.78	23.16	28.62	24.88
All India	**44.68**	**35.30**	**42.07**	**60.23**	**30.09**	**39.06**	**44.87**	**34.94**	**41.98**

TABLE B5b Total Loss of Per Day Income Due to Ailment across Sectors and States for NSS 71st Round (2014) (in INR at 2004 prices)

State	Uninsured			Insured			All		
	Rural	Urban	Total	Rural	Urban	Total	Rural	Urban	Total
Jammu & Kashmir	129.49	48.36	117.85	10.93	47.85	11.97	109.30	48.35	101.63
Himachal Pradesh	40.70	77.21	42.10	123.28	64.54	114.03	42.85	75.79	44.22
Punjab	19.01	57.08	30.57	6.77	6.59	6.68	18.23	49.42	28.36
Uttarakhand	77.40	46.32	72.08		25.35	25.35	77.40	45.60	71.80
Haryana	48.18	52.17	50.11	44.90	0.52	11.61	48.16	50.93	49.51
Rajasthan	23.53	26.39	24.35	21.43	30.93	25.82	22.99	28.31	24.81
Uttar Pradesh	22.63	34.25	25.29	18.00	30.54	22.83	22.40	33.88	25.13
Bihar	78.41	23.26	72.26	8.48	1.88	7.16	75.59	21.61	69.35
Sikkim	3.26	0.93	2.69	0.00	0.00	0.00	3.25	0.86	2.63
Arunachal Pradesh	206.70	510.51	240.38	324.73	688.07	609.84	208.02	554.72	256.91
Nagaland	129.59	60.20	127.40	73.88	162.45	134.18	119.18	156.07	130.18
Manipur	239.08	38.29	221.93		0.00	0.00	239.08	37.66	221.61
Mizoram	21.89	23.28	22.08	83.96	112.51	100.66	59.60	106.49	82.05
Tripura	181.40	84.07	131.67	139.99	60.31	134.63	166.18	83.15	132.36
Meghalaya	86.10	157.45	105.24	0.00	250.00	1.04	51.32	158.16	70.61
Assam	44.35	16.78	38.48	0.00	29.99	7.80	43.24	17.20	37.67
West Bengal	25.01	11.89	21.07	13.91	13.79	13.87	22.32	12.33	19.34
Jharkhand	30.76	14.45	25.42	105.42	0.00	21.23	31.14	13.86	25.35
Odisha	59.68	66.78	60.80	41.01	2.29	36.47	53.38	49.67	52.84
Chhattisgarh	53.06	39.87	50.25	10.84	20.70	10.95	34.78	39.26	35.39
Madhya Pradesh	44.27	56.07	48.16	67.41	10.62	12.66	44.31	51.57	46.87
Gujarat	64.13	36.44	47.72	51.21	388.10	134.69	60.01	70.15	65.31
Maharashtra	55.05	44.62	51.95	49.62	55.77	54.11	54.97	45.64	52.04
Andhra Pradesh	27.51	15.46	21.92	14.94	12.62	14.21	18.68	13.88	16.91
Karnataka	26.58	31.19	28.33	53.25	25.87	34.84	28.60	30.04	29.20
Goa	0.66	0.22	0.43	15.14	6,591.10	4,550.74	2.43	1,460.28	804.72
Kerala	29.50	18.84	24.20	29.32	18.37	24.25	29.41	18.61	24.23
Tamil Nadu	24.81	34.46	29.70	14.58	28.84	22.81	22.67	33.00	28.08
All India	**37.51**	**33.59**	**36.20**	**21.13**	**48.36**	**31.64**	**33.77**	**37.59**	**35.09**

TABLE B6 Median Usual Monthly Per Capita Consumption Expenditure across Sectors and States (in INR at 2004 prices)

State	NSS 60th Round			NSS 71st Round		
	Sector			Sector		
	Rural	Urban	Total	Rural	Urban	Total
Jammu & Kashmir	1,248.87	1,719.87	1,303.17	1,214.29	1,875.00	1,250.00
Himachal Pradesh	1,221.72	1,805.86	1,259.73	1,500.00	2,666.67	1,500.00
Punjab	1,466.06	1,651.08	1,551.39	1,900.00	2,400.00	2,000.00
Uttarakhand	992.89	2,063.84	1,067.87	1,166.67	1,600.00	1,200.00
Haryana	1,390.05	1,774.91	1,447.96	1,500.00	2,000.00	1,600.00
Rajasthan	977.38	1,605.21	1,085.97	1,333.33	1,727.27	1,400.00
Uttar Pradesh	868.78	1,238.31	928.73	1,000.00	1,450.00	1,066.67
Bihar	781.90	1,114.48	800.91	1,000.00	1,200.00	1,000.00
Sikkim	1,085.97	1,981.29	1,140.27	1,500.00	2,000.00	1,500.00
Arunachal Pradesh	1,085.97	1,547.88	1,126.70	1,000.00	1,666.67	1,062.50
Nagaland	1,809.96	2,407.82	2,012.25	1,666.67	2,000.00	1,714.29
Manipur	1,241.11	1,424.05	1,303.17	1,071.43	1,440.00	1,200.00
Mizoram	1,628.96	2,063.84	1,772.31	1,416.67	2,400.00	1,750.00
Tripura	917.04	1,547.88	941.18	1,346.00	1,950.00	1,425.00
Meghalaya	1,157.65	2,040.26	1,199.58	1,250.00	2,250.00	1,300.00
Assam	1,042.53	1,857.46	1,085.97	1,166.67	1,666.67	1,200.00
West Bengal	904.98	1,651.08	999.10	1,125.00	1,666.67	1,250.00
Jharkhand	799.28	1,444.69	859.93	912.00	1,376.67	966.67
Odisha	651.58	1,375.90	705.88	825.00	1,500.00	880.00
Chhattisgarh	655.20	1,313.36	695.02	833.33	1,400.00	900.00
Madhya Pradesh	796.38	1,191.87	868.78	1,000.00	1,428.57	1,050.00
Gujarat	1,085.97	1,916.43	1,303.17	1,400.00	2,000.00	1,571.43
Maharashtra	959.28	1,857.46	1,172.85	1,261.25	2,250.00	1,500.00
Andhra Pradesh	931.22	1,547.88	1,031.92	1,483.75	2,050.00	1,583.33
Karnataka	912.22	1,547.88	1,015.39	1,187.50	1,800.00	1,300.00
Goa	2,389.14	1,733.63	1,990.95	2,000.00	2,400.00	2,000.00
Kerala	1,368.33	1,599.48	1,444.34	2,000.00	2,300.00	2,142.86
Tamil Nadu	1,006.91	1,547.88	1,140.27	1,433.40	2,166.67	1,700.00
All India	**920.91**	**1,547.88**	**1,031.92**	**1,166.67**	**1,875.00**	**1,285.71**

TABLE C1   Knowledge about Male Contraceptive Methods across Age Groups: National Family Health Survey-4 (2014–15)

State	Female Respondents						Male Respondents					
	Urban			Rural			Urban			Rural		
	15–34	35–64	Total	15–34	35–64	Total	15–34	35–64	Total	15–34	35–64	Total
Andhra Pradesh	48.69	48.00	48.41	42.92	41.50	42.35	41.48	42.54	41.94	38.96	38.44	38.71
Arunachal Pradesh	50.38	56.69	52.32	49.73	49.46	49.63	32.56	44.22	37.35	39.02	43.08	40.91
Assam	55.42	60.54	57.45	53.58	56.94	54.73	42.75	56.89	49.55	44.19	52.67	47.84
Bihar	56.97	62.02	58.58	50.27	54.04	51.42	43.67	54.11	47.68	40.22	44.81	42.00
Chhattisgarh	61.71	64.87	62.78	56.46	57.55	56.82	47.25	52.79	49.52	42.46	45.83	43.77
Goa	58.87	64.19	61.18	57.56	60.72	58.98	38.85	51.79	45.45	39.64	45.22	42.39
Gujarat	60.57	66.18	62.68	54.35	58.37	55.79	45.98	52.16	48.40	42.21	44.77	43.29
Haryana	60.89	63.36	61.71	61.47	63.31	62.06	50.61	59.66	53.91	53.09	57.13	54.53
Himachal Pradesh	57.65	64.62	60.52	52.57	59.76	55.50	38.51	51.54	44.27	37.68	48.58	42.77
Jammu & Kashmir	61.21	64.47	62.44	57.04	60.89	58.26	50.27	58.14	53.70	47.39	52.41	49.37
Jharkhand	58.66	62.83	60.04	53.14	54.41	53.54	49.00	56.24	52.02	42.89	44.59	43.54
Karnataka	55.81	59.98	57.33	52.12	53.00	52.44	43.49	50.93	46.80	36.27	39.49	37.65
Kerala	56.55	60.76	58.40	57.07	59.61	58.18	36.54	46.37	41.18	36.33	47.18	41.50
Madhya Pradesh	58.24	62.10	59.55	52.85	54.60	53.44	43.31	49.84	45.89	40.60	44.72	42.21
Maharashtra	59.08	63.67	60.78	55.10	56.86	55.72	41.79	52.12	45.82	40.38	44.26	41.93
Manipur	52.84	63.37	57.07	48.38	59.05	52.26	40.46	51.11	44.89	36.93	52.31	43.65
Meghalaya	45.76	53.33	48.15	42.48	48.01	44.23	31.85	43.27	36.13	24.31	33.50	27.96
Mizoram	56.90	62.55	58.97	49.83	55.84	51.86	49.67	57.72	52.86	43.38	49.02	45.69
Nagaland	39.51	56.38	44.98	35.75	48.20	40.36	25.38	41.61	32.33	19.38	31.05	24.65
Odisha	55.83	61.60	58.03	53.44	58.01	55.07	46.87	56.27	51.25	43.45	47.94	45.50
Punjab	62.60	66.20	63.99	62.03	65.69	63.37	55.26	60.65	57.39	52.95	59.51	55.42
Rajasthan	60.63	63.99	61.75	57.68	59.61	58.27	50.24	54.34	51.75	45.46	49.43	46.92
Sikkim	57.70	63.01	59.40	58.85	61.86	59.85	47.15	49.96	48.24	47.23	48.22	47.69
Tamil Nadu	63.01	68.03	65.08	62.28	64.26	63.05	53.20	60.03	56.28	49.23	54.61	51.67
Telangana	43.63	45.96	44.46	39.73	37.96	39.09	36.29	37.36	36.74	36.61	35.33	36.09
Tripura	55.47	61.79	58.02	48.90	53.94	50.66	37.21	48.26	42.21	34.18	35.03	34.53
Uttar Pradesh	59.34	65.46	61.25	54.84	60.24	56.47	46.84	55.83	50.22	41.86	48.20	44.17
Uttarakhand	60.89	65.40	62.37	58.39	62.20	59.63	50.51	58.66	53.88	46.88	52.63	48.99
West Bengal	52.51	60.68	55.62	52.71	57.56	54.38	41.13	50.98	45.81	42.44	48.60	45.21
All India	57.82	62.42	59.50	53.79	56.68	54.77	45.48	52.91	48.54	42.28	46.83	44.14

Note: For definitions of key terms, see the notes at the end of the tables.

TABLE C2 Knowledge about Female Contraceptive Methods across Age Groups: National Family Health Survey-4 (2014–15)

State	Female Respondents						Male Respondents					
	Urban			Rural			Urban			Rural		
	15–34	35–64	Total	15–34	35–64	Total	15–34	35–64	Total	15–34	35–64	Total
Andhra Pradesh	29.46	27.56	28.69	25.80	20.53	23.69	38.02	34.28	36.37	34.21	28.44	31.41
Arunachal Pradesh	34.42	35.97	34.90	32.15	29.83	31.29	30.96	36.66	33.30	31.60	31.38	31.50
Assam	43.54	49.90	46.07	39.05	42.20	40.13	41.24	49.27	45.10	38.50	45.31	41.44
Bihar	32.81	37.58	34.33	26.36	29.11	27.20	33.41	39.83	35.87	29.40	31.91	30.37
Chhattisgarh	42.21	45.28	43.25	36.23	36.27	36.24	39.97	43.96	41.60	35.21	37.20	35.98
Goa	43.71	48.90	45.96	47.09	48.46	47.70	38.08	46.91	42.58	39.92	43.48	41.67
Gujarat	37.61	41.02	38.89	28.58	27.41	28.16	38.73	40.97	39.61	34.83	32.69	33.93
Haryana	42.42	45.68	43.50	40.33	41.54	40.72	40.11	46.16	42.31	40.23	41.93	40.84
Himachal Pradesh	41.94	46.78	43.93	37.45	40.50	38.69	34.65	43.62	38.62	33.99	39.21	36.43
Jammu & Kashmir	44.84	50.26	46.88	40.49	45.07	41.94	45.72	50.20	47.67	43.18	47.44	44.87
Jharkhand	37.25	40.57	38.35	30.46	29.82	30.26	36.28	44.32	39.63	32.11	31.75	31.97
Karnataka	33.28	33.83	33.48	26.69	24.53	25.90	37.17	41.80	39.22	31.75	30.92	31.39
Kerala	39.76	39.22	39.53	38.62	37.73	38.23	40.18	47.11	43.45	37.84	44.88	41.19
Madhya Pradesh	41.92	45.71	43.21	35.82	36.74	36.13	37.59	41.97	39.32	34.69	36.21	35.28
Maharashtra	38.69	41.21	39.62	32.68	30.67	31.98	39.42	43.11	40.86	33.62	32.93	33.35
Manipur	38.06	45.89	41.20	33.58	40.68	36.17	36.51	45.05	40.06	33.63	41.27	36.98
Meghalaya	30.44	34.80	31.82	28.56	31.20	29.40	29.09	34.53	31.13	24.42	27.81	25.76
Mizoram	31.86	35.67	33.26	24.79	27.02	25.55	30.85	32.12	31.35	24.80	26.44	25.48
Nagaland	31.68	40.09	34.41	26.43	30.33	27.87	29.04	38.15	32.94	23.62	27.57	25.40
Odisha	43.78	49.50	45.96	39.03	43.50	40.62	40.90	50.25	45.26	38.18	43.16	40.46
Punjab	43.65	48.76	45.62	41.67	46.53	43.44	44.85	48.41	46.26	41.32	44.90	42.67
Rajasthan	43.87	47.70	45.14	39.16	40.70	39.64	42.14	45.87	43.52	36.83	37.91	37.23
Sikkim	36.42	36.98	36.60	34.77	34.73	34.76	41.78	42.73	42.15	36.94	36.64	36.80
Tamil Nadu	41.75	47.06	43.94	40.05	41.62	40.66	44.15	48.62	46.17	40.33	43.51	41.77
Telangana	27.09	25.87	26.65	22.35	16.45	20.20	33.09	36.20	34.39	31.19	24.64	28.56
Tripura	45.48	48.01	46.50	38.65	39.13	38.82	40.09	46.91	43.18	35.92	37.56	36.58
Uttar Pradesh	39.38	47.68	41.97	35.94	41.91	37.75	38.23	44.76	40.69	35.21	39.22	36.67
Uttarakhand	45.00	49.71	46.55	40.17	43.03	41.10	42.83	47.85	44.91	38.50	42.33	39.91
West Bengal	43.14	47.86	44.94	39.95	41.91	40.63	44.25	49.88	46.92	40.54	45.48	42.76
All India	**39.00**	**42.66**	**40.33**	**34.36**	**35.72**	**34.82**	**39.58**	**44.33**	**41.53**	**35.58**	**37.57**	**36.40**

Note: For definitions of key terms, see the notes at the end of the tables.

TABLE C3 Knowledge about Male Contraceptive Methods across Number of Children: National Family Health Survey-4 (2014–15)

State	Female Respondents						Male Respondents					
	Urban			Rural			Urban			Rural		
	0	1–2	>2	0	1–2	>2	0	1–2	>2	0	1–2	>2
Andhra Pradesh	44.41	50.97	46.61	40.19	43.67	41.55	41.73	43.56	38.35	38.64	38.34	39.57
Arunachal Pradesh	46.79	56.65	55.23	43.57	52.39	52.13	31.97	44.54	41.12	35.20	45.95	44.60
Assam	50.38	61.82	59.09	47.22	59.19	56.27	40.80	57.76	51.73	41.33	52.80	52.37
Bihar	52.09	62.61	61.00	44.04	54.58	54.18	42.43	54.50	51.20	36.40	47.35	45.45
Chhattisgarh	57.79	65.59	65.28	51.31	60.86	58.21	45.60	52.60	52.85	38.70	48.18	45.91
Goa	55.76	64.89	61.64	56.96	61.16	58.30	38.24	52.20	47.27	39.46	46.38	42.53
Gujarat	55.92	66.15	64.53	47.46	60.66	57.73	42.84	52.85	51.69	36.81	50.02	44.39
Haryana	57.67	63.97	62.32	57.57	64.52	63.01	47.51	60.80	55.47	49.71	59.75	55.70
Himachal Pradesh	52.16	65.31	62.53	42.64	61.27	57.99	36.82	52.24	48.68	33.38	49.71	47.47
Jammu & Kashmir	59.31	65.09	64.14	54.00	61.38	60.80	49.79	59.83	53.99	45.57	54.49	52.25
Jharkhand	54.53	63.27	62.63	46.51	57.03	55.63	47.92	56.84	53.26	39.93	48.57	43.81
Karnataka	50.28	61.13	59.75	45.76	55.58	54.10	43.48	53.27	46.31	35.18	41.26	38.68
Kerala	50.48	61.88	61.34	51.72	61.39	59.61	34.97	47.77	44.09	34.52	47.98	46.29
Madhya Pradesh	53.46	62.96	61.90	48.17	56.13	54.97	41.86	49.47	48.99	37.73	45.98	44.09
Maharashtra	55.16	64.22	62.59	48.52	59.05	57.06	39.26	53.51	47.95	38.27	45.24	43.08
Manipur	47.69	62.62	63.68	40.90	59.20	57.59	38.88	50.22	51.72	36.21	51.93	50.41
Meghalaya	42.56	53.20	53.29	35.01	46.96	50.30	28.45	48.21	38.87	21.50	33.37	32.63
Mizoram	53.77	63.16	63.01	45.43	54.67	55.32	47.10	59.90	57.12	40.43	49.88	49.27
Nagaland	33.61	52.25	57.19	26.96	45.37	48.56	24.52	40.94	43.61	16.06	33.27	32.86
Odisha	48.98	62.77	61.37	46.56	59.51	58.12	45.22	55.69	55.87	40.73	50.23	46.02
Punjab	59.36	66.21	65.70	58.11	66.12	65.48	51.62	62.76	58.61	49.32	62.03	57.72
Rajasthan	57.18	64.70	63.18	52.99	61.54	59.75	48.56	56.13	51.95	43.23	51.06	48.27
Sikkim	55.28	62.28	62.37	54.87	63.45	62.18	43.98	52.80	52.53	42.99	53.36	47.09
Tamil Nadu	56.10	69.13	66.89	54.30	67.02	65.43	51.20	60.94	58.81	46.95	56.38	52.24
Telangana	40.09	46.83	44.90	36.76	40.68	38.56	35.81	38.56	35.48	35.43	37.27	35.33
Tripura	49.52	61.58	60.53	38.60	55.06	53.21	37.26	46.38	42.16	32.35	36.42	34.23
Uttar Pradesh	55.31	65.30	65.17	48.97	61.09	60.41	44.72	56.17	54.47	38.87	48.39	48.60
Uttarakhand	57.36	65.74	64.89	54.16	63.39	61.48	48.34	59.30	56.80	44.26	55.65	50.56
West Bengal	44.53	60.35	59.77	42.42	58.22	57.87	39.41	51.39	50.33	38.75	50.30	47.62
All India	**53.16**	**62.92**	**61.87**	**47.99**	**58.16**	**56.96**	**43.54**	**53.91**	**50.86**	**39.44**	**48.58**	**46.30**

Note: For definitions of key terms, see the notes at the end of the tables.

TABLE C4   Knowledge about Female Contraceptive Methods across Number of Children: National Family Health Survey-4 (2014–15)

State	Female Respondents						Male Respondents					
	Urban			Rural			Urban			Rural		
	0	1–2	>2	0	1–2	>2	0	1–2	>2	0	1–2	>2
Andhra Pradesh	26.86	30.77	25.26	24.79	25.07	20.08	37.36	37.44	31.21	33.12	31.78	27.88
Arunachal Pradesh	31.56	38.16	35.67	27.33	34.30	31.87	30.66	37.32	34.38	29.14	34.17	32.56
Assam	37.45	51.80	46.96	31.32	45.87	41.34	39.39	50.25	47.18	36.04	46.44	44.06
Bihar	27.39	40.77	35.29	20.94	30.88	29.00	32.48	42.53	36.38	26.93	34.01	32.32
Chhattisgarh	36.52	48.48	44.45	30.98	40.75	37.03	38.70	45.25	42.21	32.19	39.98	37.07
Goa	41.93	50.24	42.27	45.50	52.29	40.37	36.89	47.96	43.88	39.06	45.32	41.31
Gujarat	33.46	43.42	36.80	24.43	32.82	26.24	37.44	42.18	39.12	31.46	38.30	32.36
Haryana	36.70	48.01	43.34	34.00	45.39	40.81	37.51	47.41	43.64	38.11	44.42	40.67
Himachal Pradesh	37.66	48.10	43.73	29.88	43.65	38.44	32.54	45.95	39.15	31.56	41.23	36.68
Jammu & Kashmir	41.12	53.13	48.03	35.64	47.64	44.74	45.64	50.82	47.88	41.44	49.66	47.30
Jharkhand	31.66	44.16	39.21	24.25	34.23	31.29	35.29	44.83	40.79	29.61	35.79	31.74
Karnataka	29.52	37.27	30.87	22.89	28.52	24.47	38.34	41.92	37.50	31.79	33.01	28.04
Kerala	36.10	41.77	37.52	34.50	41.05	34.89	38.53	49.39	43.01	36.58	45.83	42.91
Madhya Pradesh	36.50	48.37	43.96	30.43	39.82	37.19	36.14	43.29	40.39	32.00	39.03	35.95
Maharashtra	35.49	43.61	38.22	27.97	35.14	30.84	37.76	45.91	38.73	32.48	35.27	31.75
Manipur	33.81	46.64	44.63	27.89	41.96	39.26	35.01	45.76	43.79	31.42	43.45	41.77
Meghalaya	28.91	35.31	33.32	24.35	32.06	31.88	27.52	37.72	31.16	21.96	29.02	28.48
Mizoram	28.34	38.26	36.12	21.51	27.52	27.57	30.35	35.13	30.40	23.00	24.55	29.18
Nagaland	27.41	41.10	39.67	21.19	32.42	30.66	28.87	37.80	38.39	20.22	32.34	29.40
Odisha	35.56	51.99	48.47	30.74	46.40	43.28	39.28	50.15	48.54	36.10	44.55	41.25
Punjab	38.17	49.89	46.63	35.50	48.15	45.64	43.12	50.00	44.45	39.03	46.25	44.71
Rajasthan	38.79	50.30	45.77	32.98	44.25	41.08	40.16	48.79	42.81	34.35	41.52	37.48
Sikkim	35.48	38.06	35.06	32.83	36.79	34.26	40.11	45.35	40.49	36.10	39.59	33.03
Tamil Nadu	33.20	48.90	45.63	31.71	45.04	42.37	41.81	50.30	47.71	38.42	45.33	41.66
Telangana	24.79	29.24	23.46	20.72	22.24	16.81	34.23	36.72	30.23	30.22	29.74	24.18
Tripura	41.67	49.23	44.16	31.62	42.82	36.69	39.08	46.77	41.54	33.46	39.36	35.98
Uttar Pradesh	33.13	49.47	46.49	28.63	43.99	42.19	36.16	46.00	43.79	32.40	41.26	39.65
Uttarakhand	39.92	52.44	47.99	34.68	46.52	42.37	40.68	50.00	45.82	36.38	46.17	39.99
West Bengal	35.62	49.81	45.90	30.77	44.81	41.59	42.20	51.65	48.39	37.77	46.67	44.68
All India	**33.90**	**44.84**	**40.78**	**28.50**	**38.93**	**35.85**	**38.20**	**46.09**	**41.18**	**33.49**	**40.24**	**36.52**

Note: For definitions of key terms, see the notes at the end of the tables.

TABLE C5 Knowledge about Male Contraceptive Methods across Quintiles of Frequency of Reading Newspaper, Listening Radio, and Watching Television: National Family Health Survey-4 (2014–15)

| State | Female Respondents | | | | | | | | Male Respondents | | | | | | | |
| | Urban | | | | Rural | | | | Urban | | | | Rural | | | |
	1	2	3	4	1	2	3	4	1	2	3	4	1	2	3	4
Andhra Pradesh	39.82	45.26	50.37	53.35	39.05	40.82	44.92	48.05	37.37	40.37	46.95	39.61	37.38	39.24	40.27	38.62
Arunachal Pradesh	46.85	52.94	53.11	57.85	46.77	52.97	52.86	50.87	34.34	40.26	37.70	43.79	39.53	45.15	41.89	46.85
Assam	55.10	56.67	58.21	60.15	52.85	56.73	57.54	58.80	45.03	48.08	56.40	53.09	46.44	49.69	50.49	50.89
Bihar	54.85	59.99	59.97	60.93	49.80	54.28	55.34	57.45	39.01	43.79	53.61	59.15	38.32	45.67	48.88	50.42
Chhattisgarh	59.42	62.93	62.41	64.20	52.58	59.10	59.37	60.72	45.19	49.05	53.74	47.22	41.16	44.23	49.82	47.50
Goa	54.87	59.95	61.11	63.13	52.51	51.21	60.52	62.00	34.94	41.05	49.86	46.10	30.11	35.21	49.12	43.03
Gujarat	57.98	61.80	63.50	65.10	50.58	57.93	60.26	59.27	41.61	48.55	53.53	50.04	37.19	46.83	52.70	50.34
Haryana	56.01	59.65	63.70	64.11	57.64	62.62	63.36	63.98	50.29	48.90	58.16	58.05	49.95	54.96	58.22	57.87
Himachal Pradesh	54.82	60.90	60.94	61.15	51.42	55.01	56.12	58.43	33.49	42.52	51.33	48.98	35.24	42.25	47.50	47.03
Jammu & Kashmir	60.32	61.61	62.21	63.71	55.33	58.59	60.14	61.20	50.07	52.22	54.24	57.07	45.17	49.73	50.19	54.94
Jharkhand	56.16	59.59	61.01	62.38	51.75	57.78	58.31	59.80	45.39	50.38	55.84	61.92	40.79	47.58	50.22	54.60
Karnataka	53.88	56.06	56.27	59.49	48.65	53.05	53.81	53.12	41.63	45.98	42.17	53.72	31.13	36.15	39.85	47.39
Kerala	57.45	54.43	56.58	60.08	51.64	54.94	57.20	60.26	27.20	35.35	45.67	41.75	36.17	35.79	44.64	44.32
Madhya Pradesh	55.61	58.74	60.03	61.36	50.54	55.80	57.16	58.30	38.68	42.18	48.53	54.12	38.84	43.61	49.95	50.04
Maharashtra	57.46	60.04	61.47	61.88	53.02	56.32	57.59	57.01	40.19	44.09	48.91	48.16	36.40	41.98	47.30	45.99
Manipur	54.05	56.54	55.58	58.60	45.85	51.48	52.98	56.99	37.61	39.54	44.47	48.33	29.79	38.83	45.55	52.30
Meghalaya	40.32	40.69	50.33	52.11	43.00	44.95	44.13	47.85	25.85	35.62	40.13	41.45	29.61	25.09	28.02	28.55
Mizoram	48.11	57.27	59.16	59.93	35.04	51.81	58.34	59.15	40.84	50.16	56.81	56.89	34.26	48.54	54.40	50.14
Nagaland	43.75	45.97	43.75	47.02	39.70	41.90	40.23	42.83	25.55	33.42	39.69	38.18	22.11	28.27	30.93	28.45
Odisha	54.15	57.94	58.50	60.10	52.93	56.50	56.08	57.61	46.11	48.86	54.92	54.41	42.02	47.99	50.02	54.22
Punjab	61.73	64.22	63.65	64.58	63.23	63.65	62.74	64.13	53.17	55.94	62.03	57.24	51.89	55.71	61.61	51.49
Rajasthan	59.29	60.91	62.02	63.33	56.24	59.88	60.52	60.78	46.80	49.88	55.36	53.24	42.35	49.18	55.18	53.68
Sikkim	51.83	60.85	59.06	60.87	57.43	59.97	60.30	60.61	38.55	50.11	50.35	58.57	42.46	50.17	55.00	60.80
Tamil Nadu	61.10	64.65	65.11	65.88	59.12	63.07	62.80	64.57	50.18	52.21	59.04	57.77	48.46	49.57	56.63	51.34
Telangana	36.54	41.45	45.45	48.31	36.03	37.67	41.60	44.84	32.62	35.53	36.79	41.39	33.82	36.57	36.99	40.88
Tripura	53.48	57.80	58.35	61.18	48.90	51.17	52.62	53.91	35.28	39.90	48.06	43.64	30.06	39.10	43.89	36.66
Uttar Pradesh	58.83	60.99	61.47	63.46	55.08	58.28	58.61	59.81	44.69	47.92	56.11	54.92	41.55	46.17	48.96	49.84
Uttarakhand	57.96	61.42	62.36	65.09	56.94	60.00	60.79	62.61	44.44	51.59	57.95	58.01	42.55	47.33	55.45	54.96
West Bengal	54.35	55.77	54.94	57.15	52.67	56.09	54.53	55.44	39.96	41.36	52.63	54.64	42.45	46.82	50.96	51.40
All India	**56.21**	**58.58**	**59.75**	**61.43**	**52.40**	**55.60**	**56.81**	**58.55**	**42.43**	**46.23**	**52.04**	**52.68**	**40.38**	**45.36**	**49.13**	**49.27**

Note: For definitions of key terms, see the notes at the end of the tables.

TABLE C6 Knowledge about Female Contraceptive Methods across Quintiles of Frequency of Reading Newspaper, Listening Radio, and Watching Television: National Family Health Survey-4 (2014–15)

State	Female Respondents								Male Respondents							
	Urban				Rural				Urban				Rural			
	1	2	3	4	1	2	3	4	1	2	3	4	1	2	3	4
Andhra Pradesh	21.67	23.30	31.41	35.60	16.88	20.53	29.63	33.74	26.91	38.24	39.30	38.75	24.47	34.80	36.37	37.70
Arunachal Pradesh	29.41	34.78	35.84	42.64	27.81	34.04	36.99	38.26	30.20	36.19	32.98	41.61	30.16	36.06	32.53	34.42
Assam	42.49	45.10	46.55	50.70	37.87	41.97	44.07	46.19	41.98	44.21	49.07	48.32	39.05	44.36	45.82	47.49
Bihar	29.31	33.88	36.30	39.90	25.10	30.95	32.31	34.82	27.77	34.93	40.95	43.39	27.09	33.79	36.12	37.94
Chhattisgarh	38.34	41.37	42.88	47.14	32.14	38.23	38.28	42.45	36.86	40.46	43.69	44.37	33.20	36.63	41.39	40.99
Goa	35.47	40.68	46.52	50.55	36.46	39.56	48.31	52.92	39.42	39.66	47.08	38.16	31.62	36.20	46.76	42.59
Gujarat	29.20	36.16	41.20	44.22	21.38	29.27	34.88	37.05	33.36	38.91	43.44	45.19	27.14	37.55	44.48	42.99
Haryana	35.18	41.48	45.19	47.17	32.46	41.54	42.81	45.47	39.34	36.62	47.91	44.36	37.80	39.83	45.42	42.51
Himachal Pradesh	37.35	42.08	44.69	45.61	31.78	37.32	39.73	44.35	27.17	38.01	46.15	41.32	30.42	35.70	40.30	40.37
Jammu & Kashmir	41.62	44.49	47.01	49.63	38.39	42.06	44.30	45.78	41.62	47.53	49.46	50.58	40.33	46.20	46.45	49.09
Jharkhand	33.10	36.08	39.36	43.60	28.07	34.79	36.52	39.82	33.11	39.65	43.57	44.59	29.27	35.90	39.06	42.14
Karnataka	26.10	27.42	32.87	39.79	20.78	23.62	29.73	31.91	31.57	36.75	37.24	46.93	23.84	29.28	35.66	40.93
Kerala	33.09	31.84	36.58	42.91	26.60	30.94	35.97	42.63	32.16	39.72	46.78	43.65	33.03	37.29	44.08	43.77
Madhya Pradesh	36.68	41.06	43.54	47.21	32.84	38.20	40.57	43.35	34.13	36.37	42.87	43.53	32.13	37.07	41.86	42.03
Maharashtra	33.39	36.74	39.87	43.75	27.62	31.95	34.95	36.38	35.90	40.34	44.04	41.39	28.46	33.99	37.76	36.03
Manipur	36.13	38.39	39.28	43.90	30.21	35.05	36.25	41.26	35.01	35.98	38.66	42.88	29.57	34.47	37.20	41.89
Meghalaya	23.53	26.01	32.61	36.37	26.57	28.80	32.03	34.17	25.61	29.25	36.04	33.55	24.83	25.93	27.80	27.65
Mizoram	23.73	27.92	32.47	36.03	17.26	23.44	28.53	33.16	23.44	29.75	32.97	35.50	21.08	26.52	27.71	29.24
Nagaland	30.52	34.26	35.01	38.15	25.55	30.57	31.38	34.09	25.30	35.90	38.91	40.08	23.32	28.34	31.48	27.03
Odisha	41.89	44.81	46.33	49.72	37.89	41.65	43.04	45.09	38.39	42.35	49.44	50.39	37.31	42.51	45.73	47.14
Punjab	41.64	44.02	44.45	49.08	42.43	42.87	43.26	46.12	42.51	45.15	49.89	47.61	40.77	42.75	45.99	41.77
Rajasthan	40.68	42.78	45.63	48.68	37.40	40.99	42.24	43.67	36.33	40.89	47.06	48.46	32.31	40.49	44.56	44.13
Sikkim	31.19	34.42	37.43	40.25	29.92	33.61	36.39	37.81	35.46	42.46	44.09	50.78	32.53	38.90	43.40	46.65
Tamil Nadu	37.05	41.36	44.70	46.58	35.36	39.35	41.02	44.99	41.08	40.38	49.39	47.81	36.53	40.15	46.22	42.79
Telangana	17.02	21.21	28.69	32.25	13.96	17.85	25.24	29.84	28.22	32.10	36.03	39.62	21.74	29.81	35.60	34.95
Tripura	39.27	45.68	47.72	51.41	34.69	39.97	43.41	46.57	37.53	41.61	48.11	32.96	32.71	40.18	46.89	34.92
Uttar Pradesh	38.27	40.99	42.42	45.85	36.23	39.47	39.98	42.41	35.77	38.75	45.32	46.12	34.14	38.56	41.65	41.79
Uttarakhand	39.88	44.09	46.88	51.06	37.10	41.18	42.96	46.36	38.30	40.38	48.58	49.71	34.39	39.28	45.56	43.04
West Bengal	40.97	43.97	45.26	49.14	38.25	41.92	42.82	44.31	42.07	43.09	54.06	52.05	40.42	44.57	47.01	47.25
All India	**35.06**	**37.73**	**40.87**	**44.39**	**31.96**	**35.11**	**37.76**	**40.60**	**35.44**	**39.48**	**45.04**	**45.36**	**32.27**	**37.94**	**41.75**	**41.70**

Note: For definitions of key terms, see the notes at the end of the tables.

TABLE C7 Knowledge about Male Contraceptive Methods across Educational Attainments: National Family Health Survey-4 (2014–15)

State	Female Respondents							
	Urban				Rural			
	No education	Primary	Secondary	Above secondary	No education	Primary	Secondary	Above secondary
Andhra Pradesh	41.80	46.78	49.62	54.09	39.24	41.73	44.66	47.76
Arunachal Pradesh	46.66	53.54	52.35	57.38	43.78	54.27	52.03	57.33
Assam	54.23	58.65	56.86	60.52	51.92	55.05	55.54	58.90
Bihar	56.40	58.03	58.53	62.82	49.76	52.41	52.51	60.94
Chhattisgarh	61.54	63.88	61.74	65.59	54.04	58.72	57.48	63.02
Goa	54.56	63.61	60.60	64.49	47.27	59.37	58.91	63.49
Gujarat	59.60	63.01	61.99	66.36	52.73	57.13	56.33	62.98
Haryana	59.32	59.48	61.38	65.20	60.95	62.69	61.83	65.13
Himachal Pradesh	58.63	63.91	59.93	61.01	51.27	56.94	55.33	57.71
Jammu & Kashmir	63.20	61.97	61.28	64.49	58.84	58.90	57.39	60.95
Jharkhand	57.85	59.92	59.42	63.92	50.97	55.74	54.93	62.78
Karnataka	56.08	57.14	55.98	61.45	50.71	51.62	53.20	56.26
Kerala	54.31	52.42	56.80	62.24	46.73	51.00	57.35	61.93
Madhya Pradesh	58.54	59.38	58.65	62.84	51.48	55.07	54.06	61.56
Maharashtra	58.29	61.13	60.25	63.05	51.45	55.15	56.67	60.13
Manipur	58.33	59.05	54.68	61.63	49.99	49.42	51.65	60.84
Meghalaya	39.37	44.20	46.18	55.77	43.45	43.51	44.35	49.08
Mizoram	44.33	57.90	58.66	62.00	26.60	53.05	56.15	64.29
Nagaland	43.05	48.48	44.36	46.49	38.35	41.46	40.57	41.55
Odisha	56.19	57.57	57.92	60.23	54.09	57.70	54.69	56.75
Punjab	64.00	64.26	63.39	64.96	64.76	64.51	62.51	63.93
Rajasthan	60.47	61.50	60.96	64.52	57.41	59.73	58.02	62.43
Sikkim	56.50	59.94	58.63	63.17	56.50	61.02	59.67	63.56
Tamil Nadu	63.93	65.39	65.07	65.43	60.41	65.02	63.49	63.74
Telangana	38.73	42.65	44.83	48.58	36.58	38.82	41.34	43.29
Tripura	56.40	58.62	57.04	61.44	46.35	51.52	50.90	60.16
Uttar Pradesh	61.36	59.69	59.65	64.38	57.05	56.74	54.64	61.02
Uttarakhand	62.03	61.83	61.02	64.76	58.30	60.18	58.91	64.03
West Bengal	56.39	56.19	54.61	57.83	53.67	56.92	53.62	55.45
All India	**57.55**	**59.27**	**58.82**	**62.46**	**52.68**	**55.65**	**55.19**	**60.05**

(Cont'd) ⟶

TABLE C7 (*Contd*) →

State	Male Respondents							
	Urban				Rural			
	No education	Primary	Secondary	Above secondary	No education	Primary	Secondary	Above secondary
Andhra Pradesh	38.13	38.38	41.34	45.34	37.13	40.59	37.50	42.94
Arunachal Pradesh	19.93	39.97	36.55	44.85	32.80	41.73	41.49	55.51
Assam	45.85	44.84	47.28	59.17	46.11	47.96	47.23	55.82
Bihar	32.71	34.02	46.55	61.64	34.89	37.99	43.60	56.34
Chhattisgarh	45.89	48.98	48.31	53.18	41.15	41.42	43.91	53.80
Goa	36.18	38.06	44.35	53.09	30.20	37.01	41.18	53.78
Gujarat	38.31	41.93	47.46	55.60	34.70	39.07	44.12	54.24
Haryana	50.64	52.35	50.79	61.84	49.31	49.80	54.76	59.72
Himachal Pradesh	29.59	37.55	39.80	53.57	37.98	41.22	41.19	49.45
Jammu & Kashmir	52.76	53.65	52.30	57.75	46.22	50.25	48.44	56.78
Jharkhand	46.26	43.75	50.13	61.09	36.23	40.99	45.46	54.98
Karnataka	34.85	40.09	45.49	56.47	32.73	34.29	38.08	46.31
Kerala	39.48	30.47	39.79	46.66	17.46	40.03	40.23	46.67
Madhya Pradesh	37.13	40.68	44.87	54.20	38.89	40.95	41.97	54.63
Maharashtra	37.59	43.50	43.77	53.31	34.92	38.61	41.44	50.30
Manipur	41.23	35.81	41.88	52.86	37.85	36.85	42.41	53.47
Meghalaya	28.43	21.58	32.92	57.84	25.80	23.12	29.85	38.73
Mizoram	53.93	45.62	51.82	59.17	29.87	44.04	45.85	63.61
Nagaland	27.44	26.90	29.92	41.32	21.73	20.79	25.04	39.09
Odisha	49.21	48.65	49.67	56.68	40.29	44.47	45.92	53.96
Punjab	52.60	50.75	56.70	62.28	52.37	53.27	55.88	58.22
Rajasthan	45.32	46.82	50.21	57.38	41.67	43.73	46.87	56.62
Sikkim	46.45	40.43	48.34	53.89	35.01	41.88	50.06	59.33
Tamil Nadu	50.86	55.39	54.85	60.44	47.41	53.35	50.82	56.23
Telangana	35.21	35.02	36.07	39.04	33.65	35.19	36.04	42.05
Tripura	32.17	36.66	41.60	47.69	22.65	29.28	36.24	43.88
Uttar Pradesh	44.86	46.66	49.33	57.02	39.63	43.05	43.80	52.73
Uttarakhand	42.43	48.51	53.48	59.58	43.50	43.26	48.41	59.67
West Bengal	38.91	41.58	44.40	56.09	43.13	45.76	44.57	53.01
All India	**42.12**	**44.62**	**47.03**	**55.39**	**39.18**	**42.31**	**44.20**	**52.59**

Note: For definitions of key terms, see the notes at the end of the tables.

TABLE C8 Knowledge about Female Contraceptive Methods across Educational Attainments: National Family Health Survey-4 (2014–15)

State	Female Respondents							
	Urban				Rural			
	No education	Primary	Secondary	Above secondary	No education	Primary	Secondary	Above secondary
Andhra Pradesh	20.05	24.97	30.14	37.34	17.87	22.75	27.70	35.04
Arunachal Pradesh	27.67	34.64	34.64	43.36	24.74	34.31	34.03	45.49
Assam	40.77	45.59	45.89	49.67	36.23	39.64	41.41	47.03
Bihar	29.53	33.38	34.39	43.02	24.80	28.82	29.01	38.13
Chhattisgarh	39.45	42.29	42.28	48.90	32.81	37.78	37.36	43.92
Goa	33.10	40.90	46.19	52.19	33.66	45.31	47.17	55.95
Gujarat	30.99	34.25	38.17	48.32	21.54	26.64	30.80	42.54
Haryana	39.13	40.65	42.37	50.57	37.11	39.86	41.25	47.77
Himachal Pradesh	34.34	42.93	42.98	46.95	29.86	35.98	39.18	44.63
Jammu & Kashmir	45.47	45.78	45.32	52.05	41.60	42.53	41.25	47.03
Jharkhand	32.74	36.70	37.84	45.92	26.80	32.17	32.50	42.14
Karnataka	25.38	28.68	31.78	44.57	20.56	23.55	28.26	37.17
Kerala	20.82	27.75	36.21	47.55	20.11	25.36	36.13	46.29
Madhya Pradesh	39.99	41.85	42.05	49.93	34.06	37.28	36.87	46.49
Maharashtra	31.61	36.45	38.79	46.74	24.97	29.47	33.71	40.59
Manipur	37.87	39.23	38.81	48.12	32.57	32.44	35.82	45.66
Meghalaya	22.14	26.55	30.15	39.48	26.58	26.41	30.93	37.53
Mizoram	17.81	28.30	32.65	39.37	13.62	24.05	27.92	37.33
Nagaland	30.65	32.28	33.71	38.84	23.19	26.09	29.08	35.63
Odisha	43.23	45.55	45.33	50.42	38.94	42.52	40.65	44.79
Punjab	42.85	44.07	44.13	49.78	43.49	44.05	42.80	45.69
Rajasthan	42.00	44.01	43.83	51.08	38.47	41.01	39.33	46.29
Sikkim	30.87	31.92	36.26	43.55	29.13	33.20	35.28	42.68
Tamil Nadu	40.49	42.24	43.31	47.19	36.90	40.82	41.39	43.73
Telangana	16.84	22.40	27.15	34.29	14.67	18.86	24.87	31.97
Tripura	40.54	45.26	45.91	51.60	32.51	37.78	40.23	49.30
Uttar Pradesh	41.28	39.06	39.96	47.09	38.83	37.53	35.36	43.06
Uttarakhand	43.85	44.51	44.73	51.52	38.15	40.69	40.58	48.60
West Bengal	41.63	43.39	44.76	50.07	37.40	42.01	41.16	47.43
All India	**35.56**	**38.15**	**39.36**	**46.76**	**31.51**	**35.26**	**35.81**	**43.08**

(Cont'd) ⟶

TABLE C8 (*Cont'd*) →

Male Respondents

State	Urban				Rural			
	No education	Primary	Secondary	Above secondary	No education	Primary	Secondary	Above secondary
Andhra Pradesh	20.90	28.32	36.44	43.37	22.48	29.65	33.66	41.48
Arunachal Pradesh	21.33	32.34	31.71	41.85	25.22	31.52	32.12	42.74
Assam	41.45	41.88	43.72	51.45	38.96	39.86	41.55	49.56
Bihar	22.50	31.02	35.24	45.35	24.13	28.29	31.62	41.78
Chhattisgarh	36.05	36.80	40.43	47.46	32.27	33.83	36.53	44.83
Goa	39.10	37.97	41.08	49.32	31.36	35.50	41.20	49.13
Gujarat	29.16	32.17	38.50	47.67	22.39	30.20	34.79	47.33
Haryana	38.86	38.15	39.77	49.97	34.71	37.98	40.73	46.84
Himachal Pradesh	20.55	26.14	34.42	49.05	29.34	32.63	34.69	44.95
Jammu & Kashmir	44.30	45.25	46.54	52.83	41.65	43.33	44.28	51.74
Jharkhand	33.06	32.55	37.43	49.36	25.56	29.96	33.73	41.14
Karnataka	27.91	33.35	38.32	47.36	24.11	27.30	31.98	43.34
Kerala	32.66	36.96	41.17	50.29	19.69	34.75	40.23	46.52
Madhya Pradesh	32.06	34.47	38.11	47.41	31.02	34.34	35.51	46.04
Maharashtra	30.07	36.87	39.56	47.75	24.77	28.79	33.23	41.87
Manipur	36.24	35.36	37.49	46.45	31.44	31.66	36.15	44.34
Meghalaya	18.61	22.93	27.92	49.06	23.48	22.48	27.37	33.39
Mizoram	25.23	21.86	30.66	37.44	21.73	24.09	25.45	33.35
Nagaland	29.00	29.77	30.32	41.43	19.72	21.67	26.71	37.49
Odisha	40.05	40.90	43.97	51.27	35.71	39.45	40.62	49.57
Punjab	42.15	41.76	45.16	51.19	40.12	42.04	42.58	46.97
Rajasthan	35.53	38.89	41.52	50.26	29.60	33.39	37.66	48.51
Sikkim	34.24	37.95	42.61	46.50	24.95	31.12	39.13	47.58
Tamil Nadu	40.47	45.19	44.00	51.76	37.32	40.90	41.36	46.89
Telangana	24.94	31.29	33.44	40.51	19.92	23.55	31.41	39.79
Tripura	37.17	38.97	41.42	50.11	28.10	32.32	37.30	48.92
Uttar Pradesh	36.73	36.48	39.75	47.05	33.36	34.90	36.42	43.75
Uttarakhand	37.53	39.60	43.17	52.10	32.00	35.38	39.67	49.30
West Bengal	39.37	43.69	45.59	56.53	41.47	42.03	42.42	50.26
All India	**33.65**	**37.50**	**40.12**	**48.66**	**30.34**	**34.17**	**36.78**	**45.21**

Note: For definitions of key terms, see the notes at the end of the tables.

TABLE C9 Knowledge about Male Contraceptive Methods across Religion: National Family Health Survey-4 (2014–15)

State	Female Respondents						Male Respondents					
	Urban			Rural			Urban			Rural		
	Hindu	Muslim	Others	Hindu	Muslim	Others	Hindu	Muslim	Others	Hindu	Muslim	Others
Andhra Pradesh	48.11	49.59	50.37	42.56	41.04	41.30	41.80	39.81	53.14	38.86	39.11	36.07
Arunachal Pradesh	55.34	51.71	50.68	56.90	48.22	47.52	40.04	31.26	36.06	46.55	33.58	39.46
Assam	58.20	54.46	56.15	56.86	50.75	55.85	50.90	43.12	53.30	48.25	46.72	50.33
Bihar	59.17	56.54	56.97	51.91	48.79	38.05	49.47	39.41	66.67	42.15	41.16	40.07
Chhattisgarh	62.77	62.71	63.25	56.86	58.68	52.23	49.74	51.25	40.53	43.82	43.29	39.05
Goa	60.61	59.48	64.24	58.58	54.99	60.60	45.34	42.69	47.71	41.88	40.91	44.68
Gujarat	63.06	59.41	65.49	55.99	53.01	49.40	48.93	42.92	53.49	43.23	43.11	51.49
Haryana	62.25	52.91	64.87	62.56	54.08	64.89	54.75	43.49	63.88	55.41	41.42	55.18
Himachal Pradesh	61.29	55.05	53.54	55.53	50.83	58.56	43.92	43.87	48.89	42.68	41.01	50.53
Jammu & Kashmir	62.81	62.51	59.01	57.04	58.80	58.14	56.49	52.81	55.26	52.30	47.72	59.81
Jharkhand	60.30	59.64	58.36	53.99	54.63	50.31	51.33	52.98	58.83	43.42	44.97	42.94
Karnataka	57.89	55.52	57.41	52.75	49.73	48.21	47.92	42.66	50.54	37.76	36.07	39.24
Kerala	59.19	57.17	58.12	58.41	56.78	59.33	41.09	38.80	46.86	41.27	42.32	41.13
Madhya Pradesh	59.78	57.72	62.43	53.34	55.81	58.68	46.39	41.90	51.22	42.12	45.12	49.85
Maharashtra	60.75	60.17	61.90	55.65	55.55	56.47	45.91	44.85	47.01	41.81	40.55	43.74
Manipur	58.72	54.95	54.49	55.84	53.31	49.46	48.68	37.99	39.30	48.76	51.03	39.30
Meghalaya	44.28	42.09	49.51	46.66	61.43	42.75	45.21	30.61	33.71	35.49	33.54	26.23
Mizoram	49.13	54.10	59.08	42.25	62.28	51.84	18.74	7.69	53.79	46.98	66.67	45.65
Nagaland	44.68	38.82	45.33	36.29	32.59	40.69	32.29	30.56	32.51	19.19	19.92	24.88
Odisha	58.65	48.96	59.31	55.13	51.80	54.64	51.75	43.56	47.42	45.60	58.23	39.96
Punjab	63.82	59.50	64.43	63.47	58.87	63.43	57.68	48.97	57.58	50.25	52.13	57.39
Rajasthan	61.96	60.28	64.50	58.39	55.42	61.59	51.77	50.60	55.21	47.09	40.97	54.96
Sikkim	58.78	46.02	61.14	59.94	59.93	59.72	48.67	53.37	46.97	47.95		47.45
Tamil Nadu	65.40	63.14	63.11	62.98	65.19	64.26	56.46	55.06	55.11	51.79	52.69	48.78
Telangana	44.41	44.25	46.46	38.85	43.27	40.80	37.04	35.28	38.91	35.84	40.46	38.80
Tripura	58.17	57.30	55.65	51.44	47.91	47.64	43.41	29.92	36.97	35.16	30.36	32.36
Uttar Pradesh	62.32	59.02	64.36	56.59	55.71	62.49	50.84	48.69	52.75	43.98	45.38	46.09
Uttarakhand	63.25	59.08	63.72	59.87	57.51	60.40	54.58	50.19	58.12	49.23	45.66	59.11
West Bengal	56.39	52.87	60.94	55.17	52.85	50.36	45.59	46.43	47.43	45.47	44.77	42.60
All India	**59.93**	**57.40**	**60.43**	**54.93**	**53.22**	**55.53**	**49.01**	**45.77**	**50.79**	**43.99**	**44.02**	**46.86**

Note: For definitions of key terms, see the notes at the end of the tables.

TABLE C10　Knowledge about Female Contraceptive Methods across Religion: National Family Health Survey-4 (2014–15)

State	Female Respondents						Male Respondents					
	Urban			Rural			Urban			Rural		
	Hindu	Muslim	Others	Hindu	Muslim	Others	Hindu	Muslim	Others	Hindu	Muslim	Others
Andhra Pradesh	28.87	26.64	30.78	23.74	21.54	24.67	37.16	31.42	37.15	31.72	30.76	27.62
Arunachal Pradesh	36.94	34.68	33.77	36.53	30.10	29.77	35.43	22.60	32.57	35.34	27.89	30.47
Assam	46.48	44.48	44.18	41.54	37.59	40.12	45.62	41.92	53.34	42.67	39.47	36.57
Bihar	34.94	32.19	34.85	27.42	26.01	19.28	37.11	30.61	25.00	30.16	31.49	43.51
Chhattisgarh	43.16	43.41	45.09	36.31	38.42	30.05	41.55	44.13	38.98	36.03	39.06	28.29
Goa	45.86	40.61	49.85	46.71	42.71	51.50	42.06	40.29	46.20	40.79	39.08	45.64
Gujarat	39.40	34.30	44.91	28.14	28.50	27.94	39.99	35.62	42.11	33.76	36.13	41.07
Haryana	43.86	36.93	47.26	41.54	28.62	43.66	42.33	41.51	44.62	41.51	31.33	40.11
Himachal Pradesh	44.41	36.96	40.48	38.81	30.75	38.82	38.93	41.43	33.22	36.46	34.14	36.99
Jammu & Kashmir	53.16	44.97	49.82	44.32	40.89	42.12	53.46	45.97	48.02	47.10	43.60	52.85
Jharkhand	39.00	36.57	36.62	31.01	31.10	25.71	39.72	38.69	41.68	31.74	34.85	30.73
Karnataka	34.50	30.23	33.47	25.96	25.16	25.53	40.18	36.44	38.69	31.47	30.47	30.85
Kerala	41.06	36.29	41.07	37.97	35.94	42.14	43.52	42.71	44.83	40.84	41.25	42.57
Madhya Pradesh	43.37	41.33	48.67	36.05	37.76	41.54	39.70	36.39	43.04	35.23	37.36	38.86
Maharashtra	39.69	37.88	42.00	31.98	31.73	32.11	40.58	42.04	40.50	33.27	33.31	34.01
Manipur	42.98	37.54	39.17	39.84	34.51	33.80	41.13	33.61	40.15	39.58	39.63	34.98
Meghalaya	32.09	27.52	31.84	33.55	42.26	28.09	35.48	28.86	29.96	31.02	31.62	24.40
Mizoram	22.07	20.47	33.42	18.61	21.89	25.57	20.36	18.96	31.63	27.23	16.67	25.48
Nagaland	34.98	33.12	34.37	30.61	27.07	27.81	33.59	29.60	33.14	27.13	26.28	25.35
Odisha	46.41	41.58	43.21	40.69	37.81	39.51	45.53	38.15	47.66	40.55	48.58	35.53
Punjab	45.71	36.72	45.92	43.22	40.25	43.57	47.12	30.85	46.14	40.68	34.39	43.64
Rajasthan	45.51	42.71	48.75	39.72	36.86	44.07	43.82	40.36	47.45	37.73	29.56	33.68
Sikkim	35.98	30.50	37.92	35.09	36.47	34.29	42.18	40.98	42.20	37.61		36.03
Tamil Nadu	43.95	43.13	44.84	40.55	43.56	42.88	46.55	44.99	41.73	41.87	41.55	39.56
Telangana	27.04	25.03	26.30	20.11	21.33	21.54	34.20	33.86	42.66	28.47	32.07	26.25
Tripura	46.61	44.04	46.95	39.51	37.17	35.43	43.77	37.03	40.76	36.49	37.43	36.78
Uttar Pradesh	43.49	38.80	47.17	37.95	36.46	45.18	41.19	39.24	49.09	36.55	37.45	38.82
Uttarakhand	47.64	42.22	50.62	41.35	38.37	44.75	45.90	40.08	43.97	40.37	35.03	48.10
West Bengal	46.07	41.12	50.48	40.98	39.67	40.74	47.16	46.07	49.59	42.58	43.30	42.94
All India	**40.91**	**37.44**	**41.91**	**34.74**	**34.67**	**36.45**	**41.84**	**39.93**	**42.39**	**36.14**	**37.86**	**37.61**

Note: For definitions of key terms, see the notes at the end of the tables.

TABLE C11 Knowledge about Male Contraceptive Methods across Social Groups: National Family Health Survey-4 (2014–15)

State	Female Respondents						Male Respondents					
	Urban			Rural			Urban			Rural		
	Scheduled caste	Scheduled tribe	Others	Scheduled caste	Scheduled tribe	Others	Scheduled caste	Scheduled tribe	Others	Scheduled caste	Scheduled tribe	Others
Andhra Pradesh	48.46	42.68	66.67	42.48	40.09	33.33	42.09	35.94	38.90	39.04	34.63	33.33
Arunachal Pradesh	53.91	51.94	50.18	58.04	47.90	44.84	35.34	38.06	38.38	45.34	40.68	32.39
Assam	57.60	59.44	55.79	54.76	57.44	53.29	49.67	49.28	49.13	47.36	49.64	48.23
Bihar	58.87	40.17	55.74	51.65	44.06	49.65	48.39	53.97	32.66	41.96	32.10	49.65
Chhattisgarh	62.94	61.28	64.71	58.63	53.20	52.98	50.03	44.72	51.78	45.49	40.78	37.22
Goa	61.26	63.50	60.33	59.30	54.78	59.38	43.40	33.63	59.89	41.58	47.90	46.79
Gujarat	62.92	58.67	60.54	56.82	51.64	46.68	48.92	33.56	47.93	45.27	34.56	34.69
Haryana	61.78	49.03	48.61	62.08	35.85	54.81	53.96		46.67	54.53	59.47	
Himachal Pradesh	60.74	66.67	51.64	55.44	52.17	60.77	43.73	66.67	47.35	42.77	46.12	34.51
Jammu & Kashmir	61.65	63.13	62.86	56.89	57.93	60.08	56.15	55.11	52.06	50.38	48.24	48.31
Jharkhand	60.10	59.40	61.55	54.10	51.58	57.83	52.24	51.05	48.18	44.32	40.78	36.88
Karnataka	56.17	61.68	60.95	52.47	52.91	51.94	43.49	51.45	56.03	37.02	44.48	40.70
Kerala	58.42	46.27	58.05	58.28	41.77	57.52	41.55	0.00	38.53	41.95	15.78	38.09
Madhya Pradesh	59.65	57.50	59.62	54.35	49.48	51.56	45.50	49.80	53.03	42.96	39.18	38.57
Maharashtra	60.89	59.62	58.43	56.17	53.24	52.14	45.87	43.76	46.67	42.27	38.80	36.41
Manipur	57.58	52.92	58.06	55.65	47.22	53.51	46.50	40.73	40.42	48.73	35.19	47.11
Meghalaya	43.58	49.52	43.13	41.64	43.06	60.25	30.23	34.09	50.62	45.10	27.08	35.49
Mizoram	49.78	59.19	53.69	40.81	51.98	46.72	17.53	53.14	46.75	62.38	45.51	45.26
Nagaland	44.68	45.22	42.64	31.48	40.72	34.15	34.62	32.55	23.72	13.87	24.86	28.87
Odisha	58.31	57.22	52.13	55.94	51.11	52.31	51.97	43.44	49.44	46.39	41.51	46.26
Punjab	63.98	66.67	66.41	63.39	66.67	59.89	57.32	66.67	66.67	55.54		46.33
Rajasthan	61.78	62.58	55.48	58.57	56.23	54.79	51.70	52.71	54.28	47.35	44.49	34.85
Sikkim	58.78	62.75	62.06	59.62	59.88	64.61	48.27	45.60	66.67	46.07	52.72	57.25
Tamil Nadu	65.11	55.08	61.68	63.13	58.53	54.99	56.27	60.60	56.35	51.72	49.31	47.13
Telangana	44.66	39.90	39.16	39.25	37.78	37.12	36.87	28.97	32.15	36.45	32.27	54.26
Tripura	57.88	59.26	57.77	52.31	47.53	51.84	44.13	44.24	32.15	36.52	33.06	28.55
Uttar Pradesh	61.26	61.44	56.06	56.57	47.03	54.11	50.19	44.45	60.59	44.18	40.05	46.13
Uttarakhand	62.38	63.68	55.22	59.81	57.01	60.60	53.18	61.50	55.86	48.49	51.61	56.10
West Bengal	55.80	55.96	55.13	55.07	49.39	53.00	45.47	33.58	48.15	45.43	37.82	45.99
All India	**59.66**	**57.21**	**57.86**	**55.22**	**50.80**	**53.51**	**48.56**	**44.60**	**50.04**	**44.58**	**39.15**	**45.02**

Note: For definitions of key terms, see the notes at the end of the tables.

TABLE C12 Knowledge about Female Contraceptive Methods across Social Groups: National Family Health Survey-4 (2014–15)

| State | Female Respondents | | | | | | Male Respondents | | | | | |
| | Urban | | | Rural | | | Urban | | | Rural | | |
	Scheduled caste	Scheduled tribe	Others	Scheduled caste	Scheduled tribe	Others	Scheduled caste	Scheduled tribe	Others	Scheduled caste	Scheduled tribe	Others
Andhra Pradesh	28.71	25.65	53.85	23.72	23.28	7.69	36.84	11.50	34.67	31.67	27.92	33.33
Arunachal Pradesh	37.16	34.00	33.48	37.55	29.96	28.32	33.16	33.24	34.00	34.98	30.70	31.33
Assam	46.71	43.47	43.72	40.59	41.60	38.02	45.50	42.01	45.01	41.61	42.13	40.50
Bihar	34.49	22.39	33.60	27.34	21.04	29.04	35.79	30.38	38.41	30.42	20.89	30.76
Chhattisgarh	43.52	41.45	38.21	37.83	33.12	29.57	41.89	38.56	58.33	37.67	33.05	31.75
Goa	46.86	47.45	40.81	48.49	42.32	45.02	40.93	32.58	54.32	40.77	38.66	49.70
Gujarat	39.15	34.17	37.02	29.00	24.48	24.61	40.07	28.56	35.25	35.58	26.32	30.58
Haryana	43.58	27.93	30.12	40.74	32.53	32.32	42.34		38.33	40.84	41.84	
Himachal Pradesh	43.98	56.39	38.97	38.69	34.54	40.57	38.36	58.33	36.95	36.44	36.80	34.71
Jammu & Kashmir	50.48	47.00	44.81	43.20	37.35	40.61	53.51	46.29	44.20	47.79	37.92	42.02
Jharkhand	38.56	36.49	39.98	31.11	27.50	31.95	39.81	38.07	41.64	32.19	31.24	27.51
Karnataka	32.32	34.75	38.13	25.67	26.08	28.01	36.46	50.16	45.45	30.46	39.68	36.77
Kerala	39.77	22.62	35.47	38.31	24.71	37.57	43.30	33.33	44.61	41.22	22.52	43.17
Madhya Pradesh	43.26	41.15	44.67	36.84	33.13	33.91	39.39	36.65	41.60	35.89	32.94	31.36
Maharashtra	39.75	36.94	38.19	32.44	29.44	28.38	41.15	36.42	33.53	33.85	28.19	27.34
Manipur	41.66	37.50	42.12	39.24	31.94	35.17	40.17	40.32	39.30	39.12	33.57	38.01
Meghalaya	33.80	31.92	29.82	30.48	28.49	41.05	31.81	29.70	38.80	31.11	25.16	31.84
Mizoram	25.18	33.48	22.87	18.78	25.67	17.57	13.32	31.71	18.86	32.49	25.54	17.11
Nagaland	35.34	34.24	34.93	28.47	27.85	28.46	32.25	33.17	31.80	24.54	25.43	25.52
Odisha	46.23	43.97	43.36	41.39	37.19	37.33	45.50	41.11	46.13	41.17	37.08	42.23
Punjab	45.61	51.16	46.52	43.46	47.45	40.20	46.27	61.52	36.88	42.76		36.01
Rajasthan	45.15	45.36	44.03	39.97	37.35	35.94	43.50	43.38	45.34	37.57	35.01	42.99
Sikkim	35.84	41.14	34.21	34.15	36.93	34.92	42.01	40.63	60.89	36.21	39.04	37.81
Tamil Nadu	43.95	25.41	44.84	40.72	36.99	36.56	46.22	50.44	41.70	41.91	32.52	31.64
Telangana	26.71	23.93	27.51	20.44	18.62	14.71	34.69	17.46		28.87	25.15	45.70
Tripura	46.90	47.25	44.30	40.67	36.22	38.54	44.82	42.01	36.67	38.08	35.24	33.00
Uttar Pradesh	41.98	42.26	39.68	37.81	32.28	35.19	40.65	38.11	51.50	36.69	30.47	37.60
Uttarakhand	46.49	49.94	36.59	40.89	42.51	44.13	44.72	46.84	47.14	40.04	38.51	39.73
West Bengal	44.92	43.63	45.03	41.19	34.97	39.76	47.27	45.06	45.91	42.50	38.95	44.53
All India	**40.34**	**37.07**	**41.90**	**35.06**	**31.30**	**36.89**	**41.51**	**37.43**	**43.83**	**36.59**	**32.16**	**40.57**

Note: For definitions of key terms, see the notes at the end of the tables.

TABLE C13 Tuberculosis: National Family Health Survey-4 (2014–15)

State	Female Respondents								Male Respondents							
	Urban				Rural				Urban				Rural			
	Know	Spread	Cure	Disclose	Know	Spread	Cure	Disclose	Know	Spread	Cure	Disclose	Know	Spread	Cure	Disclose
Andhra Pradesh	87.84	86.25	74.58	59.85	82.25	85.99	67.59	54.12	83.40	85.95	74.66	48.56	76.01	87.84	66.05	42.58
Arunachal Pradesh	91.32	83.86	81.39	77.45	85.42	83.24	66.27	71.52	88.65	84.21	81.52	69.77	82.82	84.25	72.04	54.89
Assam	90.79	83.09	81.48	82.64	89.21	81.11	69.83	81.84	93.36	84.93	81.92	85.01	91.31	83.16	77.53	83.47
Bihar	89.86	84.37	85.65	85.86	79.51	81.72	71.55	69.40	90.67	84.29	87.03	83.42	84.56	84.55	78.29	74.54
Chhattisgarh	97.81	80.95	92.32	87.65	90.20	81.60	78.80	80.80	97.91	82.24	94.96	91.78	95.60	81.61	89.49	85.95
Goa	98.04	84.47	90.69	78.33	94.17	86.23	88.87	76.72	94.89	89.43	93.09	84.72	88.79	86.65	86.48	80.75
Gujarat	87.88	85.20	79.23	74.96	74.03	84.56	60.15	60.20	90.72	87.55	79.75	75.74	81.53	86.25	70.05	66.29
Haryana	90.57	82.23	88.04	73.97	89.19	80.95	85.84	73.94	89.95	83.75	87.59	72.34	94.73	80.97	92.12	76.21
Himachal Pradesh	96.64	83.24	91.49	87.81	93.36	81.78	84.91	85.43	94.04	80.07	90.52	85.30	94.69	80.87	89.61	84.56
Jammu & Kashmir	91.93	85.79	87.22	77.92	88.22	84.62	79.43	70.72	83.97	87.36	80.47	73.40	85.77	85.04	78.87	72.66
Jharkhand	96.23	78.46	91.28	88.80	86.16	78.83	77.62	77.52	92.31	83.45	89.44	76.30	87.59	81.00	81.84	72.15
Karnataka	68.47	82.99	60.26	41.43	59.23	83.20	46.90	40.04	67.47	84.46	60.58	37.91	61.97	85.20	53.36	33.74
Kerala	97.24	93.29	81.18	77.18	96.36	92.60	79.79	78.18	88.80	92.96	76.43	70.76	87.78	92.27	72.46	76.35
Madhya Pradesh	92.99	83.59	87.67	82.75	83.98	82.54	73.13	73.58	92.66	86.26	87.41	73.84	85.40	83.87	76.53	65.21
Maharashtra	86.42	90.86	81.30	69.50	78.36	89.82	67.96	63.87	92.62	91.54	88.78	80.72	86.93	90.78	78.23	67.42
Manipur	96.76	89.29	86.52	92.23	95.11	88.09	80.30	89.53	92.80	88.23	84.35	87.14	86.03	88.67	75.04	79.54
Meghalaya	92.89	84.84	88.15	75.15	89.24	82.67	76.83	73.09	89.76	85.21	83.42	76.20	90.44	81.89	82.86	79.75
Mizoram	98.51	94.02	95.74	94.47	87.85	90.88	81.97	83.32	96.37	92.35	95.11	89.43	90.19	90.27	86.65	84.06
Nagaland	93.22	86.13	78.74	80.31	81.95	84.91	60.65	67.96	86.73	87.36	79.57	79.23	86.75	87.12	69.12	76.76
Odisha	95.04	87.54	90.59	87.86	90.29	86.26	81.99	81.88	88.15	88.45	81.34	80.00	89.92	87.29	81.33	77.95
Punjab	97.72	80.65	94.02	92.88	97.16	81.10	93.33	92.08	97.51	82.04	94.71	92.83	96.42	79.90	92.18	87.81
Rajasthan	96.98	81.75	92.07	89.56	91.32	81.14	82.88	84.45	95.81	81.63	92.01	86.49	90.39	82.03	85.01	80.75
Sikkim	95.39	90.87	92.63	84.30	94.90	90.15	91.74	83.03	92.07	82.15	88.48	81.44	94.13	81.41	90.79	84.19
Tamil Nadu	88.81	87.62	69.19	50.67	84.77	87.56	59.77	47.55	86.78	87.72	68.23	32.19	80.82	86.15	62.54	28.38
Telangana	79.97	87.39	70.07	49.06	64.85	86.59	49.59	32.79	75.33	85.84	65.36	25.21	70.92	85.05	57.51	29.69
Tripura	99.04	82.39	95.18	96.52	95.87	81.02	82.52	90.77	98.98	83.40	95.82	96.60	92.59	83.88	84.86	88.26
Uttar Pradesh	98.00	79.77	93.35	87.27	94.09	79.60	85.35	80.44	94.85	82.45	88.87	84.93	90.97	81.14	85.29	79.25
Uttarakhand	95.88	83.01	91.01	87.67	92.52	81.89	85.18	81.87	97.69	77.47	95.38	91.12	96.12	77.40	93.53	85.93
West Bengal	95.90	80.78	91.63	92.88	91.68	78.95	83.28	88.57	96.30	82.27	90.86	93.06	95.86	82.68	88.35	93.08
All India	**90.35**	**84.83**	**82.50**	**73.63**	**85.51**	**82.94**	**74.56**	**71.79**	**89.43**	**86.13**	**81.82**	**69.31**	**86.41**	**84.47**	**77.81**	**69.16**

Note: For definitions of key terms, see the notes at the end of the tables.

TABLE C14 Knowledge about Tuberculosis across Highest Educational Level Attained: National Family Health Survey-4 (2014–15)

Female Respondents

State	Urban				Rural			
	No education	Primary	Secondary	Above secondary	No education	Primary	Secondary	Above secondary
Andhra Pradesh	73.14	86.40	92.06	95.53	71.94	81.75	89.93	96.91
Arunachal Pradesh	84.00	89.41	92.94	94.21	78.58	86.80	89.82	91.02
Assam	85.65	88.24	91.48	92.41	83.60	86.95	91.81	95.38
Bihar	83.32	89.18	92.53	93.28	73.90	81.53	85.86	90.49
Chhattisgarh	93.81	97.18	98.75	98.64	80.72	89.76	96.10	99.14
Goa	93.26	97.90	98.63	98.57	81.96	89.63	94.82	98.64
Gujarat	73.93	84.14	89.04	95.79	59.56	70.80	81.27	94.09
Haryana	81.51	85.89	92.23	96.12	81.89	87.40	92.15	94.47
Himachal Pradesh	93.23	98.79	95.28	98.66	82.43	87.73	95.07	98.12
Jammu & Kashmir	86.59	89.22	93.09	94.87	83.15	87.88	90.44	93.93
Jharkhand	91.28	95.10	97.33	98.49	80.51	88.09	91.01	95.83
Karnataka	53.50	62.30	68.79	79.51	46.15	53.22	66.55	76.13
Kerala	90.42	95.12	96.86	98.29	75.24	85.98	96.66	98.38
Madhya Pradesh	88.32	90.33	93.94	96.50	77.31	84.35	89.86	95.19
Maharashtra	72.49	80.58	87.36	92.94	66.02	73.56	81.99	90.01
Manipur	95.92	97.41	96.80	96.74	91.78	92.35	95.99	97.06
Meghalaya	86.40	95.09	92.44	94.46	82.42	88.26	91.55	94.43
Mizoram	96.69	94.24	98.72	99.49	47.83	87.53	95.93	99.68
Nagaland	88.98	90.62	92.60	97.75	72.22	77.74	84.91	95.23
Odisha	90.74	93.54	96.26	96.16	84.34	89.41	93.56	96.84
Punjab	94.00	97.01	98.16	98.74	94.55	97.29	97.64	99.03
Rajasthan	94.30	95.90	98.06	98.18	87.24	92.24	95.34	98.37
Sikkim	86.06	93.15	96.69	97.79	89.16	95.03	95.96	95.81
Tamil Nadu	79.45	83.19	89.26	93.64	75.90	80.44	87.22	93.59
Telangana	66.50	81.55	81.50	86.50	52.86	60.97	75.41	89.54
Tripura	98.08	100.00	98.76	99.60	90.69	95.42	97.11	100.00
Uttar Pradesh	96.67	97.40	98.33	99.00	91.41	93.12	96.15	98.17
Uttarakhand	89.35	95.75	97.29	97.77	87.10	90.28	94.33	97.59
West Bengal	91.16	93.01	97.48	97.54	86.34	90.28	94.51	97.38
All India	**83.42**	**87.89**	**91.05**	**94.60**	**78.53**	**84.46**	**89.49**	**95.03**

(Contd) —→

TABLE C14 (Cont'd) ⟶

State	Male Respondents							
	Urban				Rural			
	No education	Primary	Secondary	Above secondary	No education	Primary	Secondary	Above secondary
Andhra Pradesh	86.75	85.03	86.33	86.21	85.82	85.82	86.43	84.88
Arunachal Pradesh	82.74	83.39	83.96	84.94	82.44	82.40	83.93	85.14
Assam	80.89	82.62	83.00	84.76	80.10	80.34	81.65	82.38
Bihar	82.84	84.11	84.69	86.21	81.47	81.30	82.06	83.28
Chhattisgarh	81.56	81.99	81.54	78.43	81.36	81.70	81.83	80.44
Goa	84.27	84.95	83.84	85.94	82.63	85.27	86.89	85.77
Gujarat	84.71	84.52	85.26	85.68	84.06	83.66	85.03	85.41
Haryana	82.91	83.59	82.52	80.54	81.53	81.41	81.01	78.72
Himachal Pradesh	82.00	79.91	82.42	85.16	80.98	81.00	81.73	83.10
Jammu & Kashmir	84.24	83.29	86.15	86.90	82.95	83.30	85.35	87.35
Jharkhand	77.95	76.90	78.92	78.39	78.80	78.42	78.94	79.24
Karnataka	84.48	83.91	83.09	81.45	83.96	83.48	82.86	81.78
Kerala	80.51	87.29	92.56	95.45	83.50	87.04	92.18	94.99
Madhya Pradesh	82.89	83.35	84.09	83.14	82.83	82.47	82.41	81.02
Maharashtra	88.81	90.27	90.83	92.11	88.64	88.68	90.39	90.48
Manipur	84.86	86.75	89.89	89.88	85.38	85.91	88.75	89.89
Meghalaya	86.72	82.39	85.14	84.71	83.13	82.75	82.59	81.44
Mizoram	83.10	89.74	94.12	96.18	84.39	87.64	93.17	95.14
Nagaland	81.99	82.74	86.01	89.32	83.34	84.32	85.19	88.66
Odisha	85.05	86.28	88.02	89.10	83.64	85.55	87.73	89.71
Punjab	81.19	80.37	80.75	80.30	81.90	81.41	81.11	79.39
Rajasthan	81.32	81.02	82.33	81.51	81.02	81.01	81.48	80.64
Sikkim	89.63	91.26	90.78	91.64	88.52	89.79	90.81	88.76
Tamil Nadu	87.57	86.98	87.86	87.37	87.11	86.78	87.89	87.77
Telangana	86.20	86.86	87.96	87.28	86.59	86.17	86.84	85.86
Tripura	82.05	80.18	82.38	84.30	79.26	79.95	81.92	79.93
Uttar Pradesh	80.33	80.14	80.17	78.45	79.97	79.73	79.62	77.88
Uttarakhand	82.21	82.35	83.24	83.37	80.70	81.13	82.45	82.66
West Bengal	78.43	79.95	81.42	81.52	78.25	78.38	79.43	80.21
All India	**83.26**	**84.04**	**85.34**	**85.11**	**82.11**	**82.32**	**83.63**	**83.77**

Note: For definitions of key terms, see the notes at the end of the tables.

TABLE C15 Knowledge about Cure for Tuberculosis across Highest Educational Level Attained: National Family Health Survey-4 (2014–15)

Female Respondents

State	Urban				Rural			
	No education	Primary	Secondary	Above secondary	No education	Primary	Secondary	Above secondary
Andhra Pradesh	56.78	66.68	78.55	90.24	55.84	65.84	75.91	89.00
Arunachal Pradesh	68.73	80.23	82.64	90.67	50.78	65.44	76.44	88.10
Assam	65.20	77.91	82.53	88.25	56.36	63.58	75.83	89.49
Bihar	76.85	84.71	88.79	91.69	64.54	73.88	79.33	87.14
Chhattisgarh	84.27	88.47	93.69	96.89	65.19	77.64	87.08	95.72
Goa	71.85	81.92	93.24	94.83	71.93	75.11	90.25	96.76
Gujarat	62.68	72.52	79.81	91.87	45.31	56.04	67.28	84.78
Haryana	77.08	81.42	90.09	95.03	77.02	82.29	89.59	93.09
Himachal Pradesh	78.66	94.93	88.93	96.44	68.80	76.53	87.03	93.62
Jammu & Kashmir	79.71	79.53	88.73	92.34	71.25	76.66	82.85	91.14
Jharkhand	83.00	88.03	93.24	95.35	70.43	79.07	83.96	91.19
Karnataka	42.98	53.25	60.28	73.83	32.38	39.54	54.62	69.78
Kerala	48.79	64.69	78.52	88.46	30.61	57.79	78.48	89.01
Madhya Pradesh	79.66	82.71	89.11	94.46	64.43	73.62	80.51	91.06
Maharashtra	62.16	72.33	82.91	89.91	52.38	60.18	72.71	84.47
Manipur	74.35	81.94	85.63	93.28	67.76	70.16	82.42	93.41
Meghalaya	74.81	86.07	87.48	93.25	60.32	72.82	82.94	91.85
Mizoram	78.61	92.19	95.95	97.59	34.71	78.54	92.39	99.04
Nagaland	63.62	70.70	77.58	91.23	42.99	53.14	66.05	84.19
Odisha	82.07	88.78	92.37	94.01	72.42	80.77	87.14	93.03
Punjab	84.91	91.01	94.66	97.56	89.42	91.09	94.25	97.77
Rajasthan	84.83	89.20	94.22	96.65	76.70	83.60	88.98	94.93
Sikkim	79.83	91.46	94.51	94.51	80.99	90.92	93.88	94.56
Tamil Nadu	51.14	57.43	69.08	80.81	44.72	48.90	64.02	77.68
Telangana	54.61	65.38	70.96	81.28	36.97	44.11	60.67	77.61
Tripura	93.20	94.85	95.31	95.72	65.63	79.37	87.06	99.10
Uttar Pradesh	88.84	91.26	94.16	97.20	81.31	83.55	88.02	93.73
Uttarakhand	79.38	89.34	92.98	95.65	77.32	80.48	87.85	93.86
West Bengal	83.51	88.01	93.50	96.13	76.30	81.69	86.58	94.36
All India	**72.61**	**77.67**	**83.07**	**90.10**	**65.99**	**72.26**	**79.32**	**88.76**

(Contd) →

TABLE C15 (Cont'd) →

State	Male Respondents							
	Urban				Rural			
	No education	Primary	Secondary	Above secondary	No education	Primary	Secondary	Above secondary
Andhra Pradesh	59.90	84.86	83.47	89.76	61.28	73.61	81.34	87.19
Arunachal Pradesh	78.23	88.40	88.82	92.09	72.45	85.92	85.45	87.03
Assam	87.10	92.63	93.24	95.45	89.59	92.62	91.16	93.29
Bihar	85.76	86.40	91.77	92.16	79.27	85.54	85.66	90.20
Chhattisgarh	91.35	95.48	98.84	98.03	91.27	94.57	96.85	97.64
Goa	91.01	97.73	93.30	100.00	72.27	73.26	89.31	96.58
Gujarat	78.03	83.56	90.61	96.60	62.64	75.57	84.40	94.14
Haryana	75.79	89.23	88.45	96.70	91.25	87.75	95.93	95.94
Himachal Pradesh	78.14	78.64	94.05	98.56	79.67	85.77	95.28	98.57
Jammu & Kashmir	77.10	77.24	84.30	88.15	77.30	84.65	87.14	87.96
Jharkhand	89.68	92.14	92.00	94.14	80.07	87.09	89.60	95.57
Karnataka	36.89	63.39	67.26	78.95	51.36	54.91	64.84	71.47
Kerala	72.81	82.74	88.68	90.66	54.00	86.53	87.40	90.55
Madhya Pradesh	81.98	91.82	92.61	96.70	76.45	84.23	87.72	93.68
Maharashtra	77.24	89.34	92.84	96.96	69.28	81.17	88.98	91.09
Manipur	82.65	89.12	92.30	95.15	65.97	78.11	88.39	86.95
Meghalaya	57.83	82.59	90.99	96.14	83.85	90.75	92.11	97.10
Mizoram	37.80	95.97	96.14	100.00	72.09	86.71	92.07	97.44
Nagaland	74.17	88.52	84.58	93.97	82.02	85.95	87.02	98.71
Odisha	81.25	76.66	88.32	93.60	80.57	88.41	92.31	94.67
Punjab	95.71	98.07	97.18	98.62	93.42	95.52	96.84	98.35
Rajasthan	93.35	95.50	95.16	97.66	82.62	87.66	91.76	96.99
Sikkim	85.07	84.17	94.37	92.76	79.70	95.55	94.88	99.20
Tamil Nadu	81.49	80.94	86.12	90.93	70.48	81.09	82.42	83.27
Telangana	71.12	64.78	76.50	77.65	56.17	66.65	75.05	88.54
Tripura	100.00	100.00	98.30	100.00	79.27	88.60	94.54	97.59
Uttar Pradesh	92.48	93.50	94.85	96.98	86.45	90.03	91.89	93.84
Uttarakhand	94.37	97.10	98.74	96.71	94.66	93.51	96.34	98.19
West Bengal	92.68	91.13	97.47	99.69	93.14	95.21	96.96	96.77
All India	**81.21**	**86.07**	**89.37**	**93.44**	**77.69**	**84.57**	**88.28**	**91.25**

Note: For definitions of key terms, see the notes at the end of the tables.

TABLE C16 Willingness to Disclose Tuberculosis across Highest Educational Level Attained: National Family Health Survey-4 (2014–15)

State	Female Respondents							
	Urban				Rural			
	No education	Primary	Secondary	Above secondary	No education	Primary	Secondary	Above secondary
Andhra Pradesh	49.18	54.52	63.58	66.41	46.95	51.75	58.95	71.21
Arunachal Pradesh	69.12	81.07	78.36	80.97	62.92	75.94	75.99	80.88
Assam	71.83	79.15	83.69	86.50	73.88	78.65	85.56	90.19
Bihar	78.27	84.22	88.90	90.47	64.14	70.81	75.65	78.41
Chhattisgarh	85.39	87.84	88.08	88.07	71.59	81.01	86.19	90.82
Goa	71.84	72.52	77.02	85.96	64.19	70.37	77.20	82.68
Gujarat	62.40	70.60	75.55	83.77	48.01	56.25	66.50	78.44
Haryana	62.86	71.14	75.36	81.00	63.95	71.07	77.87	82.28
Himachal Pradesh	80.55	86.23	86.98	90.40	73.13	79.52	87.24	90.90
Jammu & Kashmir	68.33	72.44	79.68	84.05	61.72	70.24	74.37	82.56
Jharkhand	84.79	87.86	89.72	90.53	72.44	78.78	82.05	85.69
Karnataka	32.74	33.84	41.01	50.78	31.05	36.38	45.05	50.94
Kerala	85.79	79.95	75.76	79.71	53.18	62.85	78.35	81.51
Madhya Pradesh	76.23	80.87	83.80	87.28	66.73	74.20	79.61	84.15
Maharashtra	55.44	65.16	70.20	75.99	51.46	59.06	67.55	75.39
Manipur	88.29	90.72	92.08	94.10	84.83	83.35	90.93	93.88
Meghalaya	63.38	82.85	73.52	78.32	63.00	72.10	76.11	82.88
Mizoram	78.35	93.06	94.65	95.49	40.15	81.87	92.30	98.25
Nagaland	73.22	75.77	79.34	87.80	57.57	62.77	71.02	84.88
Odisha	83.01	88.59	88.98	88.48	76.89	81.03	84.74	86.59
Punjab	86.75	89.90	93.59	94.98	87.43	91.18	93.02	96.23
Rajasthan	84.64	88.44	91.13	92.02	79.94	85.02	89.08	92.22
Sikkim	74.87	83.53	86.14	84.14	75.59	80.13	84.80	87.91
Tamil Nadu	44.50	47.24	50.87	53.94	42.50	47.64	48.76	50.90
Telangana	38.30	42.86	48.75	59.64	26.64	30.55	38.05	46.52
Tripura	92.48	97.65	96.58	96.83	81.96	90.33	92.75	97.85
Uttar Pradesh	85.57	85.79	87.21	89.58	77.62	78.71	82.63	85.53
Uttarakhand	82.12	88.52	88.58	89.39	75.68	79.63	84.04	86.91
West Bengal	84.45	89.49	95.47	94.91	82.07	87.52	91.78	94.84
All India	**68.24**	**71.88**	**73.88**	**77.51**	**65.72**	**71.43**	**75.32**	**78.60**

(Contd) →

TABLE C16 (Cont'd) →

State	Male Respondents							
	Urban				Rural			
	No education	Primary	Secondary	Above secondary	No education	Primary	Secondary	Above secondary
Andhra Pradesh	25.45	61.62	48.76	50.89	34.60	44.45	43.19	52.07
Arunachal Pradesh	43.77	75.18	68.19	81.43	48.12	55.73	56.14	62.34
Assam	76.71	86.09	84.59	87.42	80.91	82.15	83.95	88.67
Bihar	77.94	73.62	83.36	89.23	69.51	75.93	75.53	79.60
Chhattisgarh	78.02	89.84	92.23	94.02	79.62	84.58	87.57	90.17
Goa	77.27	97.73	83.90	85.60	28.81	58.90	82.56	92.79
Gujarat	63.23	64.50	74.83	85.13	47.74	59.85	68.24	84.97
Haryana	64.39	68.13	70.08	80.45	69.48	64.76	76.61	85.80
Himachal Pradesh	78.14	73.55	83.85	90.72	73.11	78.10	84.51	89.04
Jammu & Kashmir	58.98	64.75	75.14	78.10	61.79	67.37	73.67	81.03
Jharkhand	76.38	75.30	74.51	80.54	62.32	73.21	74.39	82.29
Karnataka	17.35	32.69	36.63	49.54	27.89	27.19	34.29	46.80
Kerala	51.04	69.90	68.94	75.51	54.00	69.88	75.62	81.00
Madhya Pradesh	61.38	71.12	72.77	82.04	54.88	65.20	67.05	77.24
Maharashtra	62.46	68.68	80.23	90.06	46.32	67.63	67.64	76.51
Manipur	82.65	81.19	85.79	91.21	53.90	67.23	82.25	83.08
Meghalaya	44.98	70.77	78.13	79.01	69.78	80.44	82.06	90.47
Mizoram	37.80	95.09	89.95	87.91	61.66	83.79	85.04	95.24
Nagaland	70.74	82.35	75.52	89.08	75.11	75.96	75.95	91.55
Odisha	66.19	65.86	80.94	85.82	69.20	79.18	79.54	81.14
Punjab	89.11	94.69	91.97	95.33	84.25	88.37	88.02	90.45
Rajasthan	84.81	76.45	85.68	90.87	73.19	79.14	81.83	87.27
Sikkim	61.70	79.46	85.45	77.47	69.11	84.23	85.57	89.53
Tamil Nadu	30.56	21.97	30.89	37.94	26.89	27.02	29.11	28.20
Telangana	23.98	19.08	26.88	24.26	26.29	27.04	30.14	37.34
Tripura	92.68	96.17	97.19	96.06	68.55	83.73	90.43	97.59
Uttar Pradesh	80.12	82.93	84.90	88.89	72.98	78.15	79.78	86.28
Uttarakhand	83.00	89.29	91.68	92.86	77.29	79.17	87.23	90.78
West Bengal	86.48	88.85	93.79	98.17	91.03	90.74	94.55	94.72
All India	**62.03**	**65.56**	**68.71**	**74.34**	**61.37**	**68.35**	**70.52**	**74.00**

Note: For definitions of key terms, see the notes at the end of the tables.

TABLE C17 HIV/AIDS: National Family Health Survey-4 (2014–15)

Female Respondents

State	Urban				Rural			
	Know	Attitude	Cure	Disclose	Know	Attitude	Cure	Disclose
Andhra Pradesh	16.61	11.80	8.06	6.49	15.59	10.69	7.39	6.03
Arunachal Pradesh	15.05	10.27	3.97	8.94	12.75	7.15	2.93	7.05
Assam	16.97	12.15	4.11	12.54	11.83	7.31	2.34	8.52
Bihar	12.18	10.00	4.53	8.43	6.74	4.82	2.52	4.44
Chhattisgarh	15.27	12.60	4.91	8.98	12.21	8.92	3.47	7.84
Goa	48.68	43.89	25.65	29.15	45.66	39.94	25.04	26.47
Gujarat	19.93	14.17	8.38	11.11	12.60	8.25	4.87	7.06
Haryana	14.04	11.67	6.88	8.45	12.42	10.11	4.73	6.78
Himachal Pradesh	36.54	31.06	13.87	23.89	25.37	19.71	8.39	19.13
Jammu & Kashmir	31.17	21.99	11.49	18.72	26.47	15.71	9.25	16.77
Jharkhand	13.77	11.68	4.99	9.09	8.42	6.02	2.61	6.06
Karnataka	15.98	12.05	8.07	5.93	12.28	8.27	4.76	6.02
Kerala	22.15	18.16	8.44	10.31	20.43	16.79	7.33	8.93
Madhya Pradesh	13.17	10.47	5.43	7.80	8.02	5.39	2.78	5.20
Maharashtra	14.64	12.16	7.62	7.68	12.78	9.59	5.47	6.97
Manipur	14.32	12.27	10.67	12.30	15.52	12.03	9.77	13.08
Meghalaya	15.19	9.36	5.01	8.96	11.35	4.98	2.63	6.45
Mizoram	16.44	14.47	10.25	9.07	14.38	12.26	6.19	8.16
Nagaland	15.43	9.19	5.61	8.90	12.24	7.06	4.23	6.61
Odisha	18.16	15.08	9.30	12.57	13.80	10.95	6.32	9.33
Punjab	14.80	12.86	6.88	10.00	15.38	12.91	6.06	11.07
Rajasthan	13.50	11.18	4.15	7.77	9.28	6.89	2.77	5.54
Sikkim	20.15	16.31	7.57	14.43	13.55	10.81	5.14	8.76
Tamil Nadu	19.81	13.72	7.10	6.70	20.24	14.06	6.39	7.34
Telangana	15.87	11.64	7.16	5.85	14.57	8.83	5.66	5.39
Tripura	18.75	14.39	8.64	15.28	15.81	9.31	5.35	12.89
Uttar Pradesh	12.44	9.37	3.72	7.67	8.53	5.78	2.49	5.49
Uttarakhand	13.74	11.82	5.32	7.84	11.93	9.46	4.35	7.12
West Bengal	13.33	9.64	7.10	10.01	11.22	7.43	5.22	8.63
All India	**15.75**	**12.11**	**6.59**	**8.28**	**11.69**	**8.25**	**4.28**	**6.80**

(Cont'd) —→

TABLE C17 (*Cont'd*) →

State	Male Respondents							
	Urban				Rural			
	Know	Attitude	Cure	Disclose	Know	Attitude	Cure	Disclose
Andhra Pradesh	97.85	78.45	56.63	25.20	95.26	68.51	43.70	32.36
Arunachal Pradesh	96.05	72.46	26.46	62.08	80.85	53.13	18.37	47.91
Assam	94.75	74.73	37.86	64.81	87.96	57.59	25.97	62.65
Bihar	89.25	70.01	39.97	65.36	77.60	54.58	27.80	56.90
Chhattisgarh	97.16	79.66	29.51	74.23	89.87	64.04	21.57	67.69
Goa	98.83	89.70	35.07	62.94	92.70	77.11	32.35	61.20
Gujarat	85.60	66.13	22.12	55.45	66.70	45.73	19.13	39.74
Haryana	97.42	75.26	35.22	58.04	95.38	74.48	33.12	52.28
Himachal Pradesh	97.18	80.23	36.61	45.79	96.90	82.21	33.14	72.95
Jammu & Kashmir	98.79	74.33	32.13	67.49	95.92	63.71	33.72	61.65
Jharkhand	93.03	73.99	36.93	62.16	76.74	51.86	25.50	52.64
Karnataka	93.91	77.63	42.91	23.32	86.63	69.65	29.23	24.27
Kerala	98.64	81.87	31.53	38.74	98.28	80.62	26.74	46.79
Madhya Pradesh	88.58	70.96	24.66	54.03	72.29	53.72	20.66	44.16
Maharashtra	95.59	82.07	41.15	61.17	91.28	71.27	35.35	44.55
Manipur	99.71	91.11	77.86	89.92	99.59	86.31	67.41	90.37
Meghalaya	88.45	47.84	29.63	56.49	79.54	28.94	13.88	53.73
Mizoram	99.22	85.16	57.25	47.64	95.63	78.81	44.72	58.34
Nagaland	96.67	70.67	34.33	68.48	89.75	57.30	30.98	66.64
Odisha	96.96	82.59	40.18	69.59	92.88	73.13	36.63	66.25
Punjab	98.60	89.52	39.75	81.01	98.52	83.80	25.67	78.67
Rajasthan	94.60	76.97	39.77	71.96	81.43	63.59	31.00	62.63
Sikkim	96.23	80.80	23.70	78.27	92.13	73.08	25.03	76.26
Tamil Nadu	96.91	69.83	38.28	21.87	94.27	66.03	29.80	22.93
Telangana	95.64	68.91	57.72	23.84	94.68	58.39	46.03	29.26
Tripura	97.51	81.46	29.33	71.96	84.45	59.89	22.81	56.39
Uttar Pradesh	89.34	64.27	21.59	68.61	80.25	53.85	17.97	60.79
Uttarakhand	96.48	82.50	38.76	70.74	93.29	74.20	31.34	70.21
West Bengal	92.78	68.59	32.50	68.82	88.92	57.62	24.94	70.97
All India	**93.66**	**73.95**	**35.68**	**51.66**	**85.17**	**61.47**	**27.49**	**51.65**

Note: For definitions of key terms, see the notes at the end of the tables.

TABLE C18 Knowledge about HIV/AIDS across Quintiles of Frequency of Reading Newspaper, Listening Radio, and Watching Television: National Family Health Survey-4 (2014–15)

State	Female Respondents							
	Urban				Rural			
	1	2	3	4	1	2	3	4
Andhra Pradesh	17.06	16.73	16.52	16.40	13.61	14.52	17.83	17.98
Arunachal Pradesh	16.11	15.24	15.59	11.68	10.82	14.41	16.25	14.18
Assam	13.94	16.15	18.70	19.01	10.08	13.34	15.36	14.63
Bihar	8.78	9.50	15.57	16.12	5.51	8.22	10.85	10.50
Chhattisgarh	13.07	13.42	16.31	16.65	10.03	13.63	13.94	11.75
Goa	49.30	51.40	47.90	47.67	37.45	45.89	49.12	44.18
Gujarat	13.42	18.04	23.27	21.80	6.28	12.64	19.62	22.99
Haryana	12.59	13.81	15.12	13.79	8.44	12.91	14.62	12.16
Himachal Pradesh	34.58	30.14	40.81	36.55	19.08	25.49	25.73	29.80
Jammu & Kashmir	27.83	28.98	31.88	32.73	23.82	27.60	27.82	28.64
Jharkhand	9.87	12.40	14.50	17.37	6.95	10.48	14.51	13.63
Karnataka	15.79	13.23	18.48	16.78	9.57	10.77	14.18	16.41
Kerala	25.97	20.09	23.36	21.62	26.02	22.07	20.80	19.22
Madhya Pradesh	7.61	12.57	14.42	14.87	5.50	9.15	12.57	12.64
Maharashtra	12.87	15.10	14.11	15.35	9.87	12.95	14.94	14.92
Manipur	13.46	13.18	14.22	14.79	14.52	15.69	15.06	16.63
Meghalaya	15.88	14.63	18.80	11.80	9.14	10.74	13.48	15.19
Mizoram	18.31	11.13	18.70	14.72	9.57	14.31	16.99	13.49
Nagaland	14.98	14.73	14.28	18.61	11.37	13.54	13.41	14.10
Odisha	15.00	15.30	22.99	18.77	12.03	15.06	14.38	16.21
Punjab	13.26	15.33	14.05	15.44	17.22	15.55	14.53	15.45
Rajasthan	9.17	11.50	15.04	15.78	6.51	9.41	14.59	15.09
Sikkim	19.75	21.10	19.12	21.43	15.35	12.13	14.70	12.04
Tamil Nadu	19.22	21.10	19.71	18.73	17.69	19.82	20.77	21.38
Telangana	10.93	18.37	16.16	14.43	11.82	15.21	15.88	13.79
Tripura	9.63	19.29	18.57	24.37	14.05	15.44	20.97	18.12
Uttar Pradesh	8.84	12.01	13.57	14.90	6.70	10.30	12.30	12.65
Uttarakhand	8.83	12.57	15.15	15.18	8.43	11.50	14.93	14.02
West Bengal	8.18	12.34	14.10	17.91	8.51	12.20	15.35	13.82
All India	**11.45**	**15.25**	**16.65**	**17.11**	**7.83**	**13.18**	**15.54**	**16.42**

(Contd) →

TABLE C18 *(Cont'd)* →

State	Male Respondents							
	Urban				Rural			
	1	2	3	4	1	2	3	4
Andhra Pradesh	92.83	99.44	99.44	97.87	89.26	98.39	100.00	98.85
Arunachal Pradesh	93.21	97.17	100.00	99.95	78.35	90.67	82.99	78.32
Assam	90.44	94.66	98.98	98.61	83.86	92.90	96.47	97.47
Bihar	76.04	90.71	97.07	97.83	70.02	85.71	92.47	92.56
Chhattisgarh	91.66	98.21	98.23	99.04	83.17	95.26	94.94	98.03
Goa	92.76	98.11	100.00	100.00	74.01	95.91	95.80	93.09
Gujarat	71.23	87.39	95.34	88.85	47.92	84.59	87.31	81.56
Haryana	91.42	97.72	99.56	100.00	89.63	97.44	98.29	97.96
Himachal Pradesh	90.26	97.80	100.00	100.00	90.95	97.78	99.22	99.11
Jammu & Kashmir	96.96	99.56	99.68	98.71	91.28	97.49	98.44	99.35
Jharkhand	81.56	97.14	98.00	97.63	69.71	90.16	91.37	93.62
Karnataka	87.80	94.19	94.66	97.08	76.20	87.37	93.89	93.64
Kerala	94.85	98.13	99.32	98.88	94.98	97.73	98.76	99.55
Madhya Pradesh	72.52	89.96	95.90	94.82	60.53	84.03	90.31	90.75
Maharashtra	91.30	95.30	98.87	95.30	84.37	94.08	94.05	95.36
Manipur	98.82	99.18	100.00	100.00	97.76	100.00	100.00	100.00
Meghalaya	60.41	94.78	95.61	90.65	68.37	86.39	95.66	96.77
Mizoram	93.24	99.91	100.00	100.00	86.44	98.61	100.00	100.00
Nagaland	93.32	97.31	100.00	100.00	85.79	95.16	99.50	97.07
Odisha	90.98	98.07	99.42	98.34	88.82	96.48	99.30	98.59
Punjab	97.15	98.75	99.86	97.17	97.35	99.28	99.31	97.76
Rajasthan	83.60	97.73	96.45	97.63	69.52	91.61	96.13	93.96
Sikkim	89.73	97.85	100.00	100.00	87.47	96.58	97.58	97.33
Tamil Nadu	92.23	95.75	98.40	97.61	88.82	93.01	97.30	96.26
Telangana	90.32	97.35	98.02	94.10	88.10	98.33	98.64	100.00
Tripura	88.44	100.00	100.00	100.00	73.76	96.62	100.00	100.00
Uttar Pradesh	78.30	90.30	96.84	97.14	71.37	89.02	93.87	96.32
Uttarakhand	88.84	96.70	98.88	98.92	83.93	96.03	97.53	96.49
West Bengal	86.05	90.22	100.00	99.80	84.35	92.94	97.32	95.73
All India	**84.32**	**94.24**	**97.86**	**96.85**	**74.98**	**91.86**	**95.45**	**95.39**

Note: For definitions of key terms, see the notes at the end of the tables.

TABLE C19   Knowledge about HIV/AIDS across Educational Attainments: National Family Health Survey-4 (2014–15)

State	Female Respondents							
	Urban				Rural			
	No education	Primary	Secondary	Above secondary	No education	Primary	Secondary	Above secondary
Andhra Pradesh	16.32	18.37	16.71	15.66	14.22	14.74	16.44	20.11
Arunachal Pradesh	12.79	10.17	16.42	15.20	9.96	12.34	14.47	18.40
Assam	13.51	12.16	17.62	18.97	8.95	9.87	13.29	15.91
Bihar	8.08	9.13	12.77	19.16	4.45	5.93	9.56	13.97
Chhattisgarh	12.31	12.96	15.85	17.30	10.05	11.55	13.77	14.05
Goa	43.19	48.23	48.92	50.46	35.29	40.86	46.19	49.95
Gujarat	11.56	11.95	20.80	27.19	5.00	8.97	16.70	25.30
Haryana	10.12	11.41	14.23	17.80	8.88	12.55	13.90	13.65
Himachal Pradesh	45.63	31.11	32.14	42.01	16.59	22.90	26.16	29.91
Jammu & Kashmir	29.97	31.52	31.68	31.07	23.71	27.19	27.63	29.33
Jharkhand	9.05	8.72	14.88	17.54	5.96	7.05	11.09	13.58
Karnataka	10.67	13.85	17.15	17.32	8.84	11.47	14.21	15.22
Kerala	3.60	25.80	21.55	23.23	15.88	22.75	20.52	20.06
Madhya Pradesh	9.25	11.84	14.26	14.87	5.32	7.69	10.40	14.86
Maharashtra	13.78	15.16	13.90	16.64	8.16	11.13	14.13	16.91
Manipur	9.26	19.01	14.42	14.38	14.86	16.56	15.55	14.96
Meghalaya	10.52	15.59	15.57	15.23	8.02	9.82	12.45	19.08
Mizoram	25.64	17.00	16.64	14.59	6.11	14.60	16.10	14.43
Nagaland	11.93	14.69	15.42	17.10	9.42	9.95	13.54	14.91
Odisha	10.74	15.22	21.00	18.16	12.07	13.33	14.67	17.24
Punjab	15.08	12.69	14.27	16.09	13.71	15.47	15.98	15.20
Rajasthan	9.08	11.93	15.03	15.81	5.97	9.62	12.38	16.65
Sikkim	13.55	21.03	20.82	21.22	11.12	14.67	13.34	16.19
Tamil Nadu	18.17	19.67	20.41	19.32	16.68	18.93	20.84	24.81
Telangana	15.14	13.05	16.77	15.44	13.41	13.23	15.67	17.81
Tripura	14.08	16.46	18.78	22.13	10.20	14.64	17.39	20.88
Uttar Pradesh	8.17	10.50	13.87	14.99	5.76	7.50	10.10	15.07
Uttarakhand	7.85	10.64	15.10	16.29	7.51	10.08	13.31	16.47
West Bengal	9.28	12.48	13.91	15.91	6.92	10.23	13.30	17.42
All India	**11.67**	**13.87**	**16.42**	**17.83**	**7.72**	**10.57**	**13.97**	**17.90**

(Cont'd) →

TABLE C19 (*Cont'd*) →

State	Male Respondents							
	Urban				Rural			
	No education	Primary	Secondary	Above secondary	No education	Primary	Secondary	Above secondary
Andhra Pradesh	88.22	92.64	99.40	99.43	85.73	96.66	98.44	100.00
Arunachal Pradesh	81.96	92.07	97.02	99.97	60.21	81.16	86.48	96.34
Assam	93.92	87.23	94.71	99.00	76.25	85.08	90.84	99.68
Bihar	66.67	83.09	91.07	98.65	59.72	71.78	83.61	97.28
Chhattisgarh	84.16	94.00	98.41	97.98	74.94	82.76	94.91	99.67
Goa	82.99	100.00	99.62	100.00	80.81	67.92	93.85	100.00
Gujarat	52.55	70.49	86.02	97.85	22.58	46.44	74.79	97.06
Haryana	90.69	91.16	97.95	100.00	81.92	91.86	96.85	99.30
Himachal Pradesh	100.00	81.73	97.60	100.00	82.99	89.99	97.62	99.30
Jammu & Kashmir	99.36	100.00	98.10	100.00	87.70	92.35	97.12	99.87
Jharkhand	75.38	84.03	94.48	99.84	55.30	70.28	83.94	97.94
Karnataka	78.94	90.11	94.83	97.67	72.52	76.65	90.86	98.09
Kerala	100.00	98.03	98.15	99.88	73.28	94.14	98.54	99.43
Madhya Pradesh	60.82	80.21	90.05	98.81	47.23	65.23	79.76	97.73
Maharashtra	84.31	90.24	95.68	99.84	73.78	82.86	93.29	97.80
Manipur	100.00	93.77	100.00	100.00	96.73	99.69	99.66	100.00
Meghalaya	61.27	68.78	90.61	100.00	59.35	74.24	88.25	100.00
Mizoram	100.00	87.95	100.00	100.00	61.91	93.12	98.87	100.00
Nagaland	75.65	90.99	97.84	100.00	77.59	78.93	94.85	100.00
Odisha	77.42	94.18	97.92	99.38	79.19	90.53	96.40	100.00
Punjab	93.13	98.63	98.75	100.00	94.14	97.28	99.51	98.89
Rajasthan	80.70	87.56	95.18	99.28	54.91	70.05	87.77	99.21
Sikkim	73.06	88.75	99.38	100.00	62.40	84.33	98.59	100.00
Tamil Nadu	90.82	91.42	97.53	98.81	87.29	91.50	95.05	98.92
Telangana	83.56	93.23	97.27	97.69	84.55	91.22	99.42	100.00
Tripura	93.04	96.04	97.04	100.00	41.29	69.59	91.46	100.00
Uttar Pradesh	76.77	82.07	90.36	98.59	59.38	69.61	84.74	98.30
Uttarakhand	83.97	92.86	97.49	99.11	77.78	80.05	96.28	99.88
West Bengal	74.92	90.42	94.40	100.00	76.37	85.38	93.36	99.07
All India	**78.73**	**87.46**	**94.43**	**99.00**	**66.39**	**77.42**	**89.51**	**98.64**

Note: For definitions of key terms, see the notes at the end of the tables.

TABLE C20 Knowledge about Cure for HIV/AIDS across Educational Attainments: National Family Health Survey-4 (2014–15)

State	Female Respondents							
	Urban				Rural			
	No education	Primary	Secondary	Above secondary	No education	Primary	Secondary	Above secondary
Andhra Pradesh	4.73	8.87	8.44	10.48	4.90	6.35	9.17	13.32
Arunachal Pradesh	1.89	2.16	4.33	5.78	1.61	1.80	3.80	7.61
Assam	2.23	1.63	4.25	5.86	1.34	1.33	2.69	6.31
Bihar	2.04	2.26	4.68	9.63	1.55	1.81	3.74	6.37
Chhattisgarh	3.25	2.68	4.77	7.77	2.18	3.27	4.15	6.70
Goa	11.94	13.81	26.63	32.54	15.05	18.68	24.52	33.51
Gujarat	2.96	4.50	8.44	13.76	1.33	2.86	6.61	12.79
Haryana	3.42	3.50	6.69	11.39	2.53	4.44	5.35	7.37
Himachal Pradesh	9.98	8.47	10.78	19.65	2.90	5.56	8.37	14.30
Jammu & Kashmir	8.45	9.36	11.45	14.88	6.68	9.02	9.98	14.63
Jharkhand	2.07	2.17	5.25	8.39	1.54	1.90	3.73	5.75
Karnataka	3.57	6.74	8.26	10.97	2.94	3.77	5.71	7.88
Kerala	0.65	3.91	6.59	12.69	3.22	4.88	6.48	9.97
Madhya Pradesh	3.03	3.56	5.80	7.89	1.71	2.43	3.68	6.95
Maharashtra	4.35	6.91	7.60	9.45	2.93	4.42	6.12	8.73
Manipur	5.95	11.65	10.32	12.58	6.72	8.06	10.11	13.03
Meghalaya	4.85	4.72	4.64	5.94	1.35	1.13	3.32	7.13
Mizoram	3.82	7.44	10.34	11.53	0.76	4.34	7.63	12.37
Nagaland	3.56	2.91	5.48	7.80	2.49	2.66	4.83	8.10
Odisha	3.75	7.46	10.68	11.26	4.62	5.76	7.16	10.20
Punjab	5.22	4.79	6.65	8.49	4.40	5.34	6.51	7.46
Rajasthan	2.22	3.24	4.13	6.49	1.41	2.63	4.01	6.49
Sikkim	5.42	6.42	7.79	8.72	3.04	3.99	5.03	11.37
Tamil Nadu	3.78	4.32	7.31	9.01	3.91	4.15	6.83	10.76
Telangana	4.19	4.97	8.20	7.95	3.76	3.89	7.43	10.67
Tripura	5.02	5.82	8.41	12.95	2.32	4.70	6.28	6.68
Uttar Pradesh	1.83	2.84	3.79	5.76	1.45	1.81	3.06	5.42
Uttarakhand	1.56	3.34	5.40	8.11	2.25	3.51	4.62	7.89
West Bengal	3.62	5.46	7.60	10.12	3.10	4.52	6.28	8.88
All India	**3.20**	**4.77**	**6.81**	**9.18**	**2.31**	**3.43**	**5.34**	**8.41**

(*Cont'd*) →

TABLE C20 (*Cont'd*) →

State	Male Respondents							
	Urban				Rural			
	No education	Primary	Secondary	Above secondary	No education	Primary	Secondary	Above secondary
Andhra Pradesh	38.53	56.20	56.41	62.55	26.35	40.34	48.14	63.06
Arunachal Pradesh	16.87	17.31	24.43	37.75	8.68	19.19	19.42	33.97
Assam	20.01	23.79	36.43	53.14	18.80	19.37	28.09	41.27
Bihar	17.91	26.80	37.00	61.16	19.80	25.07	29.31	43.02
Chhattisgarh	24.72	18.94	24.87	45.85	11.74	15.03	23.42	43.70
Goa	19.79	20.07	31.20	54.82	5.77	11.35	30.26	58.22
Gujarat	11.69	16.08	18.41	36.51	6.25	11.29	20.65	36.19
Haryana	18.74	21.11	31.19	52.46	20.85	23.71	33.33	45.59
Himachal Pradesh	0.00	4.38	31.84	53.62	12.18	18.62	30.35	51.69
Jammu & Kashmir	29.45	36.05	31.62	33.74	25.84	36.64	32.48	46.46
Jharkhand	25.89	31.09	34.08	49.59	14.83	20.63	29.68	34.88
Karnataka	28.08	49.05	42.18	46.70	19.30	23.46	29.31	49.06
Kerala	48.34	27.97	27.33	41.63	4.96	12.42	23.40	41.30
Madhya Pradesh	11.25	14.38	23.35	38.14	11.66	15.14	22.53	42.18
Maharashtra	33.64	33.66	38.79	50.73	20.83	27.58	34.41	53.08
Manipur	51.80	68.57	76.35	84.31	45.51	48.09	67.46	83.69
Meghalaya	8.15	14.66	23.95	61.62	4.38	10.11	16.29	37.56
Mizoram	34.55	28.89	57.56	66.59	17.81	39.57	46.36	67.64
Nagaland	18.22	28.49	32.63	43.93	22.81	23.77	33.06	51.39
Odisha	21.95	38.37	37.46	51.34	25.52	31.28	38.53	54.77
Punjab	29.46	27.66	38.06	50.06	19.10	20.66	25.17	41.25
Rajasthan	28.39	22.29	35.21	55.04	17.88	23.11	32.75	47.50
Sikkim	15.90	11.07	25.01	31.06	18.58	19.46	25.19	43.30
Tamil Nadu	25.23	29.19	35.27	49.50	19.86	20.66	30.38	41.63
Telangana	27.45	47.30	56.30	74.42	28.35	33.25	52.76	67.99
Tripura	4.73	16.43	25.68	47.55	5.13	12.02	24.63	51.10
Uttar Pradesh	12.74	17.39	20.38	31.46	9.34	12.18	18.61	31.98
Uttarakhand	32.21	27.60	35.06	51.39	24.29	27.70	29.61	46.27
West Bengal	22.56	25.08	30.38	48.62	18.64	22.26	25.94	40.97
All India	**22.47**	**27.82**	**33.42**	**47.82**	**17.17**	**21.25**	**28.35**	**44.38**

Note: For definitions of key terms, see the notes at the end of the tables.

TABLE C21 Attitude towards HIV/AIDS across Educational Attainments: National Family Health Survey-4 (2014–15)

Female Respondents

State	Urban				Rural			
	No education	Primary	Secondary	Above secondary	No education	Primary	Secondary	Above secondary
Andhra Pradesh	10.06	11.94	12.16	12.84	8.24	9.67	12.45	16.39
Arunachal Pradesh	7.27	6.25	11.37	11.62	4.42	6.18	8.99	12.81
Assam	8.58	5.88	12.63	15.55	5.01	5.35	8.41	12.43
Bihar	5.45	7.13	10.69	17.35	3.03	4.02	7.02	10.76
Chhattisgarh	9.79	10.26	12.83	15.41	6.84	8.62	10.19	11.84
Goa	32.69	38.59	45.19	46.91	29.28	31.29	40.30	46.65
Gujarat	6.30	7.73	14.35	22.13	2.93	5.09	11.04	19.15
Haryana	7.15	7.97	11.88	16.30	6.31	9.63	11.64	12.47
Himachal Pradesh	27.41	20.63	26.82	39.26	9.28	14.87	20.52	27.12
Jammu & Kashmir	18.58	18.96	22.39	24.90	11.11	15.13	17.29	23.64
Jharkhand	7.10	6.97	12.69	15.43	3.85	4.59	8.32	11.90
Karnataka	5.98	9.55	13.10	14.29	5.13	6.96	9.96	12.62
Kerala	3.27	20.26	16.72	21.06	6.52	14.46	16.63	18.06
Madhya Pradesh	6.41	8.76	11.44	12.83	3.09	5.01	7.33	12.59
Maharashtra	9.36	11.79	11.40	15.47	5.55	7.44	10.77	14.54
Manipur	7.60	14.95	12.13	13.28	9.32	10.93	12.55	13.40
Meghalaya	5.73	6.54	9.23	11.50	3.24	3.48	5.72	10.40
Mizoram	19.61	13.78	14.79	12.89	3.86	11.73	14.20	13.34
Nagaland	5.24	7.49	8.82	12.55	4.11	4.93	8.17	11.45
Odisha	7.89	11.89	17.64	15.83	8.76	10.65	11.96	15.29
Punjab	11.22	8.61	12.37	15.41	9.80	12.37	13.80	14.36
Rajasthan	6.61	9.11	12.38	14.49	4.09	6.96	9.50	13.57
Sikkim	8.14	14.42	17.59	17.90	7.50	10.39	10.98	15.38
Tamil Nadu	10.02	13.03	13.76	15.35	9.83	12.70	14.62	19.90
Telangana	8.39	7.74	12.55	13.40	6.77	7.25	10.47	15.11
Tripura	9.01	10.79	14.60	18.46	4.33	6.97	10.98	18.28
Uttar Pradesh	5.46	6.78	10.41	12.48	3.44	4.71	7.00	11.92
Uttarakhand	6.53	7.49	12.81	14.96	5.42	6.98	10.69	14.51
West Bengal	6.02	8.21	9.76	13.93	3.84	6.14	9.15	15.17
All India	**7.51**	**9.68**	**12.50**	**15.43**	**4.74**	**6.94**	**10.18**	**14.88**

(Cont'd) →

TABLE C21 (Cont'd) →

Male Respondents

State	Urban				Rural			
	No education	Primary	Secondary	Above secondary	No education	Primary	Secondary	Above secondary
Andhra Pradesh	51.40	62.39	80.09	88.45	49.31	66.69	74.04	85.94
Arunachal Pradesh	47.39	65.71	71.34	86.33	32.32	45.33	58.67	82.52
Assam	59.14	62.67	74.78	84.31	41.01	50.66	62.02	77.98
Bihar	45.35	59.79	68.73	88.09	37.04	44.84	60.97	76.77
Chhattisgarh	58.03	67.32	79.93	88.44	49.61	51.91	69.21	83.66
Goa	76.49	92.46	88.88	94.73	52.69	55.65	77.15	91.72
Gujarat	36.31	48.00	65.62	81.12	14.89	29.36	50.37	76.65
Haryana	57.54	58.76	75.79	83.94	52.02	56.42	76.87	89.01
Himachal Pradesh	69.70	38.63	79.83	91.26	57.01	67.08	81.68	93.90
Jammu & Kashmir	55.59	59.85	74.56	86.47	47.00	51.60	65.09	79.30
Jharkhand	50.20	55.38	75.01	87.24	32.06	41.91	58.78	76.39
Karnataka	51.42	75.19	77.39	87.17	50.27	58.95	74.36	86.90
Kerala	66.22	73.18	80.34	87.50	39.24	73.41	79.06	88.76
Madhya Pradesh	39.65	53.94	72.61	86.88	31.04	45.74	60.16	82.57
Maharashtra	61.15	70.11	81.02	93.35	46.72	57.87	73.01	86.57
Manipur	81.89	77.37	91.59	92.87	71.90	74.19	86.93	94.54
Meghalaya	26.57	33.01	47.26	63.66	17.80	25.35	35.07	34.90
Mizoram	74.46	76.86	85.92	85.54	50.19	70.70	82.66	88.62
Nagaland	54.68	59.82	67.29	86.27	39.26	39.44	64.05	85.99
Odisha	56.00	75.01	83.21	89.09	51.40	66.23	78.47	92.08
Punjab	80.03	76.52	90.49	94.17	65.91	77.87	86.25	96.02
Rajasthan	58.62	68.52	74.96	87.58	38.95	50.37	68.35	87.08
Sikkim	48.16	70.67	83.83	90.32	42.97	57.34	81.51	88.98
Tamil Nadu	50.98	64.67	67.71	79.65	53.51	61.24	65.76	79.32
Telangana	50.92	57.10	69.71	77.33	39.79	44.66	64.51	85.41
Tripura	59.25	61.74	80.95	94.56	27.01	36.62	66.37	95.76
Uttar Pradesh	45.96	49.07	64.79	81.97	33.41	41.48	56.91	79.06
Uttarakhand	63.79	75.98	82.17	90.47	51.29	56.15	77.14	89.33
West Bengal	48.75	49.91	68.77	93.75	40.00	47.69	63.90	85.77
All India	**51.41**	**60.05**	**73.96**	**86.32**	**39.79**	**50.11**	**65.75**	**83.31**

Note: For definitions of key terms, see the notes at the end of the tables.

TABLE C22 Willingness to Disclose HIV/AIDS across Educational Attainments: National Family Health Survey-4 (2014–15)

State	Female Respondents							
	Urban				Rural			
	No education	Primary	Secondary	Above secondary	No education	Primary	Secondary	Above secondary
Andhra Pradesh	7.62	8.04	6.24	4.86	5.58	5.10	6.58	7.40
Arunachal Pradesh	8.12	5.04	9.92	8.46	5.21	7.48	8.12	9.35
Assam	7.85	7.70	13.28	14.93	6.19	7.27	9.47	13.34
Bihar	5.67	5.83	8.97	12.98	2.80	3.79	6.42	10.15
Chhattisgarh	7.11	8.41	8.96	10.68	6.44	7.52	8.72	9.99
Goa	29.96	26.00	29.49	28.97	17.59	26.82	26.98	27.97
Gujarat	7.25	5.65	11.77	14.67	3.03	5.28	9.50	11.42
Haryana	5.37	7.79	8.35	11.41	4.37	6.01	7.79	8.57
Himachal Pradesh	30.67	29.54	22.83	23.24	11.84	17.51	19.91	22.03
Jammu & Kashmir	16.90	18.94	19.17	19.36	14.50	17.69	17.56	19.76
Jharkhand	6.78	6.36	9.86	10.40	4.26	5.36	7.95	9.68
Karnataka	5.34	5.88	6.34	5.30	4.73	5.89	6.84	6.08
Kerala	0.00	11.60	9.81	11.31	6.04	11.93	9.33	7.65
Madhya Pradesh	5.73	7.27	8.31	8.77	3.44	4.88	6.80	9.55
Maharashtra	6.68	8.98	7.42	8.18	4.06	6.04	7.75	10.01
Manipur	8.25	16.24	12.44	12.18	11.61	12.63	13.24	14.29
Meghalaya	6.71	8.84	8.95	9.53	4.63	4.36	7.39	12.83
Mizoram	21.64	13.12	9.11	6.21	3.42	9.57	8.70	8.16
Nagaland	8.85	6.15	8.92	9.80	4.99	5.02	7.40	8.58
Odisha	7.66	11.95	14.40	11.94	7.88	9.01	10.07	11.84
Punjab	9.35	9.25	9.92	10.59	8.97	11.95	11.58	11.14
Rajasthan	4.84	6.80	8.73	9.37	3.60	5.99	7.36	9.31
Sikkim	10.21	16.63	14.55	15.13	7.46	9.05	8.64	10.83
Tamil Nadu	7.76	6.95	6.94	5.72	7.34	7.38	7.32	7.36
Telangana	5.13	4.98	5.79	6.77	5.39	6.92	5.16	4.52
Tripura	12.17	13.73	14.92	18.88	9.51	11.84	13.83	18.79
Uttar Pradesh	5.13	6.76	8.79	8.67	3.56	4.62	6.63	10.03
Uttarakhand	3.94	5.77	8.55	9.80	4.61	5.63	7.72	10.80
West Bengal	6.73	8.91	11.02	10.59	4.89	7.84	10.55	12.34
All India	**6.46**	**7.57**	**8.68**	**8.92**	**4.43**	**6.31**	**8.24**	**9.74**

(Contd) →

TABLE C22 (*Contd*) →

State	Male Respondents							
	Urban				Rural			
	No education	Primary	Secondary	Above secondary	No education	Primary	Secondary	Above secondary
Andhra Pradesh	21.16	28.70	24.57	26.46	30.52	30.71	33.85	32.74
Arunachal Pradesh	41.03	62.01	64.30	64.23	34.67	46.96	52.24	55.42
Assam	70.02	62.38	63.99	67.24	52.05	59.42	65.69	71.56
Bihar	47.58	67.82	65.73	72.77	45.07	50.14	61.27	71.81
Chhattisgarh	63.05	67.73	77.80	70.92	52.19	64.28	71.91	76.23
Goa	56.34	64.60	60.09	72.90	21.73	27.27	61.88	81.28
Gujarat	31.40	44.56	55.07	66.13	11.11	24.40	45.18	61.55
Haryana	63.72	49.53	58.67	58.31	49.91	52.93	51.89	55.00
Himachal Pradesh	78.75	53.24	46.19	41.54	64.55	69.82	73.06	75.06
Jammu & Kashmir	66.79	55.15	66.99	72.23	52.06	55.93	61.60	74.23
Jharkhand	55.37	49.87	64.59	63.33	37.85	48.39	56.65	73.44
Karnataka	20.34	22.55	22.42	26.81	22.66	21.46	24.37	29.27
Kerala	27.19	40.21	38.01	40.35	43.11	36.64	47.39	47.53
Madhya Pradesh	35.57	46.60	53.42	65.76	24.48	40.16	49.15	66.43
Maharashtra	47.74	56.70	62.11	63.72	31.68	45.39	45.11	47.55
Manipur	85.54	78.89	90.37	90.98	85.92	83.11	90.28	95.94
Meghalaya	45.66	45.97	59.73	55.52	39.24	47.54	58.72	83.64
Mizoram	12.41	67.66	44.66	53.78	28.26	59.52	62.19	41.98
Nagaland	54.15	57.75	70.18	70.98	56.42	58.50	70.18	80.30
Odisha	45.21	56.51	70.83	76.28	55.56	67.11	68.39	70.20
Punjab	72.87	84.42	81.36	81.87	68.35	76.37	80.17	84.28
Rajasthan	62.82	55.49	71.89	78.79	43.61	52.76	67.65	75.02
Sikkim	52.30	84.30	79.85	78.95	51.86	68.25	82.20	82.90
Tamil Nadu	27.63	18.57	21.64	21.89	27.83	23.29	22.82	19.42
Telangana	23.23	32.15	22.01	25.15	31.57	25.26	29.55	27.50
Tripura	62.82	81.13	70.21	74.05	32.42	43.35	61.23	70.68
Uttar Pradesh	59.82	63.37	68.79	76.22	44.46	53.25	64.21	74.61
Uttarakhand	67.68	65.17	72.95	68.85	50.83	60.13	72.85	77.87
West Bengal	51.09	71.32	70.84	71.00	62.67	68.41	73.36	82.14
All India	**44.84**	**50.00**	**51.49**	**54.83**	**40.37**	**47.49**	**54.44**	**58.31**

Note: For definitions of key terms, see the notes at the end of the tables.

TABLE C23 Female Sample Observations across Age Groups: National Family Health Survey-4 (2014-15)

State	Urban			Rural			Total		
	15–34	35–64	Total	15–34	35–64	Total	15–34	35–64	Total
Andhra Pradesh	5,743.61	3,884.56	9,628.17	12,489.52	8,328.68	20,818.20	18,233.13	12,213.24	30,446.37
Arunachal Pradesh	110.70	49.24	159.94	279.22	164.72	443.93	389.92	213.95	603.87
Assam	1,565.29	1,030.72	2,596.02	9,669.17	5,054.82	14,723.99	11,234.46	6,085.54	17,320.00
Bihar	5,158.48	2,414.51	7,572.98	33,893.01	14,880.08	48,773.09	39,051.49	17,294.58	56,346.07
Chhattisgarh	2,704.04	1,385.97	4,090.01	8,333.58	4,092.32	12,425.90	11,037.63	5,478.29	16,515.91
Goa	306.53	234.96	541.49	176.67	143.27	319.94	483.20	378.22	861.43
Gujarat	9,057.08	5,471.77	14,528.85	11,655.21	6,519.03	18,174.24	20,712.29	11,990.80	32,703.09
Haryana	4,143.17	2,056.78	6,199.95	6,379.15	3,017.93	9,397.08	10,522.32	5,074.71	15,597.03
Himachal Pradesh	218.06	152.10	370.16	2,058.64	1,416.25	3,474.88	2,276.70	1,568.34	3,845.04
Jammu & Kashmir	1,270.08	767.07	2,037.15	3,267.96	1,510.46	4,778.42	4,538.05	2,277.52	6,815.57
Jharkhand	3,246.71	1,594.84	4,841.55	8,768.40	4,003.09	12,771.48	12,015.11	5,597.92	17,613.03
Karnataka	9,686.73	5,527.54	15,214.26	12,479.98	7,220.58	19,700.56	22,166.71	12,748.11	34,914.82
Kerala	5,078.93	3,961.05	9,039.99	5,745.58	4,497.28	10,242.86	10,824.51	8,458.33	19,282.85
Madhya Pradesh	8,888.15	4,568.85	13,457.00	20,207.95	10,110.06	30,318.00	29,096.10	14,678.90	43,775.01
Maharashtra	20,806.01	12,295.80	33,101.81	21,812.29	11,784.07	33,596.36	42,618.30	24,079.87	66,698.17
Manipur	296.95	199.19	496.14	462.92	264.86	727.78	759.87	464.05	1,223.92
Meghalaya	252.95	116.87	369.82	833.61	387.68	1,221.28	1,086.56	504.55	1,591.11
Mizoram	223.07	129.00	352.07	154.15	78.58	232.73	377.22	207.58	584.80
Nagaland	211.18	101.25	312.43	306.20	180.16	486.35	517.37	281.41	798.79
Odisha	2,713.23	1,673.47	4,386.70	13,223.66	7,357.93	20,581.59	15,936.89	9,031.40	24,968.29
Punjab	3,705.74	2,324.49	6,030.23	5,842.37	3,351.99	9,194.36	9,548.11	5,676.48	15,224.59
Rajasthan	6,279.19	3,130.07	9,409.27	18,835.29	8,317.90	27,153.20	25,114.49	11,447.98	36,562.46
Sikkim	70.96	33.49	104.45	143.30	71.82	215.12	214.26	105.31	319.57
Tamil Nadu	15,451.70	10,822.45	26,274.15	15,447.20	9,912.82	25,360.02	30,898.90	20,735.28	51,634.17
Telangana	6,878.09	3,857.69	10,735.78	7,110.79	4,070.53	11,181.32	13,988.87	7,928.23	21,917.10
Tripura	389.77	263.47	653.24	988.31	531.81	1,520.13	1,378.08	795.29	2,173.37
Uttar Pradesh	19,074.53	8,660.16	27,734.69	54,031.34	23,416.72	77,448.06	73,105.88	32,076.88	105,182.76
Uttarakhand	1,451.27	710.50	2,161.78	2,543.45	1,228.40	3,771.86	3,994.73	1,938.91	5,933.63
West Bengal	11,150.91	6,821.51	17,972.42	24,783.42	13,014.48	37,797.90	35,934.34	19,835.99	55,770.32
All India	**154,022.72**	**88,201.84**	**242,224.56**	**302,306.64**	**155,154.80**	**457,461.44**	**456,329.35**	**243,356.64**	**699,686.00**

TABLE C24 Female Sample Observations across Number of Children: National Family Health Survey-4 (2014–15)

State	Urban				Rural				Total			
	0	1–2	>2	Total	0	1–2	>2	Total	0	1–2	>2	Total
Andhra Pradesh	2,532.66	5,259.58	1,835.92	9,628.17	4,546.55	10,759.10	5,512.55	20,818.20	7,079.21	16,018.68	7,348.48	30,446.37
Arunachal Pradesh	64.80	57.44	37.70	159.94	133.96	143.92	166.05	443.93	198.76	201.36	203.76	603.87
Assam	884.43	1,259.55	452.04	2,596.02	4,341.10	5,683.94	4,698.95	14,723.99	5,225.53	6,943.49	5,150.98	17,320.00
Bihar	2,457.61	2,214.34	2,901.04	7,572.98	13,751.24	12,224.45	22,797.40	48,773.09	16,208.85	14,438.79	25,698.44	56,346.07
Chhattisgarh	1,430.42	1,591.25	1,068.34	4,090.01	3,991.81	3,872.91	4,561.18	12,425.90	5,422.23	5,464.16	5,629.52	16,515.91
Goa	185.32	258.37	97.79	541.49	134.53	138.87	46.54	319.94	319.85	397.24	144.33	861.43
Gujarat	4,403.64	6,810.10	3,315.11	14,528.85	5,364.92	6,774.63	6,034.70	18,174.24	9,768.55	13,584.73	9,349.81	32,703.09
Haryana	1,800.19	2,772.62	1,627.14	6,199.95	2,698.48	3,824.87	2,873.73	9,397.08	4,498.67	6,597.48	4,500.87	15,597.03
Himachal Pradesh	121.74	185.87	62.55	370.16	925.07	1,689.46	860.35	3,474.88	1,046.81	1,875.33	922.90	3,845.04
Jammu & Kashmir	855.65	700.66	480.84	2,037.15	1,901.15	1,352.00	1,525.27	4,778.42	2,756.79	2,052.66	2,006.11	6,815.57
Jharkhand	1,685.05	1,724.25	1,432.24	4,841.55	3,550.56	4,024.42	5,196.51	12,771.48	5,235.61	5,748.67	6,628.75	17,613.03
Karnataka	4,954.15	7,249.40	3,010.71	15,214.26	5,531.81	9,087.76	5,080.99	19,700.56	10,485.96	16,337.16	8,091.70	34,914.82
Kerala	2,707.03	5,173.02	1,159.94	9,039.99	3,144.92	5,749.86	1,348.08	10,242.86	5,851.95	10,922.87	2,508.02	19,282.85
Madhya Pradesh	4,396.02	5,140.04	3,920.94	13,457.00	8,472.16	9,543.17	12,302.67	30,318.00	12,868.18	14,683.21	16,223.62	43,775.01
Maharashtra	11,189.00	14,274.97	7,637.84	33,101.81	8,693.44	14,678.17	10,224.75	33,596.36	19,882.44	28,953.14	17,862.60	66,698.17
Manipur	192.59	191.17	112.39	496.14	255.76	242.96	229.05	727.78	448.35	434.13	341.44	1,223.92
Meghalaya	176.17	111.31	82.35	369.82	410.78	337.48	473.02	1,221.28	586.95	448.79	555.37	1,591.11
Mizoram	155.41	93.77	102.89	352.07	77.07	66.86	88.80	232.73	232.48	160.64	191.69	584.80
Nagaland	144.03	84.79	83.61	312.43	166.16	124.47	195.73	486.35	310.19	209.26	279.34	798.79
Odisha	1,416.61	2,072.08	898.02	4,386.70	6,410.48	8,233.12	5,937.99	20,581.59	7,827.09	10,305.20	6,836.01	24,968.29
Punjab	1,867.89	2,976.46	1,185.88	6,030.23	2,988.71	4,001.08	2,204.56	9,194.36	4,856.60	6,977.54	3,390.45	15,224.59
Rajasthan	3,138.10	3,533.11	2,738.06	9,409.27	8,182.30	8,530.20	10,440.70	27,153.20	11,320.39	12,063.32	13,178.75	36,562.46
Sikkim	43.14	47.59	13.71	104.45	84.14	89.74	41.24	215.12	127.28	137.33	54.95	319.57
Tamil Nadu	7,545.52	15,075.83	3,652.80	26,274.15	7,219.62	12,632.69	5,507.71	25,360.02	14,765.14	27,708.52	9,160.52	51,634.17
Telangana	3,062.73	5,222.19	2,450.86	10,735.78	2,690.97	5,047.02	3,443.33	11,181.32	5,753.70	10,269.21	5,894.19	21,917.10
Tripura	186.49	392.93	73.82	653.24	370.50	833.72	315.90	1,520.13	556.99	1,226.65	389.72	2,173.37
Uttar Pradesh	11,119.73	7,822.14	8,792.82	27,734.69	27,680.72	17,468.03	32,299.31	77,448.06	38,800.45	25,290.17	41,092.14	105,182.76
Uttarakhand	808.40	765.23	588.15	2,161.78	1,263.16	1,186.62	1,322.08	3,771.86	2,071.55	1,951.85	1,910.23	5,933.63
West Bengal	5,260.62	9,395.68	3,316.12	17,972.42	8,979.75	18,856.74	9,961.41	37,797.90	14,240.37	28,252.42	13,277.53	55,770.32
All India	78,930.64	107,052.21	56,241.71	242,224.56	134,147.23	167,481.31	155,832.90	457,461.44	213,077.87	274,533.52	212,074.61	699,686.00

TABLE C25 Female Sample Observations across Quintiles of Frequency of Reading Newspaper, Listening Radio, and Watching Television: National Family Health Survey-4 (2014–15)

State	Urban				Rural				Total			
	1	2	3	4	1	2	3	4	1	2	3	4
Andhra Pradesh	709.87	3,559.41	3,072.64	2,286.24	2,856.52	10,512.40	5,415.03	2,034.25	3,566.39	14,071.81	8,487.68	4,320.49
Arunachal Pradesh	33.71	68.04	37.83	20.36	232.99	139.88	55.11	15.95	266.70	207.92	92.94	36.31
Assam	471.93	944.61	690.61	488.87	8,417.57	3,450.11	2,149.41	706.89	8,889.50	4,394.72	2,840.02	1,195.77
Bihar	2,363.66	1,730.78	1,872.19	1,606.34	34,674.27	5,363.06	5,547.17	3,188.59	37,037.93	7,093.84	7,419.36	4,794.94
Chhattisgarh	400.51	1,160.60	1,339.27	1,189.63	4,686.24	4,138.57	2,713.75	887.34	5,086.75	5,299.17	4,053.02	2,076.97
Goa	34.62	119.66	194.18	193.02	29.53	47.26	119.78	123.37	64.15	166.93	313.96	316.39
Gujarat	1,987.93	4,376.80	4,069.27	4,094.86	6,756.91	6,099.45	3,785.47	1,532.42	8,744.83	10,476.24	7,854.74	5,627.27
Haryana	692.63	1,924.91	1,751.57	1,830.84	1,834.55	3,455.56	2,709.49	1,397.47	2,527.19	5,380.47	4,461.06	3,228.31
Himachal Pradesh	30.23	73.32	123.72	142.90	616.00	914.80	1,187.54	756.54	646.23	988.12	1,311.26	899.44
Jammu & Kashmir	262.09	364.02	622.03	789.02	1,712.49	1,029.42	1,250.84	785.67	1,974.58	1,393.44	1,872.87	1,574.69
Jharkhand	941.39	1,307.18	1,350.52	1,242.47	9,226.47	1,917.57	1,213.57	413.88	10,167.85	3,224.75	2,564.09	1,656.35
Karnataka	1,144.09	4,669.50	3,268.78	6,131.89	3,583.42	8,229.40	4,737.48	3,150.25	4,727.51	12,898.91	8,006.26	9,282.14
Kerala	449.84	957.78	2,458.61	5,173.75	520.15	1,431.50	2,999.94	5,291.27	969.99	2,389.28	5,458.55	10,465.02
Madhya Pradesh	1,787.51	3,603.54	3,503.39	4,562.57	15,853.71	7,597.53	4,734.30	2,132.46	17,641.22	11,201.07	8237.68	6,695.04
Maharashtra	3,722.68	8,602.65	9,698.31	11,078.17	10,351.70	10,181.52	8,538.01	4,525.13	14,074.38	18,784.17	18,236.32	15,603.30
Manipur	59.95	51.98	126.41	257.80	179.55	110.41	207.38	230.45	239.49	162.39	333.79	488.25
Meghalaya	35.60	71.33	129.38	133.51	479.11	264.68	356.27	121.21	514.71	336.01	485.65	254.72
Mizoram	10.96	29.68	169.07	142.37	54.03	41.62	109.80	27.28	64.99	71.29	278.87	169.66
Nagaland	72.54	80.31	96.82	62.76	296.05	82.92	74.68	32.70	368.59	163.23	171.51	95.46
Odisha	674.31	1,470.95	1,177.63	1,063.82	8,190.83	7,395.28	3,688.48	1,306.99	8,865.15	8,866.23	4,866.11	2,370.81
Punjab	381.66	1,707.18	2,025.66	1,915.74	1,045.45	3,659.01	3,117.03	1,372.86	1,427.11	5,366.19	5,142.69	3,288.60
Rajasthan	1,390.57	2,419.92	2,585.29	3,013.49	13,289.20	7,285.27	4,638.24	1,940.48	14,679.77	9,705.19	7,223.53	4,953.97
Sikkim	7.21	30.78	48.31	18.14	27.82	75.47	85.17	26.66	35.03	106.26	133.48	44.80
Tamil Nadu	1,002.58	8,975.84	6,912.68	9,383.05	1,664.93	12,254.08	6,194.49	5,246.52	2,667.52	21,229.92	13,107.17	14,629.57
Telangana	830.71	3,302.88	3,100.39	3,501.80	2,190.23	5,014.14	2,803.83	1,173.12	3,020.94	8,317.02	5,904.23	4,674.92
Tripura	85.11	256.62	191.56	119.95	541.75	709.76	211.24	57.37	626.86	966.38	402.81	177.32
Uttar Pradesh	6,169.59	7,356.21	7,290.09	6,918.80	47,252.87	14,443.32	10,886.26	4,865.62	53,422.46	21,799.54	18,176.34	11,784.41
Uttarakhand	271.55	524.22	736.00	630.01	1,127.31	1,047.53	1,169.62	427.41	1,398.86	1,571.74	1,905.61	1,057.42
West Bengal	2,818.33	6,554.32	4,800.97	3,798.80	15,898.03	14,227.61	5,870.91	1,801.36	18,716.36	20,781.93	10,671.88	5,600.16
All India	29,796.88	70,506.87	66,701.31	75,219.49	193,689.56	131,365.16	86,713.25	45,693.47	223,486.44	201,872.03	153,414.56	120,912.97

Note: For definitions of key terms, see the notes at the end of the tables.

TABLE C26 Female Sample Observations across Educational Attainments: National Family Health Survey-4 (2014–15)

State	Urban				Rural				Total			
	No education	Primary	Secondary	Above secondary	No education	Primary	Secondary	Above secondary	No education	Primary	Secondary	Above secondary
Andhra Pradesh	2,162.88	1,113.24	4,462.56	1,889.49	8,012.68	3,231.77	8,039.16	1,534.59	10,175.56	4,345.01	12,501.72	3,424.07
Arunachal Pradesh	27.32	13.95	92.08	26.60	159.92	60.71	201.23	22.07	187.24	74.66	293.31	48.67
Assam	251.60	240.31	1,624.13	479.97	3,697.12	2,170.25	8,110.82	745.80	3,948.72	2,410.56	9,734.95	1,225.77
Bihar	2,057.11	649.11	3,685.07	1,181.70	24,687.71	5,293.49	16,975.69	1,816.19	26,744.82	5,942.60	20,660.76	2,997.89
Chhattisgarh	600.60	513.79	2,120.55	855.06	4,000.30	2,112.42	5,784.80	528.38	4,600.90	2,626.21	7,905.35	1,383.44
Goa	52.67	40.86	317.64	130.31	23.26	27.15	208.68	60.85	75.94	68.01	526.32	191.16
Gujarat	1,958.21	1,553.99	7,999.97	3,016.68	5,478.20	2,645.09	8,878.52	1,172.43	7,436.41	4,199.09	16,878.49	4,189.11
Haryana	1,142.67	562.66	3,067.28	1,427.33	2,420.66	1,135.09	4,830.78	1,010.55	3,563.33	1,697.75	7,898.06	2,437.88
Himachal Pradesh	22.29	24.20	186.46	137.21	346.03	437.38	2,155.86	535.62	368.32	461.58	2,342.32	672.83
Jammu & Kashmir	435.91	86.78	1,058.37	456.09	1,550.72	288.69	2,525.25	413.76	1,986.63	375.47	3,583.62	869.85
Jharkhand	902.48	421.48	2,586.23	931.36	5,690.37	1,498.41	5,131.13	451.57	6,592.85	1,919.88	7,717.37	1,382.93
Karnataka	2,190.94	1,259.25	8,338.42	3,425.66	6,133.53	2,380.35	9,852.42	1,334.25	8,324.48	3,639.59	18,190.84	4,759.91
Kerala	32.25	264.01	5,859.65	2,884.07	144.79	452.61	6,822.11	2,823.35	177.04	716.63	12,681.76	5,707.42
Madhya Pradesh	2,450.63	1,643.25	6,696.87	2,666.25	12,433.39	5,077.16	11,739.03	1,068.43	14,884.01	6,720.41	18,435.91	3,734.68
Maharashtra	3,321.47	3,484.11	18,792.58	7,503.65	6,476.65	4,712.04	19,760.22	2,647.45	9,798.13	8,196.15	38,552.80	10,151.10
Manipur	38.05	32.66	295.44	130.00	93.12	93.63	452.75	88.29	131.17	126.29	748.18	218.29
Meghalaya	21.57	37.15	212.06	99.04	225.30	289.22	643.39	63.37	246.87	326.37	855.45	162.41
Mizoram	4.34	24.23	266.55	56.96	31.06	50.19	142.33	9.16	35.39	74.41	408.88	66.12
Nagaland	25.28	21.99	201.55	63.61	91.92	82.38	281.32	30.73	117.20	104.37	482.87	94.34
Odisha	722.64	472.69	2,373.52	817.84	6,220.92	3,182.73	10,172.95	1,004.99	6,943.56	3,655.43	12,546.48	1,822.83
Punjab	766.69	404.78	3,088.20	1,770.56	1,786.01	1,156.59	5,157.81	1,093.95	2,552.70	1,561.36	8,246.01	2,864.51
Rajasthan	2,118.08	1,132.36	3,951.74	2,207.08	12,687.96	3,842.59	8,789.51	1,833.13	14,806.05	4,974.96	12,741.25	4,040.21
Sikkim	11.03	11.24	62.48	19.70	27.57	39.72	129.04	18.80	38.60	50.96	191.52	38.50
Tamil Nadu	2,729.94	2,563.10	14,026.16	6,954.95	5,478.41	3,242.25	13,187.19	3,452.18	8,208.35	5,805.35	27,213.35	10,407.13
Telangana	1,977.22	793.07	5,333.35	2,632.14	5,045.39	1,119.53	4,176.74	839.66	7,022.61	1,912.60	9,510.09	3,471.80
Tripura	41.89	93.67	400.19	117.49	222.01	350.40	901.25	46.47	263.90	444.07	1,301.44	163.95
Uttar Pradesh	6,635.51	2,877.34	11,249.97	6,971.86	30,704.44	9,668.07	29,611.92	7,463.63	37,339.95	12,545.42	40,861.89	14,435.50
Uttarakhand	381.86	206.95	939.33	633.65	876.05	525.92	1,866.74	503.16	1,257.90	732.86	2,806.06	1,136.81
West Bengal	2,661.11	2,629.29	9,839.49	2,842.52	9,621.28	7,699.89	18,950.19	1,526.55	12,282.39	10,329.18	28,789.68	4,369.07
All India	37,660.82	24,300.48	125,208.24	55,055.02	154,474.41	62,932.44	205,828.95	34,225.65	192,135.23	87,232.91	331,037.19	89,280.67

TABLE C27 Female Sample Observations across Religion: National Family Health Survey-4 (2014–15)

State	Urban				Rural				Total			
	Hindu	Muslim	Others	Total	Hindu	Muslim	Others	Total	Hindu	Muslim	Others	Total
Andhra Pradesh	7,909.59	1,211.89	506.69	9,628.17	17,602.19	1,287.51	1,928.50	20,818.20	25,511.78	2,499.40	2,435.18	30,446.37
Arunachal Pradesh	54.80	7.48	97.66	159.94	99.36	6.33	338.25	443.93	154.16	13.81	435.91	603.87
Assam	2,061.47	498.15	36.40	2,596.02	9,106.17	5,037.88	579.94	14,723.99	11,167.64	5,536.02	616.34	17,320.00
Bihar	5,874.34	1,683.07	15.58	7,572.98	41,252.46	7,465.40	55.22	48,773.09	47,126.80	9,148.47	70.80	56,346.07
Chhattisgarh	3,645.18	306.93	137.89	4,090.01	12,164.28	105.38	156.24	12,425.90	15,809.46	412.31	294.13	16,515.91
Goa	364.47	70.49	106.53	541.49	246.97	3.73	69.24	319.94	611.43	74.23	175.77	861.43
Gujarat	12,783.58	1,599.24	146.03	14,528.85	17,113.62	932.37	128.25	18,174.24	29,897.20	2,531.61	274.28	32,703.09
Haryana	5,596.42	414.13	189.40	6,199.95	8,335.04	662.49	399.54	9,397.08	13,931.47	1,076.62	588.94	15,597.03
Himachal Pradesh	331.72	7.52	30.92	370.16	3,372.89	52.55	49.44	3,474.88	3,704.62	60.07	80.36	3,845.04
Jammu & Kashmir	429.66	1,531.30	76.19	2,037.15	1,419.93	3,249.27	109.22	4,778.42	1,849.59	4,780.57	185.41	6,815.57
Jharkhand	3,531.99	978.72	330.84	4,841.55	9,386.00	1,555.45	1,830.03	12,771.48	12,917.99	2,534.17	2,160.87	17,613.03
Karnataka	11,122.54	3,506.33	585.39	15,214.26	17,896.42	1,392.66	411.48	19,700.56	29,018.96	4,898.99	996.87	34,914.82
Kerala	4,946.16	2,912.71	1,181.11	9,039.99	5,939.98	2,465.16	1,837.72	10,242.86	10,886.15	5,377.87	3,018.83	19,282.85
Madhya Pradesh	11,210.80	1,916.43	329.78	13,457.00	29,258.23	915.31	144.46	30,318.00	40,469.03	2,831.74	474.24	43,775.01
Maharashtra	22,602.51	6,379.74	4,119.56	33,101.81	28,749.10	1,846.71	3,000.56	33,596.36	51,351.61	8,226.45	7,120.12	66,698.17
Manipur	294.77	70.59	130.77	496.14	276.62	72.08	379.07	727.78	571.40	142.68	509.85	1,223.92
Meghalaya	86.12	6.83	276.87	369.82	88.15	78.54	1,054.59	1,221.28	174.27	85.38	1,331.46	1,591.11
Mizoram	2.90	1.84	347.33	352.07	0.45	0.75	231.53	232.73	3.35	2.60	578.86	584.80
Nagaland	42.90	12.60	256.94	312.43	14.58	11.89	459.88	486.35	57.48	24.49	716.82	798.79
Odisha	3,917.77	292.66	176.27	4,386.70	19,744.77	243.36	593.47	20,581.59	23,662.54	536.01	769.74	24,968.29
Punjab	3,402.97	117.13	2,510.12	6,030.23	2,055.02	140.02	6,999.31	9,194.36	5,458.00	257.16	9,509.43	15,224.59
Rajasthan	7,674.45	1,500.57	234.25	9,409.27	24,898.65	1,686.30	568.24	27,153.20	32,573.10	3,186.87	802.49	36,562.46
Sikkim	62.26	2.28	39.90	104.45	124.48	0.37	90.27	215.12	186.75	2.64	130.18	319.57
Tamil Nadu	22,528.35	2,061.17	1,684.63	26,274.15	24,218.23	317.44	824.36	25,360.02	46,746.58	2,378.60	2,508.99	51,634.17
Telangana	8,376.39	1,925.56	433.82	10,735.78	10,380.05	448.48	352.79	11,181.32	18,756.45	2,374.04	786.61	21,917.10
Tripura	593.53	31.91	27.80	653.24	1,197.07	152.61	170.44	1,520.13	1,790.60	184.53	198.24	2,173.37
Uttar Pradesh	18,417.45	9,111.47	205.78	27,734.69	65,940.54	11,342.51	165.01	77,448.06	84,357.99	20,453.97	370.79	105,182.76
Uttarakhand	1,660.79	458.64	42.35	2,161.78	3,294.87	400.35	76.64	3,771.86	4,955.66	858.98	118.99	5,933.63
West Bengal	13,209.94	4,414.54	347.94	17,972.42	26,412.37	9,935.36	1,450.17	37,797.90	39,622.31	14,349.90	1,798.11	55,770.32
All India	182,607.67	44,628.80	14,988.08	242,224.56	381,130.88	51,832.35	24,498.21	457,461.44	563,738.55	96,461.16	39,486.29	699,686.00

TABLE C28 Female Sample Observations across Social Groups: National Family Health Survey-4 (2014–15)

State	Urban				Rural				Total			
	Schedule Caste	Schedule Tribe	Others	Total	Schedule Caste	Schedule Tribe	Others	Total	Schedule Caste	Schedule Tribe	Others	Total
Andhra Pradesh	9,531.91	92.57	3.69	9,628.17	19,732.71	1,080.99	4.50	20,818.20	29,264.62	1,173.56	8.19	30,446.37
Arunachal Pradesh	48.40	92.32	19.22	159.94	82.66	338.17	23.10	443.93	131.06	430.48	42.33	603.87
Assam	2,049.00	164.09	382.93	2,596.02	9,820.14	1,638.96	3,264.89	14,723.99	11,869.13	1,803.05	3,647.81	17,320.00
Bihar	7,324.67	91.47	1,56.84	7,572.98	46,673.05	1,295.24	804.81	48,773.09	53,997.72	1,386.71	961.64	56,346.07
Chhattisgarh	3,613.80	432.13	44.08	4,090.01	8,278.12	4,112.27	35.51	12,425.90	11,891.92	4,544.40	79.59	16,515.91
Goa	445.92	13.83	81.74	541.49	265.50	23.34	31.10	319.94	711.42	37.17	112.84	861.43
Gujarat	13,554.23	606.87	367.75	14,528.85	14,785.36	3,158.39	230.50	18,174.24	28,339.59	3,765.26	598.25	32,703.09
Haryana	6,164.57	5.00	30.37	6,199.95	9,375.70	2.46	18.92	9,397.08	15,540.28	7.46	49.29	15,597.03
Himachal Pradesh	356.68	2.66	10.81	370.16	3,406.82	19.14	48.93	3,474.88	3,763.51	21.80	59.74	3,845.04
Jammu & Kashmir	722.64	56.82	1,257.69	2,037.15	2,637.16	141.45	1,999.81	4,778.42	3,359.79	198.28	3,257.50	6,815.57
Jharkhand	4,277.07	522.82	41.66	4,841.55	9,628.62	3,031.14	111.73	12,771.48	13,905.68	3,553.96	153.39	17,613.03
Karnataka	11,659.41	888.44	2,666.41	15,214.26	16,914.26	1,026.21	1,760.09	19,700.56	28,573.67	1,914.65	4,426.50	34,914.82
Kerala	8,543.50	4.87	491.61	9,039.99	9,699.94	36.54	506.38	10,242.86	18,243.45	41.42	997.99	19,282.85
Madhya Pradesh	12,423.60	616.06	417.34	13,457.00	24,352.54	5,348.17	617.30	30,318.00	36,776.14	5,964.23	1,034.64	43,775.01
Maharashtra	31,218.35	960.22	923.24	33,101.81	28,696.77	4,151.65	747.94	33,596.36	59,915.12	5,111.87	1,671.18	66,698.17
Manipur	398.05	58.92	39.18	496.14	400.56	280.22	47.00	727.78	798.61	339.13	86.18	1,223.92
Meghalaya	33.84	288.33	47.65	369.82	20.54	1,115.64	85.10	1,221.28	54.38	1,403.97	132.75	1,591.11
Mizoram	6.92	343.23	1.93	352.07	1.46	228.95	2.32	232.73	8.38	572.18	4.25	584.80
Nagaland	32.45	257.64	22.35	312.43	11.20	464.69	10.46	486.35	43.65	722.32	32.81	798.79
Odisha	3,899.95	350.51	136.24	4,386.70	16,793.51	3,366.64	421.44	20,581.59	20,693.46	3,717.15	557.69	24,968.29
Punjab	6,001.11	3.48	25.64	6,030.23	9134.17	2.67	57.51	9,194.36	15,135.28	6.15	83.15	15,224.59
Rajasthan	9,144.36	201.76	63.15	9,409.27	23,758.75	3,333.16	61.29	27,153.20	32,903.10	3,534.92	124.44	36,562.46
Sikkim	87.93	15.35	1.16	104.45	162.63	44.81	7.69	215.12	250.56	60.16	8.85	319.57
Tamil Nadu	26,040.90	23.96	209.29	26,274.15	25,015.39	225.16	119.46	25,360.02	51,056.29	249.13	328.75	51,634.17
Telangana	10,318.59	278.50	138.69	10,735.78	10,022.88	1,025.12	133.32	11,181.32	20,341.47	1,303.62	272.01	21,917.10
Tripura	466.65	74.80	111.79	653.24	736.42	494.61	289.10	1,520.13	1,203.07	569.41	400.89	2,173.37
Uttar Pradesh	27,596.72	70.28	67.70	27,734.69	76,449.11	681.77	317.18	77,448.06	104,045.83	752.05	384.87	105,182.76
Uttarakhand	2,048.96	93.01	19.80	2,161.78	3,390.10	278.89	102.87	3,771.86	5,439.06	371.91	122.67	5,933.63
West Bengal	12,639.47	237.48	5,095.47	17,972.42	27,825.92	1,481.58	8,490.41	37,797.90	40,465.38	1,719.06	13,585.88	55,770.32
All India	**222,117.75**	**6,882.88**	**13,223.93**	**242,224.56**	**398,579.21**	**38,507.01**	**20,375.22**	**457,461.44**	**620,696.96**	**45,389.89**	**33,599.15**	**699,686.00**

TABLE C29 Male Sample Observations across Age Groups: National Family Health Survey-4 (2014–15)

State	Urban			Rural			Total		
	15–34	35–64	Total	15–34	35–64	Total	15–34	35–64	Total
Andhra Pradesh	909.56	716.91	1,626.47	1,583.90	1,495.65	3,079.54	2,493.46	2,212.55	4,706.02
Arunachal Pradesh	14.19	9.89	24.09	35.42	30.88	66.30	49.62	40.77	90.39
Assam	230.77	213.84	444.60	1,217.19	922.14	2,139.33	1,447.96	1,135.98	2,583.93
Bihar	795.96	495.81	1,291.77	3,487.45	2,208.94	5,696.39	4,283.41	2,704.75	6,988.16
Chhattisgarh	377.16	261.95	639.12	1,138.07	720.47	1,858.54	1,515.23	982.42	2,497.65
Goa	129.56	134.75	264.31	80.15	77.98	158.12	209.71	212.72	422.43
Gujarat	2,544.69	1,637.08	4,181.77	2,735.98	1,985.99	4,721.97	5,280.67	3,623.07	8,903.75
Haryana	680.94	390.64	1,071.59	936.18	521.74	1,457.92	1,617.13	912.38	2,529.51
Himachal Pradesh	89.58	70.89	160.47	434.60	381.34	815.93	524.18	452.23	976.41
Jammu & Kashmir	328.28	253.53	581.82	707.14	462.15	1,169.29	1,035.42	715.69	1,751.11
Jharkhand	440.08	315.15	755.24	1,068.27	661.40	1,729.67	1,508.35	976.55	2,484.91
Karnataka	1,411.46	1,128.52	2,539.98	1,738.46	1,315.03	3,053.48	3,149.91	2,443.55	5,593.46
Kerala	889.78	795.71	1,685.49	988.35	898.75	1,887.09	1,878.12	1,694.46	3,572.58
Madhya Pradesh	1,326.21	868.17	2,194.38	2,843.86	1,822.20	4,666.05	4,170.07	2,690.37	6,860.43
Maharashtra	3,452.21	2,206.31	5,658.52	3,313.92	2,195.65	5,509.57	67,66.13	4,401.96	11,168.08
Manipur	37.07	26.43	63.49	56.67	44.06	100.74	93.74	70.49	164.23
Meghalaya	28.07	16.84	44.90	98.40	64.81	163.21	126.47	81.65	208.11
Mizoram	30.57	20.01	50.58	18.11	12.63	30.74	48.68	32.65	81.32
Nagaland	24.28	18.18	42.46	37.43	30.79	68.22	61.71	48.97	110.68
Odisha	387.27	337.85	725.11	1,431.77	1,206.63	2,638.40	1,819.03	1,544.48	3,363.51
Punjab	620.73	406.06	1,026.79	954.87	576.92	1,531.79	1,575.60	982.98	2,558.58
Rajasthan	970.89	568.40	1,539.29	2,417.15	1,416.82	3,833.96	3,388.04	1,985.21	5,373.25
Sikkim	12.96	8.13	21.09	14.84	12.98	27.82	27.80	21.11	48.91
Tamil Nadu	2,670.28	2,201.15	4,871.43	2,439.79	2,024.41	4,464.19	5,110.07	4,225.56	9,335.62
Telangana	947.52	679.48	1,627.00	1,045.18	700.69	1,745.87	1,992.70	1,380.17	3,372.87
Tripura	68.08	56.30	124.38	167.08	113.78	280.86	235.15	170.09	405.24
Uttar Pradesh	2,819.53	1,701.82	4,521.35	6,515.33	3,722.41	10,237.74	9,334.86	5,424.23	14,759.09
Uttarakhand	194.63	137.48	332.11	307.78	178.94	486.72	502.41	316.41	818.82
West Bengal	1,467.44	1,326.98	2,794.42	2,981.59	2,438.87	5,420.46	4,449.03	3,765.85	8,214.88
All India	**25,266.98**	**17,685.53**	**42,952.51**	**40,871.82**	**28,297.67**	**69,169.49**	**66,138.80**	**45,983.20**	**112,122.00**

TABLE C30 Male Sample Observations across Number of Children: National Family Health Survey-4 (2014–15)

State	Urban				Rural				Total			
	0	1–2	>2	Total	0	1–2	>2	Total	0	1–2	>2	Total
Andhra Pradesh	665.71	690.02	270.75	1,626.47	1,049.18	1,375.04	655.32	3,079.54	1,714.88	2,065.06	926.07	4,706.02
Arunachal Pradesh	12.53	6.98	4.58	24.09	28.38	16.53	21.39	66.30	40.91	23.51	25.96	90.39
Assam	193.53	190.15	60.92	444.60	903.38	685.43	550.53	2,139.33	1,096.91	875.58	611.45	2,583.93
Bihar	629.40	293.14	369.23	1,291.77	2,388.81	1,044.54	2,263.04	5,696.39	3,018.21	1,337.68	2,632.27	6,988.16
Chhattisgarh	286.58	202.59	149.95	639.12	710.67	499.44	648.43	1,858.54	997.25	702.02	798.38	2,497.65
Goa	114.65	112.28	37.37	264.31	84.55	61.77	11.81	158.12	199.20	174.05	49.18	422.43
Gujarat	1,769.21	1,637.05	775.51	4,181.77	1,817.32	1,521.48	1,383.17	4,721.97	3,586.53	3,158.53	2,158.68	8,903.75
Haryana	469.30	386.35	215.93	1,071.59	607.29	479.48	371.16	1,457.92	1,076.59	865.83	587.09	2,529.51
Himachal Pradesh	78.97	64.24	17.26	160.47	322.68	318.90	174.35	815.93	401.66	383.14	191.61	976.41
Jammu & Kashmir	286.25	177.02	118.55	581.82	591.83	262.49	314.97	1,169.29	878.07	439.51	433.52	1,751.11
Jharkhand	342.69	250.11	162.44	755.24	676.91	454.90	597.87	1,729.67	1,019.59	705.01	760.30	2,484.91
Karnataka	1,362.48	732.34	445.15	2,539.98	1,551.79	890.79	610.91	3,053.48	2,914.27	1,623.13	1,056.06	5,593.46
Kerala	816.12	690.34	179.03	1,685.49	884.39	808.02	194.68	1,887.09	1,700.51	1,498.37	373.70	3,572.58
Madhya Pradesh	998.56	652.46	543.36	2,194.38	1,743.62	1,228.46	1,693.98	4,666.05	2,742.17	1,880.92	2,237.34	6,860.43
Maharashtra	2,691.24	2,040.45	926.82	5,658.52	2,232.03	2,038.95	1,238.59	5,509.57	4,923.27	4,079.40	2,165.41	11,168.08
Manipur	31.43	19.98	12.09	63.49	50.43	23.28	27.03	100.74	81.86	43.26	39.11	164.23
Meghalaya	23.09	12.60	9.22	44.90	70.79	34.51	57.92	163.21	93.87	47.10	67.14	208.11
Mizoram	24.44	10.48	15.67	50.58	12.94	7.33	10.48	30.74	37.37	17.81	26.14	81.32
Nagaland	23.66	10.14	8.66	42.46	33.67	12.48	22.08	68.22	57.33	22.62	30.74	110.68
Odisha	309.49	301.04	114.59	725.11	1,023.06	962.56	652.77	2,638.40	1,332.55	1,263.60	767.36	3,363.51
Punjab	440.50	439.56	146.74	1,026.79	697.73	542.53	291.53	1,531.79	1,138.23	982.08	438.27	2,558.58
Rajasthan	688.21	486.02	365.06	1,539.29	1,567.55	978.42	1,287.99	3,833.96	2,255.76	1,464.44	1,653.05	5,373.25
Sikkim	10.84	8.04	2.21	21.09	11.86	10.43	5.53	27.82	22.70	18.47	7.75	48.91
Tamil Nadu	2,225.43	2,177.09	468.92	4,871.43	1,902.66	1,818.82	742.72	4,464.19	4,128.08	3,995.90	1,211.64	9,335.62
Telangana	746.30	583.79	296.92	1,627.00	665.15	653.35	427.37	1,745.87	1,411.45	1,237.13	724.29	3,372.87
Tripura	54.05	64.29	6.05	124.38	104.77	128.53	47.55	280.86	158.82	192.82	53.60	405.24
Uttar Pradesh	2,166.73	1,133.39	1,221.23	4,521.35	4,623.52	1,873.30	3,740.92	10,237.74	6,790.25	3,006.69	4,962.15	14,759.09
Uttarakhand	146.75	108.44	76.91	332.11	219.45	121.59	145.68	486.72	366.21	230.03	222.59	818.82
West Bengal	1,267.58	1,148.04	378.80	2,794.42	2,149.39	2,239.22	1,031.86	5,420.46	3,416.97	3,387.25	1,410.66	8,214.88
All India	**19,948.60**	**15,196.73**	**7,807.18**	**42,952.51**	**28,779.89**	**21,145.63**	**19,243.97**	**69,169.49**	**48,728.49**	**36,342.36**	**27,051.14**	**112,122.00**

TABLE C31 Male Sample Observations across Quintiles of Frequency of Reading Newspaper, Listening Radio, and Watching Television: National Family Health Survey-4 (2014–15)

State	Urban					Rural				
	1	2	3	4	Total	1	2	3	4	Total
Andhra Pradesh	332.46	476.48	569.08	248.46	1,626.47	1,194.49	903.59	716.98	264.49	3,079.54
Arunachal Pradesh	11.18	6.76	4.18	1.97	24.09	48.38	12.02	3.92	1.98	66.30
Assam	149.95	132.85	91.20	70.60	444.60	1,310.55	510.22	173.18	145.39	2,139.33
Bihar	385.95	340.57	328.66	236.59	1,291.77	3,409.56	1,209.28	606.17	471.37	5,696.39
Chhattisgarh	118.96	187.16	209.57	123.43	639.12	855.62	626.44	229.74	146.74	1,858.54
Goa	26.14	63.17	116.72	58.29	264.31	18.22	35.74	68.00	36.16	158.12
Gujarat	1,188.04	1,097.69	1,375.27	520.78	4,181.77	2,337.12	1,270.97	800.57	313.31	4,721.97
Haryana	224.74	298.88	351.75	196.21	1,071.59	432.76	535.72	355.99	133.46	1,457.92
Himachal Pradesh	35.30	49.70	47.63	27.84	160.47	170.60	322.00	159.72	163.62	815.93
Jammu & Kashmir	119.95	155.69	128.86	177.32	581.82	397.16	355.15	164.14	252.83	1,169.29
Jharkhand	216.04	202.43	258.36	78.41	755.24	1,155.39	370.92	130.60	72.76	1,729.67
Karnataka	550.35	528.33	592.45	868.85	2,539.98	977.45	726.18	752.30	597.55	3,053.48
Kerala	117.35	350.60	762.49	455.06	1,685.49	191.59	472.50	835.37	387.63	1,887.09
Madhya Pradesh	525.72	542.07	620.79	505.80	2,194.38	2,581.08	1,179.15	475.82	429.99	4,666.05
Maharashtra	1,100.92	1,411.96	1,695.21	1,450.43	5,658.52	1,699.60	1,867.41	1,094.66	847.89	5,509.57
Manipur	6.40	13.08	9.01	35.00	63.49	18.29	25.48	17.20	39.77	100.74
Meghalaya	7.62	17.96	11.60	7.72	44.90	80.12	49.56	19.98	13.55	163.21
Mizoram	5.62	16.69	18.15	10.11	50.58	8.39	14.74	4.73	2.89	30.74
Nagaland	16.27	12.15	10.01	4.03	42.46	42.78	16.45	5.87	3.12	68.22
Odisha	164.36	189.14	241.66	129.95	725.11	1,409.39	719.15	315.73	194.12	2,638.40
Punjab	264.21	340.23	348.79	73.57	1,026.79	578.03	587.89	327.41	38.46	1,531.79
Rajasthan	292.59	441.75	509.73	295.22	1,539.29	1,903.69	1,148.77	556.77	224.73	3,833.96
Sikkim	6.19	7.46	3.77	3.68	21.09	14.06	8.75	2.41	2.61	27.82
Tamil Nadu	550.19	903.27	1,540.43	1,877.54	4,871.43	885.81	1,064.68	1,117.99	1,395.72	4,464.19
Telangana	280.34	450.09	536.43	360.15	1,627.00	665.73	505.82	379.91	194.41	1,745.87
Tripura	26.82	46.10	49.45	2.01	124.38	154.30	94.63	25.94	5.99	280.86
Uttar Pradesh	1,413.14	1,201.58	1,363.44	543.19	4,521.35	5,704.11	2,669.24	1,132.01	732.38	10,237.74
Uttarakhand	62.20	81.06	112.58	76.27	332.11	125.75	182.17	98.89	79.90	486.72
West Bengal	940.98	710.62	709.59	433.24	2,794.42	2,951.42	1,509.86	545.40	413.79	5,420.46
All India	**9,734.69**	**10,823.37**	**13,013.22**	**9,381.23**	**42,952.51**	**31,369.33**	**19,016.42**	**11,142.09**	**7,641.66**	**69,169.49**

(Cont'd) →

TABLE C31 *(Contd)* →

State	1	2	Total 3	4	Total
Andhra Pradesh	1,526.95	1,380.07	1,286.06	512.94	4,706.02
Arunachal Pradesh	59.56	18.78	8.10	3.95	90.39
Assam	1,460.50	643.07	264.38	215.99	2,583.93
Bihar	3,795.51	1,549.85	934.83	707.96	6,988.16
Chhattisgarh	974.58	813.59	439.32	270.17	2,497.65
Goa	44.35	98.91	184.72	94.45	422.43
Gujarat	3,525.16	2,368.65	2,175.84	834.09	8,903.75
Haryana	657.50	834.60	707.74	329.67	2,529.51
Himachal Pradesh	205.90	371.70	207.35	191.46	976.41
Jammu & Kashmir	517.11	510.84	293.00	430.15	1,751.11
Jharkhand	1,371.43	573.35	388.96	151.17	2,484.91
Karnataka	1,527.80	1,254.50	1,344.75	1,466.41	5,593.46
Kerala	308.94	823.10	1,597.86	842.69	3,572.58
Madhya Pradesh	3,106.80	1,721.22	1,096.62	935.79	6,860.43
Maharashtra	2,800.52	3,279.37	2,789.87	2,298.32	11,168.08
Manipur	24.69	38.56	26.21	74.77	164.23
Meghalaya	87.74	67.52	31.58	21.27	208.11
Mizoram	14.01	31.43	22.88	13.00	81.32
Nagaland	59.05	28.60	15.87	7.16	110.68
Odisha	1,573.75	908.29	557.39	324.08	3,363.51
Punjab	842.24	928.12	676.20	112.03	2,558.58
Rajasthan	2,196.28	1,590.51	1,066.50	519.96	5,373.25
Sikkim	20.24	16.21	6.17	6.29	48.91
Tamil Nadu	1,436.00	1,967.95	2,658.42	3,273.26	9,335.62
Telangana	946.07	955.91	916.34	554.55	3,372.87
Tripura	181.12	140.73	75.39	7.99	405.24
Uttar Pradesh	7,117.26	3,870.82	2,495.45	1,275.56	14,759.09
Uttarakhand	187.95	263.23	211.47	156.17	818.82
West Bengal	3,892.40	2,220.47	1,254.99	847.02	8,214.88
All India	**41,104.02**	**29,839.78**	**24,155.31**	**17,022.89**	**112,122.00**

Note: For definitions of key terms, see the notes at the end of the tables.

TABLE C32 Male Sample Observations across Educational Attainments: National Family Health Survey-4 (2014–15)

State	Urban					Rural				
	No education	Primary	Secondary	Above secondary	Total	No education	Primary	Secondary	Above secondary	Total
Andhra Pradesh	137.13	147.38	878.66	463.30	1,626.47	755.12	502.23	1,373.14	449.05	3,079.54
Arunachal Pradesh	2.11	1.77	14.38	5.83	24.09	14.50	9.79	35.93	6.08	66.30
Assam	21.35	51.75	273.30	98.21	444.60	376.54	375.35	1,217.61	169.82	2,139.33
Bihar	167.08	100.48	690.95	333.26	1,291.77	1,370.23	780.44	2,979.48	566.24	5,696.39
Chhattisgarh	28.19	74.34	374.00	162.58	639.12	300.13	332.34	1,085.96	140.10	1,858.54
Goa	14.13	15.46	177.30	57.42	264.31	5.43	9.84	119.61	23.24	158.12
Gujarat	242.03	349.16	2,597.49	993.08	4,181.77	542.29	722.55	2,981.45	475.69	4,721.97
Haryana	67.44	99.21	615.72	289.21	1,071.59	133.72	138.29	966.76	219.15	1,457.92
Himachal Pradesh	3.19	13.33	87.35	56.60	160.47	21.80	71.41	558.42	164.30	815.93
Jammu & Kashmir	65.33	34.29	347.19	135.00	581.82	158.02	72.80	781.61	156.86	1,169.29
Jharkhand	79.29	58.69	425.01	192.24	755.24	390.73	239.34	956.92	142.68	1,729.67
Karnataka	181.71	247.08	1,511.89	599.30	2,539.98	511.95	440.77	1,723.12	377.65	3,053.48
Kerala	9.30	99.76	1,099.72	476.70	1,685.49	16.75	104.36	1,332.59	433.39	1,887.09
Madhya Pradesh	163.32	293.04	1,231.45	506.58	2,194.38	889.01	873.72	2,527.16	376.16	4,666.05
Maharashtra	370.07	440.17	3,379.72	1,468.56	5,658.52	393.47	677.46	3,628.20	810.43	5,509.57
Manipur	1.37	2.93	40.05	19.14	63.49	4.50	10.71	66.94	18.58	100.74
Meghalaya	1.45	6.34	28.18	8.94	44.90	33.85	42.47	74.06	12.83	163.21
Mizoram	0.45	3.28	37.07	9.78	50.58	1.84	5.91	21.01	1.99	30.74
Nagaland	2.08	3.78	26.15	10.45	42.46	10.84	11.46	41.80	4.12	68.22
Odisha	33.58	69.30	446.97	175.27	725.11	427.21	483.08	1,479.12	248.99	2,638.40
Punjab	86.48	78.21	588.30	273.80	1,026.79	205.71	140.16	1,021.78	164.13	1,531.79
Rajasthan	133.41	121.23	805.37	479.28	1,539.29	656.92	495.80	2,149.48	531.76	3,833.96
Sikkim	1.52	2.74	12.81	4.02	21.09	2.45	6.65	15.98	2.75	27.82
Tamil Nadu	343.15	424.93	2,649.15	1,454.19	4,871.43	592.77	567.43	2,490.14	813.86	4,464.19
Telangana	169.60	129.47	865.96	461.97	1,627.00	443.22	221.34	858.26	223.05	1,745.87
Tripura	5.66	12.68	74.51	31.53	124.38	16.27	61.29	181.45	21.85	280.86
Uttar Pradesh	667.71	561.46	2,184.19	1,107.99	4,521.35	1,783.87	1,268.51	5,825.27	1,360.10	1,0237.74
Uttarakhand	26.52	27.68	185.44	92.47	332.11	39.25	60.65	316.66	70.16	486.72
West Bengal	301.90	497.39	1,397.01	598.12	2,794.42	1,003.40	1,180.86	2,821.31	414.89	5,420.46
All India	**3,473.66**	**4,170.29**	**24,298.44**	**11,010.12**	**42,952.51**	**11,117.03**	**9,920.67**	**39,710.68**	**8,421.11**	**69,169.49**

(Cont'd) ⟶

TABLE C32 (*Cont'd*) →

State	Total				
	No education	Primary	Secondary	Above secondary	Total
Andhra Pradesh	892.25	649.61	2,251.81	912.36	4,706.02
Arunachal Pradesh	16.61	11.56	50.31	11.90	90.39
Assam	397.89	427.10	1,490.91	268.03	2,583.93
Bihar	1,537.30	880.92	3,670.43	899.50	6,988.16
Chhattisgarh	328.33	406.68	1,459.96	302.68	2,497.65
Goa	19.56	25.30	296.91	80.67	422.43
Gujarat	784.32	1,071.71	5,578.95	1,468.77	8,903.75
Haryana	201.16	237.50	1,582.48	508.36	2,529.51
Himachal Pradesh	24.99	84.74	645.77	220.91	976.41
Jammu & Kashmir	223.35	107.10	1,128.80	291.86	1,751.11
Jharkhand	470.02	298.03	1,381.93	334.92	2,484.91
Karnataka	693.66	687.84	3,235.02	976.94	5,593.46
Kerala	26.06	204.12	2,432.31	910.09	3,572.58
Madhya Pradesh	1,052.32	1,166.76	3,758.61	882.75	6,860.43
Maharashtra	763.54	1,117.64	7,007.92	2,278.99	11,168.08
Manipur	5.87	13.64	107.00	37.73	164.23
Meghalaya	35.29	48.81	102.24	21.77	208.11
Mizoram	2.28	9.19	58.08	11.77	81.32
Nagaland	12.92	15.24	67.95	14.57	110.68
Odisha	460.79	552.38	1,926.08	424.26	3,363.51
Punjab	292.19	218.37	1,610.08	437.94	2,558.58
Rajasthan	790.33	617.03	2,954.85	1,011.04	5,373.25
Sikkim	3.97	9.38	28.79	6.77	48.91
Tamil Nadu	935.92	992.37	5,139.29	2,268.04	9,335.62
Telangana	612.82	350.81	1,724.22	685.02	3,372.87
Tripura	21.93	73.97	255.96	53.38	405.24
Uttar Pradesh	2,451.58	1,829.97	8,009.45	2,468.09	14,759.09
Uttarakhand	65.76	88.33	502.10	162.64	818.82
West Bengal	1,305.30	1,678.25	4,218.32	1,013.01	8,214.88
All India	**14,590.68**	**14,090.96**	**64,009.13**	**19,431.23**	**112,122.00**

TABLE C33   Male Sample Observations across Religion: National Family Health Survey-4 (2014–15)

State	Urban				Rural				Total			
	Hindu	Muslim	Others	Total	Hindu	Muslim	Others	Total	Hindu	Muslim	Others	Total
Andhra Pradesh	1,342.33	224.07	60.07	1,626.47	2,677.54	214.82	187.18	3,079.54	4,019.87	438.89	247.25	4,706.02
Arunachal Pradesh	8.68	0.72	14.68	24.09	14.78	1.44	50.08	66.30	23.46	2.16	64.76	90.39
Assam	356.07	79.76	8.78	444.60	1,386.33	675.16	77.84	2,139.33	1,742.39	754.92	86.62	2,583.93
Bihar	1,049.97	237.50	4.29	1,291.77	4,867.07	822.37	6.96	5,696.39	5,917.04	1,059.87	11.25	6,988.16
Chhattisgarh	583.44	34.65	21.03	639.12	1,822.09	17.88	18.57	1,858.54	2,405.53	52.53	39.60	2,497.65
Goa	188.44	29.97	45.90	264.31	127.80	1.18	29.15	158.12	316.24	31.15	75.05	422.43
Gujarat	3,787.61	377.95	16.21	4,181.77	4,463.41	224.53	34.03	4,721.97	8,251.01	602.48	50.25	8,903.75
Haryana	936.83	104.37	30.38	1071.59	1,327.43	90.76	39.73	1,457.92	2,264.26	195.13	70.12	2,529.51
Himachal Pradesh	143.87	5.42	11.19	160.47	789.89	13.90	12.14	815.93	933.76	19.32	23.33	976.41
Jammu & Kashmir	125.73	433.75	22.33	581.82	361.00	785.26	23.03	1,169.29	486.73	1,219.01	45.36	1,751.11
Jharkhand	576.30	140.10	38.83	755.24	1,291.22	203.84	234.61	1,729.67	1,867.52	343.94	273.44	2,484.91
Karnataka	1,814.94	602.42	122.62	2,539.98	2,784.85	223.38	45.26	3,053.48	4,599.79	825.79	167.88	5,593.46
Kerala	908.70	536.18	240.61	1,685.49	1,167.46	437.72	281.91	1,887.09	2,076.16	973.90	522.52	3,572.58
Madhya Pradesh	1,845.59	299.14	49.65	2,194.38	4,553.44	94.27	18.35	4,666.05	6,399.03	393.40	68.00	6,860.43
Maharashtra	3,994.56	1,094.51	569.44	5,658.52	4,674.95	300.30	534.32	5,509.57	8,669.51	1,394.81	1,103.76	11,168.08
Manipur	38.77	6.68	18.05	63.49	32.40	11.26	57.08	100.74	71.17	17.93	75.13	164.23
Meghalaya	9.62	0.60	34.69	44.90	22.14	10.47	130.60	163.21	31.76	11.07	165.29	208.11
Mizoram	0.72	0.48	49.38	50.58	0.16	0.05	30.53	30.74	0.88	0.53	79.91	81.32
Nagaland	6.14	3.14	33.17	42.46	1.39	1.60	65.23	68.22	7.53	4.74	98.41	110.68
Odisha	670.33	32.85	21.93	725.11	2,557.92	11.41	69.06	2,638.40	3,228.25	44.26	91.00	3,363.51
Punjab	578.17	29.49	419.13	1,026.79	399.35	32.49	1,099.95	1,531.79	977.52	61.98	1,519.08	2,558.58
Rajasthan	1,279.15	198.54	61.59	1,539.29	3,564.99	197.87	71.10	3,833.96	4,844.14	396.42	132.69	5,373.25
Sikkim	13.00	0.72	7.37	21.09	13.49		14.33	27.82	26.49	0.72	21.70	48.91
Tamil Nadu	4,250.85	354.48	266.10	4,871.43	4,232.05	46.92	185.22	4,464.19	8,482.90	401.41	451.32	9,335.62
Telangana	1,246.40	331.39	49.22	1,627.00	1,637.20	69.90	38.77	1,745.87	2,883.59	401.29	87.99	3,372.87
Tripura	111.24	9.18	3.96	124.38	232.07	20.58	28.21	280.86	343.32	29.76	32.17	405.24
Uttar Pradesh	3,132.90	1,344.39	44.05	4,521.35	8,867.05	1,344.24	26.45	10,237.74	11,999.96	2,688.63	70.50	14,759.09
Uttarakhand	273.40	55.45	3.25	332.11	426.79	52.52	7.40	486.72	700.20	107.97	10.65	818.82
West Bengal	2,100.25	666.96	27.21	2,794.42	3,955.55	1,296.14	168.77	5,420.46	6,055.81	1,963.10	195.97	8,214.88
All India	**33,019.42**	**7,583.69**	**2,349.40**	**42,952.51**	**58,370.40**	**7,206.15**	**3,592.94**	**69,169.49**	**91,389.82**	**14,789.84**	**5,942.34**	**112,122.00**

TABLE C34 Male Sample Observations across Social Groups: National Family Health Survey-4 (2014–15)

State	Urban				Rural				Total			
	Schedule Caste	Schedule Tribe	Others	Total	Schedule Caste	Schedule Tribe	Others	Total	Schedule Caste	Schedule Tribe	Others	Total
Andhra Pradesh	1,580.43	28.65	17.39	1,626.47	2,846.85	222.49	10.20	3,079.54	4,427.28	251.14	27.59	4,706.02
Arunachal Pradesh	6.56	14.92	2.60	24.09	11.63	49.95	4.72	66.30	18.19	64.87	7.32	90.39
Assam	338.43	41.15	65.02	444.60	1,396.28	276.13	466.92	2,139.33	1,734.71	317.29	531.94	2,583.93
Bihar	1,218.26	11.19	62.32	1,291.77	5,593.20	30.57	72.61	5,696.39	6,811.46	41.76	134.93	6,988.16
Chhattisgarh	575.96	61.62	1.53	639.12	1,180.43	674.16	3.95	1,858.54	1,756.39	735.78	5.48	2,497.65
Goa	224.42	4.47	35.42	264.31	134.70	5.94	17.48	158.12	359.12	10.42	52.90	422.43
Gujarat	3,966.71	136.69	78.37	4,181.77	3,845.06	798.05	78.87	4,721.97	7,811.77	934.74	157.24	8,903.75
Haryana	1,064.62		6.97	1,071.59	1,455.65	2.28		1,457.92	2,520.26	2.28	6.97	2,529.51
Himachal Pradesh	150.23	2.58	7.67	160.47	793.38	15.93	6.63	815.93	943.60	18.50	14.30	976.41
Jammu & Kashmir	209.77	31.40	340.64	581.82	602.60	37.18	529.51	1,169.29	812.37	68.58	870.15	1,751.11
Jharkhand	648.72	91.94	14.58	755.24	1,355.90	366.63	7.14	1,729.67	2,004.63	458.57	21.71	2,484.91
Karnataka	1,825.02	124.94	590.03	2,539.98	2,668.60	140.79	244.10	3,053.48	4,493.61	265.72	834.13	5,593.46
Kerala	1,489.88	0.58	195.03	1,685.49	1,753.54	15.49	118.07	1,887.09	3,243.41	16.07	313.10	3,572.58
Madhya Pradesh	2,040.25	97.76	56.37	2,194.38	3,752.22	821.77	92.06	4,666.05	5,792.47	919.53	148.43	6,860.43
Maharashtra	5,374.01	179.63	104.87	5,658.52	5,038.96	362.54	108.07	5,509.57	10,412.97	542.18	212.93	11,168.08
Manipur	46.27	8.30	8.92	63.49	50.84	36.13	13.77	100.74	97.12	44.42	22.69	164.23
Meghalaya	3.20	35.41	6.29	44.90	1.77	148.27	13.17	163.21	4.97	183.68	19.46	208.11
Mizoram	0.20	49.28	1.10	50.58	0.34	29.90	0.50	30.74	0.55	79.17	1.60	81.32
Nagaland	6.77	33.06	2.63	42.46	1.84	64.97	1.42	68.22	8.61	98.02	4.05	110.68
Odisha	631.15	47.09	46.87	725.11	2,090.99	478.06	69.35	2,638.40	2,722.14	525.15	116.22	3,363.51
Punjab	1,019.23	2.17	5.39	1,026.79	1,512.53		19.25	1,531.79	2,531.76	2.17	24.65	2,558.58
Rajasthan	1,482.47	41.17	15.64	1,539.29	3,293.77	530.16	10.03	3,833.96	4,776.25	571.33	25.68	5,373.25
Sikkim	18.00	2.74	0.36	21.09	21.62	5.34	0.86	27.82	39.62	8.08	1.22	48.91
Tamil Nadu	4,795.25	11.15	65.03	4,871.43	4,401.84	39.78	22.57	4,464.19	9,197.10	50.94	87.59	9,335.62
Telangana	1,599.07	27.94		1,627.00	1,517.75	213.01	15.12	1,745.87	3,116.81	240.94	15.12	3,372.87
Tripura	89.91	14.39	20.08	124.38	154.59	99.09	27.18	280.86	244.50	113.48	47.26	405.24
Uttar Pradesh	4,500.30	4.06	16.99	4,521.35	10,172.01	41.29	24.43	10,237.74	14,672.32	45.35	41.42	14,759.09
Uttarakhand	303.00	27.30	1.81	332.11	432.33	37.32	17.07	486.72	735.33	64.61	18.88	818.82
West Bengal	2,121.42	58.13	614.87	2,794.42	4,078.39	237.78	1,104.29	5,420.46	6,199.81	295.91	1,719.15	8,214.88
All India	**39,293.13**	**1,199.52**	**2,459.86**	**42,952.51**	**60,260.96**	**5,803.87**	**3,104.66**	**69,169.49**	**99,554.09**	**7,003.39**	**5,564.52**	**112,122.00**

Notes

Relevant Tables	Concepts	Definitions
C1, C3, C5, C7, C9, C11	Knowledge about male contraceptive methods	Individuals were asked whether they know about the three male contraceptive methods of male sterilization, condom or nirodh, and withdrawal. The proportion of affirmative answers by individuals in the respective categories are tabulated.
C2, C4, C6, C8, C10, C12	Knowledge about female contraceptive methods	Individuals were asked whether they know about female contraceptive methods that include female sterilization, intrauterine contraceptive device (IUD) or postpartum intrauterine contraceptive device (PPIUD), injectables, pill, female condom, emergency contraception pills, diaphragm, foam/jelly, standard days method, lactational amenorrhoea method, and rhythm method. The proportion of affirmative answers by individuals in the respective categories are tabulated.
C5, C6, C25, C31	Quintiles of frequency of reading newspaper, listening radio, and watching television	Individuals are assigned a score of 0, 1, 2, or 3 based on their frequency of reading the newspaper, listening to the radio, or watching television where: 0: not at all, 1: less than once a week, 2: at least once a week, and 3: almost every day. These scores are added for each individual for the three categories of media. Finally the individuals are divided into five categories based on their quintile scores, and the average statistic of the respective headings for the individuals is given in the table.
C13, C14	Knowledge about tuberculosis	Percentage of individuals in the respective categories who have heard of tuberculosis.
C13	Spread of tuberculosis	Seven questions were asked to individuals regarding the spread of tuberculosis. These questions were: whether tuberculosis can spread through the air when coughing or sneezing, through sharing utensils, through touching a person with tuberculosis, through food, through sexual contact, through mosquito bites, and through other means. The proportion of correct answers by individuals in the respective categories are tabulated.
C13, C15	Cure for tuberculosis	Percentage of individuals in the respective categories who know that tuberculosis can be cured by medication.
C13, C16	Willingness to disclose tuberculosis	Percentage of individuals in the respective categories who are willing to disclose that themselves or their family members are affected by tuberculosis.
C17, C18, C19	Knowledge about HIV/AIDS	Percentage of individuals in the respective categories who have heard of HIV and/or AIDS.
C17, C21	Attitude towards HIV/AIDS	Individuals were asked whether she/he is willing to care for a relative with AIDS; whether a female teacher infected with HIV but who is not sick, should be allowed to continue to teach; whether a male teacher infected with HIV but who is not sick, should be allowed to continue to teach; whether she/he would buy vegetables from a vendor with HIV; whether a child with HIV should be allowed to attend school with students who do not have HIV; whether people with HIV be treated in the same public hospital with patients who do not have HIV; and whether people with HIV be allowed to work in the same office with people who do not have HIV. The proportion of affirmative answers by individuals in the respective categories are tabulated.
C17, C20	Cure for HIV/AIDS	Infection of HIV/AIDS can be checked by the infected person taking medications and its spread can be stopped by preventing infection to an unborn child. Individuals were asked about these two methods of combating the spread of the infection. The proportion of affirmative answers by individuals in the respective categories are tabulated.
C17, C22	Willingness to disclose HIV/AIDS	Percentage of individuals in the respective categories who are willing to disclose that themselves or their family members are affected by HIV/AIDS.

Blogspeak

Cross-Section of Opinions among Different Stakeholders

FROM THE EDITORS

During the course of drafting this report, we conducted a series of interviews with the different stakeholders associated with the healthcare system. Our interviewees included doctors, technicians, nurses, and administrative officials of public and private hospitals and nursing homes; representatives from pharmaceutical companies; general retail shop owners and proprietors; fair price shop owners and proprietors; medical representatives; and finally of course, patients and their family members in both rural and urban areas of Bankura, Birbhum, Durgapur, Kolkata, Murshidabad, Nadia, Purba Medinipur, and Purulia. In the following blogspeak, we put together their opinions related to a diverse array of problems and concerns that plague this system, and their possible solutions. The opinions put together in the blogspeak are expressed by the survey participants and are solely their personal views. We neither endorse nor reject the qualitative and quantitative validity of the same.

WHY DO DOCTORS PREFER THE PRIVATE SECTOR?

Poaching by the Private Sector

The government did set up medical colleges in small towns with the hope that local doctors would work in these medical colleges, which in the long-run will help these colleges to flourish. However, private hospitals with their deep pockets poach these young doctors away from the public sector.

—Orthopaedic Doctor, Kolkata, Chief Medical Officer

Remuneration

Nowadays to become a doctor in India, people have to make large investments. As a result, they prefer private sector jobs to public sector jobs. Working in a public hospital, a doctor's annual earnings are around one-and-a-half to two crores of rupees a year. Compared to this, a starting doctor in a private health facility is likely to earn at least 2–3 times more.

—Orthopaedic Doctor, Kolkata;
Doctor in a Block Rural Hospital

Quality of Medical Education in Rural Areas Is Poor

Medical students from rural areas are disadvantaged because the quality of medical education close to their residence is poor. As a result, many do not finish their education.

—Block Medical Officer (Health) of a Rural Hospital

Bleak Future Opportunities

If a doctor gets posted to a rural hospital as his first posting, it is very difficult for him to get posted out of that hospital in the future. He either retires from the rural hospital or resigns from his post. Few opportunities arise to get leave for higher studies. As a result, he can never be posted to district hospitals or to the rank of a deputy officer.

—Several Block Medical Officers (Health) of Rural Hospitals

Problem of Plenty with No Commitment

There are enough doctors in the public sector but they are not committed to their jobs. Even though the duty hours of the doctors are from 10 a.m. to 6 p.m., they leave at 2 p.m. The Superintendent of the hospital is also helpless.

—Laboratory Technician

Arduous Recruitment Process

Recruitment process in public hospitals is arduous.

—Superintendent, Super Speciality Hospital

Recruitment process is politically tainted. Often bribes have to be paid to get a comfortable posting.

—Retired Professor, Medical College

Overwork

In public hospitals, doctors often work round-the-clock, especially if they live in the residential accommodation provided by the hospital. This not only frustrates the doctors, but also puts their patients at risk. In public hospitals, it is mandatory for every doctor to do post mortem services. Due to paucity of doctors in government hospitals, a public hospital doctor often serves two separate public hospitals at the same time (The respondent was referring to the district of Malda where this practice has started recently). The

order has been given from the health department through a circular which has also been forwarded to the local police station. The police station can then check on the doctor as to whether he/she is following the circular properly. In public hospitals with quarter facilities for doctors, they had to work for 24 hours which is very unscientific and risky.

—Chief Medical Officer of Health

Greed

Most doctors employed in public hospitals also attend to patients in their private chambers—often during OPD hours of public hospitals. The modus operandi is to attend to 10–15 patients in their private OPD chamber, visit the public hospital, and then return to their private practice as the number of patients waiting increases. No one opposes this malpractice. Patients in government hospitals are frustrated because of the long wait that leads them to create a ruckus in the hospitals.

—Fair Price Shop Proprietor

Pharmaceutical companies often pander to the whims of doctors so that they prescribe medicines produced by their company. Doctors are given gift cards of large amounts, they are gifted white goods like top-end refrigerators and paid family vacations to places like Dubai. In return, the doctor ensures that he prescribes medicines produced by the pharmaceutical companies that sponsor their trips and luxuries.

—Fair Price Shop Proprietor

At times, doctors make patients wait the entire day only to ask them to visit again the next. What happens then is that agents hired by private hospitals get active in luring patients away from public hospitals. Such instances need to be monitored, but unfortunately, monitoring in public hospitals is dismal.

—Pharmacist, Medical College

Overcrowding of Rural Hospitals

The number of beds in the specific rural hospital that the interviewer visited is 30, but on average, the number of admitted patients is more than double this figure. The interviewer herself confirmed that the day when she visited the hospital, 75 patients were admitted there. In the month of May, this easily goes up to 100. This often compromises the quality of healthcare delivery. For example, ligation patients are by protocol supposed to be admitted in a health facility for seven days, but due to overcrowding they are often discharged after three days. Lack of space also forces them to keep new-borns on the floor many a times. High institutional rate of deliveries can be attributed to the free ambulance service provided by them. Besides when ambulances aren't available, cars are rented for the patients free of cost to serve the same purpose. The hospital is also faced with a shortage of nursing staff so much so that at night there is only 1 nurse [on duty]. Moreover, instances of snakebites are not uncommon, and they only escalate during summers.

—Nursing Staff, Rural Hospital

Nursing staff take help from relatives of the patients due to patient overload. To give one example, relatives inform the nurses about exhaustion of saline, and in this way help in monitoring the patients.

—Health Instructor

Lack of Infrastructure in Rural Hospitals

Poor infrastructure and lack of security of doctors are other reasons for government hospitals facing a shortage of doctors. In many block and rural hospitals, there are no residential quarters for doctors. As a result, they have to commute long distances. Even if there are residential quarters, they are only for doctors and not for their families. Therefore, their families have to stay in their native place while the doctor has to continue to serve without the support of his/her family. The respondent relates an incident where a doctor in a rural hospital travelled long distances to reach his workplace. Due to the poor public transport system in the rural areas, he often reported late for duty. The media instead of understanding his problems campaigned that he was irresponsible. Fed up with the unhelpful system and incorrect allegations against him, the doctor quit his government hospital job and joined the private sector.

—Block Rural Hospital Health Officer; Health Inspector

Lack of Support Staff in Rural Hospitals

In the specific rural hospital that the interviewer visited, there were only nine nursing personnel overseeing 70–80 patients.

At night time, the situation is worse with only one nurse attending to all the patients. In emergency delivery cases, we often have to use the help of the patient party.

—Nursing Staff, Rural Hospital

SOLUTION TO THIS ISSUE

Tier System

Create a tier system in the outpatient department. First, the junior doctors screen all the patients. Based on their evaluation, each patient is designated to a department that will handle their medical problem. In these departments, senior doctors should take over the treatment if some complicated health issue arises. This would not only reduce the pressure on everyone, but also make the entire process more systematic. The doctors would perhaps not avoid the government hospitals as the proposed system would reduce the workload. This system will also help students to get first-hand experience about diagnosis. Such an experience in the early stages of their career will be of great benefit not only to them, but also to their patients in the future.

—Retired Professor, Medical College

Controlled Private Sector Practice

A possible solution to retain doctors in public sector hospitals is to allow them to practice in the private sector for a specified number of hours in a week. This would discourage doctors in government hospitals from neglecting their duties towards their patients in public hospitals. They would not have to squeeze in time for private practice in between the hours designated for serving in public sector hospitals as they will have specific hours allotted for the former.

—Orthopaedic Doctor, Kolkata

Regulation of the Private Sector

Presently, the wage gap existing between the private and public sectors is appalling. The gap is more than it appears to be if one takes into account the difference in patient load doctors in the two sectors are faced with. The private health sector should be regulated so that the wage discrepancy between the doctors in the government and private hospitals is reduced. The private–public partnership model should be encouraged by the government.

—Chief Medical Officer

DO PATIENTS PREFER PRIVATE HOSPITALS OVER PUBLIC HOSPITALS?

Diversion of Patients to Private Hospitals and Sabotaging of Machines

Long waiting [times] in public hospitals to either avail services or visit the doctor is the main factor pushing patients to opt for private hospitals. There are high costs, both implicit and explicit, associated with waiting in hospitals which the poor cannot afford. To give one example, a certain patient was able to get an X-ray done after waiting for nearly 3 months. Other times, hospital staff deliberately sabotage machines and divert patients to private clinics and thus, in return pocket commissions. Such practices need to be curbed.

—Health Instructor

Affordable High-Quality Services in Public Hospitals

If while delivery, the mother or the new-born is faced with any complication, private hospitals charge exorbitant amounts for dealing with the same, but we don't face this in public hospitals. Private hospitals are driven by the profit motive, but this is not the case with public hospitals that exist for the sole purpose of providing affordable healthcare to all. Nursing and other staff have also become more courteous. They have shed their old image of being rude and impolite. All in all, public hospitals don't need to fret about campaigning; they are providing high quality services and word-of-mouth advertising will act as their biggest promoter.

—Patient

Improvement in Services Provided and Increasing Faith

Services of public hospitals have improved a lot, which in turn is attracting several people to avail their services. Rooms, too, are well maintained. Equipment is also well kept. The introduction of different government schemes, primarily the Janani Suraksha, helped mitigate the malpractice of nursing homes in which they positioned agents outside public hospitals with the motive of luring inpatients to the private sector. Moreover, people in the surrounding areas are poor and cannot afford the expensive treatments offered by private hospitals. Coupled with the fact that services itself are improving in public hospitals, attracting patients is no longer difficult. Public hospitals are working slowly but effectively in building the public's faith in their system and care.

—Block Public Health Nurse, Rural Hospital

PATIENTS SPEAK!

Role of ASHA Workers

I am admitted to treat my diarrhoea. I had to come to the hospital because there is no ASHA worker in my locality to give me ORS packets.

—Patient, Rural Hospital

Uninformed Cardholders

My seven-month-old child is suffering from diarrhoea for the last five days. I have admitted her to the hospital. I have a health card but I do not know what I am entitled to as a cardholder. I come to this hospital when [any] health issue arises in my household. The nursing staff are overworked because of the large number of patients that they have to attend to.

—Patient, Rural Hospital

Establishment of More Hospitals

I am visiting the hospital to get my two-year-old child checked. Earlier near my village, there was only a block hospital conducting normal deliveries. Caesarean cases were referred to another hospital. However, with the opening of this super speciality hospital, people can come here for any kind of delivery cases.

—Patient, Super Speciality Hospital

Refusing Admissions

I am a 68-year-old patient who was suffering from severe burns. I was first taken to a zilla hospital. On refusal of admittance there, I was referred to Burdwan hospital that also turned my case down stating that they did not take 65 per cent burnt cases since their hospital was not equipped to treat the same. I was then referred to a private hospital in Durgapur. They said that I had only 40 per cent burns, and they could treat me but the costs will be high. My family took me to another private hospital that promised to treat me for INR 16,000 per day but which later rose to INR 35,000 per day. Also, the hospital refused to release me to the Durgapur sub-divisional hospital claiming that it was against medical protocol to release a patient to a sub-divisional hospital once he had been referred to a district hospital.

—Patient in a Big Private Hospital

Private vs Public Sector

I visit the doctor's private chambers for OPD, but the public hospital for in-hospitalization treatment because of the high costs that we have to bear in private hospitals and the fear that they will keeping us longer than necessary. I use the fair price medicine shop and am happy though a lot of people try to dissuade me against the same. They recommend that I buy branded medicines. I feel that the doctors generally are not rude to patients, but because of the crowded nature of the OPDs it is impossible for them to give adequate time to each patient.

—Patient Party, Sub-divisional Hospital

High Opportunity Cost

I am a casual worker, and have an ESI card. I have come for my wife's delivery case. I visit the doctor's private chamber for check-up and/or consultation. I come to the hospital only if I have to admit someone. If I use the OPD facilities in the sub-divisional hospital, I would have to spend the entire day there and thus, forego my earnings for the day. I think over the last few years, the conditions of public hospitals have improved significantly. Hospitals are a lot cleaner; seating arrangements for family attendants and quality of food have improved. Finally, hospital staff are more friendly and helpful. The number of nursing staff has increased. My only complaint is about the doctors who continue not to be diligent with the patients, and are always in a hurry.

—ESI Cardholder in Sub-divisional Hospital

Shortage in Medicine Supply

I am very poor so I have to use government hospitals for health issues. I have to wait for a long time to see a doctor. Sometimes I have to buy medicines from outside, as the supply of medicines in the hospital is inadequate. Many times several patients return without any medicines for similar reasons.

—Patient

INDISCRIMINATE USE OF PUBLIC HEALTH FACILITIES BY NON-INDIAN NATIONALS!

Fake Identity Cards

Patients from neighbouring countries like Nepal and Bangladesh use public sector health facilities. They often use fake identity cards to avail the services.

—Regional Manager, Pharmaceutical Company

Irregular Maintenance of Registers

Neither OPD patients nor patients admitted to the hospital are required to show identity proof. The register of patients maintained by the hospital is not regularly updated. The interviewer herself checked the register and confessed that she could not comprehend the entries in it. However, access to healthcare under different schemes requires identity proof; the patients treated under these are not foreign nationals.

—Block Medical Officer of Health, Rural Hospital

Identity Proof Is Not Needed

No identity proof is required to admit a patient except under the Janani Suraksha project. Only the name, age of the patient is required for OPD, and for hospitalization, an address is required. Official records will not show admittance of foreign nationals in a public sector hospital since no identity is required. But the staff of the hospital can figure out that the patient is from Bangladesh from the language that they speak in.

—Staff, Rural Hospital

SHORTAGE OF MEDICINES IN PUBLIC HOSPITALS

Tie-Ups with Local Medical Shops

Supply of medicines to the hospital is good and timely. We have a tie-up with some local medicine shops which provide us medicines as and when required. I want to establish a Fair Price Shop within the hospital premises but am yet to find a suitable space for its location.

—Block Medical Officer of Health, Rural Hospital

Additional Problems in Summer

Supply of medicines is generally good but during summer and monsoons, there is a critical shortage of ORS packets. Sometimes we even have to rent a car to pick up the medicines from the depot which is a hassle for the hospital.

—Block Public Health Nurse

Dependence on a Single Supplier

While general medicines are available, supply of emergency medicines like those used for snake bites, dog bites, or DOTS (Directly Observed Treatment, Short-Course) is irregular. The irregular supply of DOTS medicines is a cause for worry because if the course is not completed, the patient will develop a resistance to the medicine that can in the long-run create a health hazard. Dependence on a single supplier is not wise. Further, if there is shortage of a particular medicine in the hospital, the suppliers tend to provide medicines with short expiration dates.

—Pharmacist, Rural Hospital

Corruption

Requisitioned medicines are sold off in the open market. Consider medicines under the DOTS programme. Medical personnel are expected to visit households and distribute free medicines. But numbers are fudged to show an increased number of visits so as to sell the medicines in the open market.

—Doctor, Block Rural Hospital

FAIR PRICE MEDICINE SHOPS AND FREE MEDICINES: GOOD OR BAD?

Double Dosages and Health Risks

The belief among doctors that free medicines are not good leads them to prescribe double dosages of the same, which naturally creates health risks for such patients. Such wrong prescriptions also create resistance in the patients for medicines that would be otherwise affordable. Production of different quality medicines for cities and villages also needs monitoring.

—Retired Professor, Medical College

False Propaganda by Pharmacies

There are two pharmacies near the sub-divisional hospital which with the help of hired people spread lies about the quality of medicine in our shop, encouraging people to go for branded medicine from pharmacies. This is why the number of customers received by us is much less relative to the number of patients in the sub-divisional hospital. The patients who buy from our shop are mostly previous buyers or very poor. Quality check of the medicines of our shop is done every six months by the drug control department. We have a total of 118 listed medicines available. The doctors don't write the generic name in the prescriptions. We try our best to cross check the drug name with the generic name and give the medicine to the patients, but they aren't receptive of these alternatives. We try to convince them to double check with the doctors.

—Fair Price Shop

Questionable Authenticity

How are fair price shops able to sell the medicines for such low prices? I don't trust the government's products as they never test them prior to selling. For example, a medicine to treat diarrhoea which was banned internationally was not banned by the Indian government for a very long time.

—Doctor

Requesting Prescription with Branded Names

Other medicine shops in the surrounding areas started telling the patients that the medicines in the fair price shops are not good and are in fact, fatal. As a result, the patients request the doctors to write the brand name of the medicines. Though the hospitals use the same medicines, doctors don't want to recommend them as they are missing out on commission from the medicine companies. When patients come to us, we try to convince them that these medicines are the same as the branded ones but to little or no avail.

—Fair Price Shop Workers

Discounts and Parallel Businesses

I think GST is being used as an excuse to deny discounts on medicines. Competition enables a chemist to get good commission from a stockist. It has definitely increased from the earlier 20–26 per cent. Therefore, the chemist can in fact give discounts of up to 15–16 per cent to consumers and still make a profit. Apart from commissions, they get a lot of other offers like buy one, get three free. I also feel that medicines in the fair price shops are of a very low quality. They are sold at discounts of up to 60–70 per cent most of the time. Most medicines are not even approved by Bureau of Indian Standards. Everyone involved in spreading these types of medicines including local political parties and strongmen make money from selling them. While the big nursing homes don't use these medicines, public healthcare facilities and fair price shops don't hesitate in using them. Lower awareness among patients in villages allows doctors to use these medicines there. Medical representatives have also developed a parallel business comprising these medicines in small towns and villages.

—Regional Manager, Medicine Company

THE PUBLIC–PRIVATE PARTNERSHIP MODE

News Channels

The public–private partnership model opens channels that enable patients to avail services like dialysis, ECG, etc., 24x7. This was not possible previously. The cost for keeping a trained set of staff was steep and not always feasible, but with the introduction of public–private partnership, this problem no longer persists.

—Chief Medical Officer of Health

Checking Qualifications

The concept of the public–private partnership model is good, but one needs to make sure that both the technicians and the pathologists are qualified.

—Orthopaedic Doctor

Providing Standard Diagnostic Tests

The PPP model can become very effective if all standard diagnostics can be provided between the government hospital and the private diagnostic centre. This would help patients to avoid making trips to the district hospital to get the tests done.

—Assistant Super, Super Speciality Hospital

Increasing Efficiency of Hospitals

The public–private partnership model is a good model especially in backward areas like rural Purulia. I believe introducing the public–private partnership model in health management may increase the efficiency of hospitals and lead to better monitoring. Perhaps, introduce this type of model for doctors too!

—Doctor, Block Rural Hospital

Monitoring Is Necessary

I feel that the public–private partnership model is very good, and can change the nature of public health in West Bengal. However, I also think that it requires monitoring so that it does not fail to deliver in the future like many other schemes.

—Physical Medicine Doctor, Medical College

While the idea of a public–private partnership model is good, if there is no monitoring, private partners will take advantage of the scheme by not hiring trained pathologists and use technicians to make the diagnosis.

—Block Medical Officer of Health, Rural Hospital

Profit Motive

The public–private partnership model is good, but it leads to a compromise in quality. In order to minimise costs, they use cheap quality kits that result in incorrect reports. I, however, believe that the government may not be successful in running the public–private partnership model because private labs that are driven by profit motives may close shop.

—Retired Professor, Medical College

Encroachment of Public Sector

I don't support the public–private partnership model because as a result of it, the private sector encroaches in the public hospitals which should not be the case.

—Doctor in Medical College Hospital

SWASTHYA SATHI: GOOD OR BAD?

Need of Preventive Care

I believe that it is important to incorporate preventive medicine in the scheme. More than 80 per cent of government hospital beds occupied by patients could have been available, if an efficient preventive care programme was in place. As a result, patients requiring secondary and tertiary treatment are suffering. If a strong preventive care programme is put in place, then in the long-run, government expenses will decrease along with overcrowding of public hospitals.

—Chief Medical Officer Health

We never really pondered over the issue of inclusion of preventive care in *Swasthya Sathi* but yes, it will be beneficial to permit patients to visit the OPD. Usually, patients visit doctors privately and get the testing done. If a problem is then detected, they visit the hospitals to use their *Swasthya Sathi* cards. As a result, a lot of out-of-pocket expense is already incurred by them prior to using the scheme. This would not have been the case had OPD visits been allowed. Moreover, a couple of health check-ups a year should be incorporated in the scheme.

—Private Hospital

Exodus of Patients to Private Hospitals

[Our] Hospital is empanelled under the scheme but I don't know the number of patients that have been treated under it. I feel that it has led to an exodus of patients from the public to the private hospitals.

—Block Medical Officer of Health, Rural Hospital

Adds to Administrative Hassles

I feel that the scheme does not add anything extra to the already existing free services provided by public hospitals. In fact, it increases the administrative hassles of public hospitals. I feel that private hospitals are benefitting from it since many patients are now going to the private sector to get treated under the scheme. The only good thing about it is that it allows the cardholder's parents to be treated under it.

—Block Medical Officer of Health, Rural Hospital

Cheating the Patients

Patients who visit public hospitals under different health schemes are treated badly by the staff. This makes them apprehensive about using the card unless necessary. This attitude in public hospitals pushes patients to private nursing homes and increases their business in turn. But these nursing homes dupe the patients by charging extra under false pretences that the doctor's fee is not included under the scheme. So, they often mix and match different packages and earn higher money than is permitted under the project.

—Pharmacist, Medical College Hospital

Permission from the Health Department expedited the entire process relating to my surgery. Treatment for the entire 12-day span was good. My only complaint is that even though the hospital did not give me any medicine, they forced me to sign a document on release, stating that I was supplied with medicines for 7 days.

—Patient

Exploiting Loopholes

When I went for treatment to a private hospital, a doctor there suggested I get the *Swasthya Sathi* card made. I didn't know about such a scheme because no one in my village belonging to my economic status had any knowledge about it either. Later I learnt that families who are richer compared to us are enrolled in it. The Panchayat, Panchayat Pradhan, and a political leader in my village on listening to my request got my name listed in a SHG after which I got the card. I have since then been paying INR 50 per month which I thought was for the scheme but it was just brought to my knowledge that it is a monthly contribution to the SHG.

—Patient

Low Package Costs

[I] do not know much about the scheme. After hearing about the scheme from you, I feel that the rates for treatment packages under the scheme are very low. My fear is that quality will be compromised to provide treatment at these rates.

—Assistant Super, Super Speciality Hospital

Free Goods Are Not Valued

I feel that the government should not provide free health schemes. People misuse them. For example, distribution of free medicine often leads to enormous wastage which would not have happened if patients were made to pay a token amount.

—Physical Medicine Doctor, Medical College Hospital

Need for Token Contributions

Swasthya Sathi is a good initiative by the state government, especially the fact that the scheme covers cardholders' parents. This according to me is a unique feature of the scheme. However, I feel that health services should not be free. Patients should pay a token amount to avail of health services.

—Doctor, Rural Hospital

Lack of Awareness

The hospital has treated six patients under the scheme. This low number of treatments is because the hospital is located in an area where there are not too many cardholders. Moreover, many cardholders are unaware of the hospitals empanelled under the scheme. The *Swasthya Sathi* cardholders are treated by the resident doctors. They cannot use the visiting or consultant doctors to treat the patients under this scheme because of its low rates. I acknowledge that instead of the few tests required for treatment, we often do many more diagnostics to help the health facility.

—Desk Personnel, Private Hospital

Awareness amongst patients about the use of *Swasthya Sathi* cards is still low. I hail from Purulia, and there the awareness about the scheme is low. I feel it is important to include some provision for preventive care in the scheme. This would not only help patients but also the government in the long-run.

—Block Medical Officer of Health, Rural Hospital

Delays in Reimbursement

Since its empanelment on 2 March 2017, the hospital has treated 4,684 patients under the scheme. Earlier under the TPA, reimbursements were fast. But since it has changed to a reputed private insurance company, there are delays in reimbursements. We are yet to receive around four lakhs under the scheme, and are not sure whether we would

ever be reimbursed. Certain strictures imposed by the company are causing problems. We feel that the rates of packages under the *Swasthya Sathi* scheme need revision. For example, per-dialysis treatment is priced at INR 1,100 but the injections themselves cost INR 950.

—Private Hospital

Smooth Reimbursement

[Our] Hospital is empanelled under the *Swasthya Sathi* scheme since 29 January 2018. So far, 26 cardholders have been treated. The facility can treat patients suffering from diarrhoea, fever, and malaria. For all other ailments, they are referred to other hospitals. We have received INR 750 per patient for each of the treated patients. As of now, we have not faced any problems in getting reimbursements.

—Nurse, Rural Hospital

Delays Caused by the TPAs

The hospital is empanelled under the scheme since 21 August 2017, and has treated approximately 390 patients under the scheme. They too complained about delay in reimbursements under the new TPA and said that their hospital was yet to receive INR 1,50,000 in claims. Another issue faced by them is that they require the permission of the TPA before a surgery. The TPA delays in giving the permission, and as a result the patients suffer. Sometimes patients are charged extra and have to give an undertaking that they have not been charged under the scheme because the *Swasthya Sathi* package rates are very low.

—Private Hospital

Accessible Private Healthcare

As a *Swasthya Sathi* cardholder, I can continue treatment for my mother who is on dialysis, which would otherwise have been impossible. I even receive transport reimbursement for the treatment.

Earlier, I had to spend a lot of money for an orthopaedic operation in a private hospital. However, recently when a family member had to undergo an orthopaedic surgery, I could get free treatment in a private nursing home because I am a *Swasthya Sathi* cardholder.

—Patients Using a Private Facility

Earlier patients had to sell off their land and assets in order to receive treatment from this hospital. This scenario has changed completely after the advent of the *Swasthya Sathi* project. Now the same patients do not have to bear the financial burden of expensive treatments. They can now get good quality health service at no cost.

—Billing Clerk, Private Nursing

Supportive Health Department

My wife enrolled in *Swasthya Sathi* after becoming a self-help group member. A year later, she was diagnosed with cancer. After a couple of chemotherapy sessions, the package of INR 150,000 had been exhausted. This got us worried. As a last resort, we wrote a letter to the Health Department. The latter in turn issued a letter in our favour, instructing that my wife's cancer be treated with chemotherapy. This helped us a great deal and we are thankful to the Health Department.

—Patient

During the conduct of heart surgery, a private hospital charged us INR 9,200 for the purchase of blood but the Health Department refunded the entire amount and we did not have to bear any unnecessary expense.

—Patient

I went from one hospital to another to get a spinal cord surgery done but faced a lot of hassles. Some hospitals said that they do not perform spinal cord surgeries while some others said that the package rate is too low for the required procedure and turned me away. Finally, R.N. Tagore Hospital suggested that I contact the Health Department as the package rate of INR 150,000 won't be sufficient and if they went ahead with the treatment, I would be required to shell out money from my own pocket. The Health Department made me a generous offer of INR 600,000 for the said surgery. My surgery ultimately cost INR 360,000 which was well within the amount offered to me by the Health Department.

—Patient

Low Price, Questionable Quality?

A charge of INR 10,000 for a medical procedure worth INR 50,000 will reduce the quality of the treatment. The sole reason for private hospitals enrolling in this project is to be in the government's good books in order to avail favours from it in the future.

—Part-Time Doctor in PHCs, NGOs, and District Hospitals.

We usually associate price with quality; hence, provision of such free treatments may be viewed with scepticism. It is up to the government to ensure the project's sustainability.

—Part-Time Doctor in PHCs, NGOs, and District Hospitals

Preventive Care May Not Work

My colleagues and I conduct several one-to-one counselling sessions with many patients who are faced with the risk of soon developing a fatal disease. We try to explain to them the importance of preventive care but to no avail. For instance, I once had a patient who was a chain smoker and chewed tobacco because of which he developed an infection in his throat. He was worried it was cancer. I told him, it isn't and recommended ways to prevent the possibility of development of cancer but he did not listen. He was relieved that it was not cancer and said that he cannot quit chewing tobacco. Another time, this patient had high sugar levels with strong chances of it culminating into diabetes. I recommended that he manage his diet and take morning walks but he did not listen to any advice I had to offer. It is only when the problem becomes acute that the patients come in for treatment. In fact, they suggest procedures to us to deal with their illness. Given my experience, even if the government were to incorporate preventive care into the scheme, it would be of not much benefit as the patients themselves are not concerned.

—Superintendent, ESI Hospital

Is It Sustainable?

This scheme sounds good, patients are obviously happy, but I have my doubts regarding its sustainability. Will it remain operational in the long-run? Patients don't pay any premium, the entire cost is borne by the government; what happens when a shortage of funds results in discontinuity of the scheme? Moreover, what if a new government that comes into power decides to end the scheme? Patients have been getting services in good hospitals because of the scheme, and are developing a taste for it. They think it's their right, which it is, but what about their duty? They too should be responsible for the smooth functioning of the scheme. In this respect, I think, some minimum contribution from them is necessary.

—Superintendent, ESI Hospital

NEXUS BETWEEN PHARMACEUTICAL COMPANIES, MEDICAL REPRESENTATIVES, AND DOCTORS

Counter Sales

Medical representatives visit frequently in order to sell medicines. They form an integral part of the system. I, too, prescribe the brand name of the medicines as the patients demand it. However, it is not right to put the entire blame on doctors for doing so as the counter sales of the medicines play a pivotal role in the overall sales. The medicines shops are as much a part of it as us.

—Doctor, Block Hospital

Several Facets of Medical Representatives

This nexus leads doctors to prescribe several unnecessary medicines which create resistance to many effective drugs. Putting a stop to this nexus will prove to be a difficult task. The doctors are dependent upon MRs [medical representatives] for knowledge regarding the development of new drugs in the market. Reducing this dependency is not as easy as it may seem. But you need to look at the positives as well. This practice enables the employment of several young men and women as MRs every year. Also, I feel that patients would undoubtedly be better off if instead of getting the medicines for free from the hospital, they purchased them at a nominal price from the stockist.

—Doctor, Medical College Hospital

Gifts, Money, and More

The nexus posits a deep-rooted problem with no conceivable solution. The greed of the doctors has led them to be controlled by the medicine companies. I myself am aware of the personal profile of the doctors in my region. Gift cards and money aside, we also provide doctors with rented cars as and when demanded. We also organize several conferences and seminars for them where they are invited as guest speakers. Honorariums amounting to INR 50,000–60,000 are given in the name of such talks. But you cannot overlook the fact that we do provide employment to thousands of youngsters every year, but doctors only

look at their own self-interest, sometimes at great cost to the patients. They are now more inclined to prescribing expensive and antibiotic-related treatments.

—Regional Manager, Pharmaceutical Company

Information Problem

The nexus is the result of the incomplete and asymmetrical information that exists between the pharmaceutical companies and the doctors. The introduction of several new medicines with slightly variant compositions makes it difficult for doctors to keep track of all the medicines available in the market. This information gap can be bridged only by the medical representatives. Doctors in private chambers in turn look after the interests of the company by providing business to the latter. The web is intertwined in such a manner that it is next to impossible for the medical council or the government to untangle it.

—Block Medical Officer of Health, Rural Hospital

ROLE OF MEDICAL COUNCIL

A Pseudo Council?

The medical council has been reduced to nothing but a puppet in the hands of the doctors. They don't take responsibility for anything; instead, they provide protection to the doctors even if the latter are wrong. The pharmacists too have a council where it is mandatory for them to take two trainings in a year. Since 2011, all the managing positions are held by doctors leaving no place for pharmacists. This level of corruption in the medical profession astonishes me. I don't see the conditions changing any time soon.

—Pharmacist, Medical College Hospital

Selective Issues under the Council's Ambit

The medical council caters only to mishaps relating to treatments. Remiss on the part of the doctors falls under the ambit of the government's responsibility, not the medical council's.

—Doctor, Block Hospital

Passive Council

The role of the medical council is very passive. They show no concern regarding the happenings in the field. Many people depend on quacks but the medical council does not train these people properly.

—Doctor, Block Hospital

Role Played by Quacks

In all my years in this profession, I could not help but notice the pivotal role quacks play in providing healthcare in rural areas; however, they are not recognized by the medical community. Their importance develops from the fact that while they provide services 24x7 all year round, certified doctors visit these villages hardly once or twice in a week, that too for a couple of hours. Training by the medical council to these quacks can go a long way in improving the healthcare provision in rural areas.

—Health Instructor

Editors and Contributors

EDITORS

Jyotsna Jalan is co-director, Centre for Training and Research in Public Finance, Kolkata, and professor, economics, the Centre for Studies in Social Science, Calcutta. She has received her doctoral degree from University of California San Diego, USA.

Sugata Marjit is distinguished professor at the Indian Institute of Foreign Trade, under the Ministry of Commerce and Industries, Government of India. He has received his doctoral degree from University of Rochester, New York, USA.

Sattwik Santra is assistant professor, economics, Centre for Training and Research in Public Finance, and Policy, the Centre for Studies in Social Science, Calcutta. He has received his doctoral degree from Indian Statistical Institute, Kolkata, India.

CONTRIBUTORS

Arjun S. Bedi is professor, development economics, International Institute of Social Studies, Erasmus University Rotterdam, the Hague, the Netherlands.

Arpita Chakraborty is consultant, Oxford Policy Management, Oxford, UK.

Sisir Debnath is assistant professor, economics and public policy, Indian School of Business, Hyderabad, India.

Koushik Kumar Hati is assistant professor, economics, Department of Economics, Deshabandhu Mahavidyalaya, Chittaranjan, India.

Tarun Jain is assistant professor, economics and public policy, Indian School of Business, Hyderabad, India.

Kalyan Khan is associate professor, Pathology Department, North Bengal Medical College and Hospital, Siliguri, India.

Biswajit Mandal is assistant professor, economics, Economics and Politics Department, Visva-Bharati University, Santiniketan, India.

Anagaw Derseh Mebratie is assistant professor, the School of Public Health, Addis Ababa University, Ethiopia.

Pradeep Panda is professor, health economics, International Institute of Health Management Research (IIHMR), Delhi, India.

E. van de Poel is health economist, Global Financing Facility, World Bank Group, Washington DC, USA.

Wameq Raza is applied micro-economist, World Bank Group, Dhaka, Bangladesh.

Frans Rutten is professor, health economics, Erasmus University Rotterdam, Rotterdam Area, the Netherlands.

Sandip Sarkar is assistant professor, economics, School of Economics, Xavier School of Economics, Xavier University, Bhubaneswar, India.

Zemzem Shigute is external researcher, International Institute of Social Studies, Erasmus University Rotterdam, the Hague, the Netherlands.

Robert Sparrow is associate professor, Development Economics Group, Department of Social Sciences, Wageningen University, the Netherlands.

Revathy Suryanarayana is a current graduate student at the Policy Analysis and Management Department, Cornell University, Ithaca, USA.

Getnet Alemu Zewdu is assistant professor, Institute of Development and Policy Research, Addis Ababa University, Ethiopia.